서울대 텝스 최신기출 1200제

서울대 텝스 관리위원회 텝스 최신기출 1200제 **문제집** VOL. **3**

문제제공 서울대학교 TEPS관리위원회
펴낸이 임상진
펴낸곳 (주)넥서스

초판 1쇄 발행 2017년 1월 5일
초판 28쇄 발행 2024년 11월 1일

출판신고 1992년 4월 3일 제311-2002-2호
10880 경기도 파주시 지목로 5
Tel (02)330-5500 Fax (02)330-5555

ISBN 979-11-5752-971-1 14740
     979-11-5752-970-4 14740 (SET)

저자와 출판사의 허락 없이 내용의 일부를 인용하거나
발췌하는 것을 금합니다.
저자와의 협의에 따라서 인지는 붙이지 않습니다.

가격은 뒤표지에 있습니다.
잘못 만들어진 책은 구입처에서 바꾸어 드립니다.

www.nexusbook.com

서울대 텝스 최신기출 1200제

텝스 관리위원회

1200제

문제집

서울대학교 TEPS관리위원회 기출문제 제공

VOL. 3

넥서스

PREFACE

넥서스에서 정기 텝스 시험의 공식 출제 기관인 서울대 텝스 관리위원회가 제공하는 기출 문제를 독점 출간하게 되었다. 최초로 〈TEPS 기출 문제집〉, 〈유형별로 분석한 NEXUS 기출 800〉 등을 출간한 이후 〈서울대 텝스 관리위원회 최신기출 1000〉, 〈서울대 텝스 관리위원회 제공 최신기출 시크릿〉, 〈서울대 텝스 관리위원회 최신기출 1200 / SEASON 2, 3〉, 〈서울대 텝스 관리위원회 최신기출 Listening / Reading〉, 〈서울대 최신기출 TEPS VOCA〉, 〈서울대 텝스 관리위원회 공식기출 1000 시리즈〉에 이르기까지 연이어 대표적인 TEPS 기출 교재로 자리매김할 수 있도록 많은 사랑과 관심을 보여준 TEPS 수험생들과 학교 및 학원에서 강의하시는 선생님들께 다시 한번 감사의 마음을 전한다. 다른 영어 능력 검정시험과 달리 많은 기출문제가 공식적으로 오픈된 TEPS 시험은 그만큼 과학적인 측정 도구와 신뢰할 수 있는 콘텐츠, 뛰어난 변별력 등 공인 영어 능력 시험으로서의 자격을 충분히 인정받았다.

TEPS 수험생들로부터 이 시험이 참으로 어렵다는 얘기를 많이 듣는다. 벼락치기가 가능할 만큼 단순한 실용 영어의 측정에 그치는 것이 아니라 그야말로 기초부터 고급까지 모든 수준의 영어를 심도 있게 측정하는 것이 바로 TEPS 시험의 목표이므로 TEPS 시험 준비에도 제대로 된 전략과 교재가 필요함은 두말할 나위가 없다. 따라서 지금까지의 출제 원리와 경향 분석을 위해서는 가장 확실한 기출 문제집을 하나 골라 반복해서 풀면서 정리하는 것이 무엇보다 중요할 것이다.

이번에 출간하는 서울대 텝스 관리위원회 최신기출 시리즈는 출제 기관이 지금까지 공개한 것 중 가장 최신의 공식 기출문제 6회분으로 구성했고, 학습자 편의를 위해 문제집과 해설집을 각각 별도로 제작했다. 또한 실제 TEPS 시험장에서 접했던 문제지와 동일한 페이지로 구성했고, 청해 방송에서 듣던 MP3 음원을 고스란히 그대로 실었다. 또한 별도의 해설집에는 마치 실제 해설 강의를 듣는 것 같이 정확하게 핵심을 짚어 주는 문제 해설로 수험생들의 만족을 높이고자 했다.

새로운 TEPS 기출문제집 출간을 위해 넥서스 TEPS연구소에서 참으로 많이도 성가시게 해 드렸는데도 그간 늘 한결같이 적극적으로 도움을 주신 서울대학교 TEPS관리위원회 관계자분들께 이 자리를 통해 감사의 마음을 전한다. 본 교재를 통해 수험생 각자의 목표가 제대로 실현되기를 진심으로 바란다.

FEATURES

1

가장 최근에 공개된 공식 기출 1,200문항 독점 수록

서울대학교 TEPS관리위원회가 가장 최근에 공개한 현존 가장 최신 기출문제
1,200문항을 실제 TEPS 시험지와 동일한 페이지 구성으로 제공

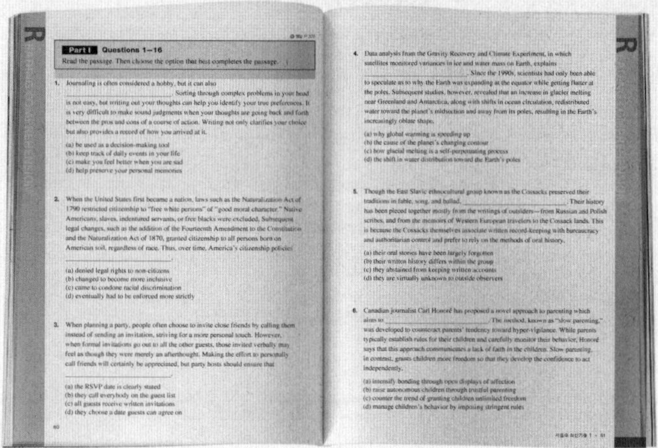

2

수험생들의 필살기 TEPS 만점 전략

청해–문법–어휘–독해 4영역 13개 파트에 대한 TEPS 출제 경향 및 고득점 대비
전략을 통합적으로 분석한 출제 비밀 노트 공개

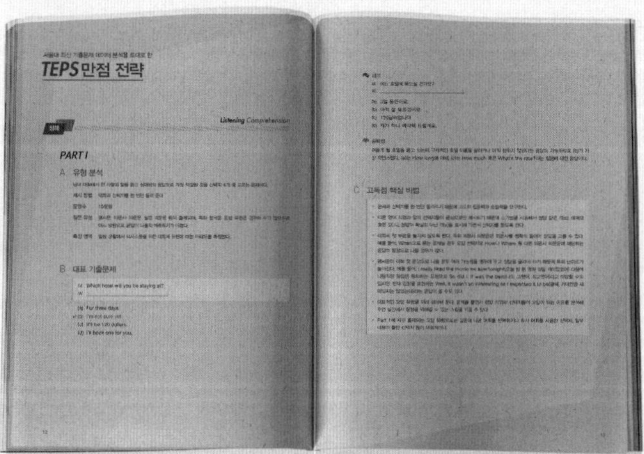

3 실제 강의를 듣는 것 같은 완전 해설

넥서스 TEPS연구소의 오랜 노하우가 살아 있는 정확한
해설로 오답과 문제 경향에 대한 속시원한 해결책 제시

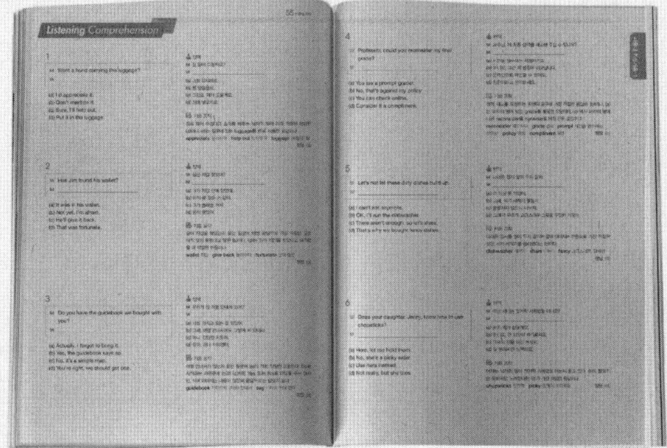

4 문제집과 해설집 별도 제작

학습자 편의를 위해 방대한 분량을 문제집과 해설집으로 별도 제작, 휴대하기 편할 뿐 아니라
학습 목적에 맞게 구매 가능

5 실제 고사장에서 듣던 청해 음성

정기 TEPS 고사장에서 청해 시험 시간에 사용했던 MP3 음원을 그대로 수록, 생생한 시험장 분위기 체험

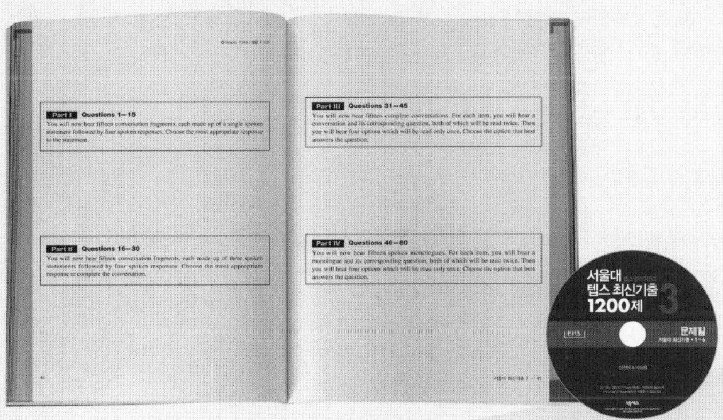

1

TEPS란?

❶ Test of English Proficiency developed by Seoul National University의 약자로 서울대학교 언어교육원에서 개발하고, TEPS관리위원회에서 주관하는 국가공인 영어시험

❷ 1999년 1월 처음 시행 이후 연 12~16회 실시

❸ 정부기관 및 기업의 직원 채용, 인사고과, 해외 파견 근무자 선발과 더불어 대학과 특목고 입학 및 졸업 자격 요건, 국가고시 및 자격 시험의 영어 대체 시험으로 활용

❹ 100여 명의 국내외 유수 대학의 최고 수준 영어 전문가들이 출제하고, 언어 테스팅 분야의 세계적인 권위자인 Bachman 교수(미국 UCLA)와 Oller 교수(미국 뉴멕시코대)로부터 타당성을 검증받음

❺ 말하기 – 쓰기 시험인 TEPS Speaking & Writing도 별도 실시 중이며, 2009년 10월부터 이를 통합한 *i*-TEPS 실시

2

TEPS 시험 구성

영역	Part별 내용	문항수	시간/배점
청해 **Listening Comprehension**	Part I : 문장 하나를 듣고 이어질 대화 고르기 Part II : 3문장의 대화를 듣고 이어질 대화 고르기 Part III : 6~8 문장의 대화를 듣고 질문에 해당하는 답 고르기 Part IV : 담화문의 내용을 듣고 질문에 해당하는 답 고르기	15 15 15 15	55분 400점
문법 **Grammar**	Part I : 대화문의 빈칸에 적절한 표현 고르기 Part II : 문장의 빈칸에 적절한 표현 고르기 Part III : 대화에서 어법상 틀리거나 어색한 부분 고르기 Part IV : 단문에서 문법상 틀리거나 어색한 부분 고르기	20 20 5 5	25분 100점
어휘 **Vocabulary**	Part I : 대화문의 빈칸에 적절한 단어 고르기 Part II : 단문의 빈칸에 적절한 단어 고르기	25 25	15분 100점
독해 **Reading Comprehension**	Part I : 지문을 읽고 빈칸에 들어갈 내용 고르기 Part II : 지문을 읽고 질문에 가장 적절한 내용 고르기 Part III : 지문을 읽고 문맥상 어색한 내용 고르기	16 21 3	45분 400점
총계	13개 Parts	200	140분 990점

☆ **IRT** (Item Response Theory)에 의하여 최고점이 990점, 최저점이 10점으로 조정됨.

3

TEPS 시험 응시 정보

현장 접수

❶ www.teps.or.kr에서 인근 접수처 확인

❷ 준비물: 응시료 39,000원(현금만 가능), 증명사진 1매(3×4 cm)

❸ 접수처 방문: 해당 접수기간 평일 12시~5시

인터넷 접수

❶ 서울대학교 TEPS관리위원회 홈페이지 접속 www.teps.or.kr

❷ 준비물: 스캔한 사진 파일, 응시료 결제를 위한 신용 카드 및 은행 계좌

❸ 응시료: 39,000원(일반) / 19,500원(군인) / 42,000원(추가 접수)

4

TEPS 시험 당일 정보

❶ 고사장 입실 완료: 9시 30분(일요일) / 2시 30분(토요일)

❷ 준비물: 신분증, 컴퓨터용 사인펜, 수정테이프, 수험표, 시계

❸ 유효한 신분증
　성인: 주민등록증, 운전면허증, 여권, 공무원증, 현역간부 신분증, 군무원증, 주민등록증 발급 신청 확인서, 외국인 등록증
　초·중고생: 학생증, 여권, 청소년증, 주민등록증(발급 신청 확인서), TEPS 신분확인 증명서

❹ 시험 시간: 2시간 20분 (중간에 쉬는 시간 없음, 각 영역별 제한시간 엄수)

❺ 성적 확인: 약 2주 후 인터넷에서 조회 가능

TEPS 만점 전략

청해

PART I

A 유형 분석

남녀 대화에서 한 사람의 말을 듣고 상대방의 응답으로 가장 적절한 것을 선택지 4개 중 고르는 문제이다.

제시 방법 대화와 선택지를 한 번만 들려준다.

문항수 15문항

질문 유형 평서문, 의문사 의문문, 일반 의문문 등이 출제되며, 특히 평서문 응답 유형은 경우의 수가 많으므로 어느 방향으로 응답이 나올지 예측하기가 어렵다.

측정 영역 일상 생활에서 의사소통을 위한 대화체 표현에 대한 이해도를 측정한다.

B 대표 기출문제

> M Which hotel will you be staying at?
> W __________________________________

  (a) For three days

✔ (b) I'm not sure yet.

  (c) It'll be 120 dollars.

  (d) I'll book one for you.

M 어느 호텔에 묵으실 건가요?
W ______________________________

(a) 3일 동안이요.
(b) 아직 잘 모르겠어요.
(c) 120달러입니다.
(d) 제가 하나 예약해 드릴게요.

머물게 될 호텔을 묻고 있는데 구체적인 호텔 이름을 말하거나 아직 정하지 않았다는 응답도 가능하므로 (b)가 가장 자연스럽다. (a)는 How long에 대해, (c)는 How much 혹은 What's the rate?라는 질문에 대한 응답이다.

C 고득점 핵심 비법

- 예전보다 Part 1도 많이 까다로워졌으며 문제와 선택지를 한 번만 들려주기 때문에 고도의 집중력과 순발력이 요구된다.

- 다른 영어 시험과 달리 선택지들이 음성으로만 제시되기 때문에 소거법을 사용해서 정답 같은 것(o), 애매모호한 것(△), 정답이 확실히 아닌 것(x)을 표시해 가면서 선택지를 듣도록 한다.

- 대화의 첫 부분을 놓치지 않도록 한다. 특히 의문사 의문문은 의문사를 정확히 들어야 정답을 고를 수 있다. 예를 들어, When으로 묻는 문제일 경우 오답 선택지로 How나 Where 등 다른 의문사 의문문에 해당하는 응답이 함정으로 나올 경우가 많다.

- 평서문이 대화 첫 문장으로 나올 경우 여러 가능성을 염두에 두고 정답을 골라야 하기 때문에 특히 난도가 높아진다. 예를 들어, I really liked the movie we saw tonight(오늘 밤 본 영화 정말 재미있었어) 다음에 동의하는 표현으로 So did I. It was the best(나도 그랬어. 최고였어)라고 대답할 수도 있지만, 반대 입장을 표현하는 Well, it wasn't so interesting as I expected it to be(글쎄, 기대만큼 재미있지는 않았는데)라는 응답이 올 수도 있다.

- 대표적인 오답 유형을 미리 정리해 둔다. 문제를 풀면서 정답 이외의 선택지들이 오답이 되는 이유를 분석해 두면 실전에서 함정을 피해갈 수 있는 스킬을 키울 수 있다.

- Part 1에 자주 출제되는 오답 유형으로는 질문에 나온 어휘를 반복하거나 유사 어휘를 사용한 선택지, 일부 내용이 틀린 선택지 등이 대표적이다.

PART II

A 유형 분석

남녀 대화에서 세 번째 대화까지 듣고 그 다음 이어질 응답으로 가장 자연스러운 것을 4개의 선택지 중에서 고르는 문제이다.

제시 방법 대화와 선택지를 한 번만 들려준다.

문항수 15문항

질문 유형 평서문, 의문사 의문문, 일반 의문문 등이 출제되며, 이 중 특히 평서문인 경우 어느 방향으로 응답이 나올지 예측하기 어렵다.

측정 영역 일상 대화 속 표현에 대한 이해도 측정이라는 점에서 Part 1과 동일한데, 이와 더불어 전반적인 대화 흐름의 이해도를 측정하기도 한다.

B 대표 기출문제

> M Nice car, Mia. It looks pretty new.
> W Really? It's actually a 2008 model.
> M It's certainly in good condition.
> W _______________________

(a) In that case, I'll buy it.

(b) I appreciate your advice.

✔ (c) Well, I take good care of it.

(d) True, but yours is no better.

💬 **해석**

M 미아, 차 좋다. 꽤 새 차 같은데.

W 정말? 실은 2008년 식이야.

M 상태가 아주 좋구나.

W _______________________

(a) 그렇다면 내가 살게.

(b) 네 충고 고마워.

(c) 음, 내가 관리를 많이 하거든.

(d) 맞아, 하지만 네 차라고 더 나을 것도 없어.

📶 공략법

여자가 연식에 비해서 차의 상태가 좋다고 칭찬을 했으므로 그만큼 많은 관리를 한다는 (c)가 남자의 응답으로 가장 적절하다. 충고가 아니라 칭찬이므로 (b)는 advice가 아닌 compliment가 되면 자연스러운 응답이 될 수 있다.

C   고득점 핵심 비법

- 한 번만 들려주는 세 줄의 대화를 정확하게 잘 듣도록 한다. 첫 문장을 잘 들어야 그 다음에 이어지는 두 줄의 대화를 잘 이해할 수 있기 때문에 Part 2 역시 고도의 집중력을 요한다.

- 만일 첫 줄을 놓쳤다면 당황하지 말고 그 다음 이어지는 두 줄의 대화를 잘 듣도록 한다. 가장 이상적인 청취는 세 줄을 다 알아듣는 것이지만, 혹시 그렇지 못하더라도 선택지가 나오기 직전의 말을 잘 들으면 자연스럽게 이어지는 응답을 고르는 데 도움이 된다.

- 소거법을 활용해서 정답을 고르는 것도 들려주기만 하는 선택지에 대처할 수 있는 한 방법이다.

- 남녀 각각 어떤 말을 했는지 구분해서 들어야 오답을 피해갈 수 있다.

- 풀어본 문제의 오답을 매번 분석해서 실전에서 신속하고 정확하게 오답을 피하도록 한다.

- Part 2의 대표적인 오답 유형으로는 대화의 앞부분을 일부 놓치고 착각해서 선택할 만한 선택지, 대화에 언급된 어휘로 만든 선택지, 대화에 등장한 어휘의 또 다른 의미를 가지고 만든 선택지, 질문한 사람이 이어서 할 만한 말로 만든 선택지 등이 있다.

PART III

A 유형 분석

남녀가 세 번씩 주고받는 대화를 듣고 4개의 선택지 중 질문에 가장 적절한 답을 고르는 문제이다.

제시 방법 대화 → 질문 → 대화 → 질문 → 선택지 순으로 들려준다.

문항수 15문항

질문 유형 대의 파악(7문항) → 세부 내용 파악(6문항) → 추론(3문항) 순으로 나온다.

측정 영역 일상 대화에 등장하는 다양한 표현에 대한 이해도를 바탕으로 전체 대의 파악, 세부 내용 파악, 추론 능력을 측정한다.

B 대표 기출문제

> M Any special plans for your two-week vacation?
> W I think I'll visit my family and relax somewhere.
> M Where do you plan on relaxing?
> W Oh, I don't know, maybe go somewhere warm.
> M What about Jeju island?
> W Actually, that sounds good. I'll put it on my list.

Q What is the main topic of the conversation?
(a) The best way to spend a vacation
✔ (b) The woman's vacation plans
(c) Popular holiday destinations
(d) Setting aside time to visit family

💬 해석

M 2주 휴가 동안 특별한 계획이 있나요?
W 집에 들렀다가 어디 가서 좀 쉴 생각이에요.
M 어디서 쉬려고 하는데요?
W 글쎄요. 모르겠어요. 아마 따뜻한 곳으로 가겠죠.
M 제주도는 어때요?
W 좋은 생각이네요. 그곳도 고려해 봐야겠어요.

Q 대화의 중심 소재는?
(a) 휴가를 보낼 가장 좋은 방법
(b) 여자의 휴가 계획
(c) 인기 있는 휴양지
(d) 가족을 방문하기 위한 시간을 남겨 놓기

🛜 공략법

대화의 중심 소재는 여자가 휴가 동안 무엇을 하는지이다. 가족을 방문하고 나서 어디로 가서 좀 쉴 거라는 말에 제주도를 권하고 있으므로 (b)가 가장 적절한 답이다. 따뜻한 곳이나 제주도라는 특정 지명을 언급하긴 했지만 인기 있는 휴양지 자체가 대화의 소재는 아니므로 (c)는 오답이다.

C 고득점 핵심 비법

- 처음 대화를 들을 때 전체 대화 내용을 파악한 뒤, 질문에 따라 집중할 부분에 더 집중하는 두 번째 듣기를 한다. 대화의 흐름을 파악해야 대의 파악 문제뿐 아니라 세부 내용 파악이나 추론 문제도 더 쉽게 풀 수 있다.

- 질문에 따라서 메모를 해야 하는 경우도 있다. 특히 세부 내용 파악 문제의 경우 숫자, 연도, 물건의 종류 등을 명확하게 기억하는 것이 유리하고, 남녀 각각 어떤 말을 했는지 구분해서 알아 두는 것이 오답을 피하는 데 많은 도움이 된다. 추론 능력은 대의 또는 세부 내용을 바탕으로 하기 때문에 세부 내용도 간과할 수 없다.

- 선택지를 한 번밖에 들려주지 않기 때문에 대화 내용을 다 이해하고도 선택지를 놓쳐서 정답을 고르지 못하는 경우가 있다. 이를 방지하기 위해 소거법을 적용해서 선택지를 차례대로 표시하면서 최종 정답을 고르도록 한다.

- 질문 종류별로 오답 확률이 높은 유형을 알아 두는 것도 도움이 된다.
  - 대의 파악 오답 유형: 대화 중 일부 세부 사항만 포함한 선택지, 너무 일반적인 내용의 선택지, 대화 중 특정 키워드를 조합한 전혀 엉뚱한 내용의 선택지 등이다.

  - 세부 내용 파악 오답 유형: 대화에서 언급된 어휘를 반복한 선택지, 대화와 전혀 무관한 선택지, 일부 내용만 사실인 선택지, 남녀의 역할이 뒤바뀐 선택지, 시제가 대화 내용과 일치하지 않는 선택지 등이 있다.

  - 추론 오답 유형: 상식적으로는 맞는 진술이지만 대화 내용과는 무관한 선택지, 대화에서 언급된 어휘로 만들었지만 대화 내용과 무관한 선택지, 추론 가능한 내용과 정반대인 선택지 등이 있다.

- 대의 파악이나 세부 내용 파악 유형에 대비해 패러프레이징(paraphrasing) 연습을 하는 것이 좋다. 대화에서 언급된 어휘가 그대로 사용된 경우는 오답일 확률이 높은 반면, 언급된 어휘를 비슷한 말로 바꾸어 만든 선택지는 정답일 확률이 높으므로 paraphrasing 연습이 많은 도움이 된다.

PART IV

A 유형 분석

담화문을 듣고 4개의 선택지 중 질문에 가장 적절한 정답을 고르는 문제이다.

제시 방법 담화문 → 질문 → 담화문 → 질문 → 선택지 순으로 들려준다.

문항수 15문항

질문 유형 대의 파악(7문항) → 세부 내용 파악(5문항) → 추론(3문항) 순으로 나온다.

측정 영역 연설, 강의, 라디오 방송 등에 나오는 다양한 표현에 대한 이해도 측정을 바탕으로 전체 대의 파악, 세부 내용 파악, 추론 능력을 측정한다.

B 대표 기출문제

Wildlife officials announced today that a tiny snail that could harm American river trout populations is spreading throughout the country. The New Zealand mud snail was first discovered in Idaho's Snake River in 1987. Since then, it has shown up in eight more rivers. The snails reproduce rapidly and destroy the habitat of trout and other aquatic life. Fishermen are being asked to clean their boots, fishing equipment and boats to prevent the snails from spreading from one river to another.

Q Which is correct according to the news report?
(a) American river trout are damaging waterways.
(b) Snails from the U.S. have been found in New Zealand.
✔ (c) It was in Snake River that the mud snail was first found.
(d) Fishermen have been asked to collect the snails they find.

🗨 해석

야생 생물 관계자는 오늘 미국 민물송어 개체군에 해를 끼칠 수 있는 작은 달팽이가 전국적으로 확산되고 있다고 발표했습니다. 뉴질랜드 진흙 달팽이는 1987년 아이다호 주 스네이크 강에서 처음으로 발견됐습니다. 그 이후 이 달팽이는 8개 강에 추가로 나타났습니다. 이 달팽이는 번식이 빠르고 송어 및 다른 수생 생물의 서식처를 파괴합니다. 이들 달팽이가 하나의 강에서 다른 강으로 확산되는 것을 막기 위해 어부에게 장화와 낚시 장비, 배를 청소하도록 요청하는 바입니다.

Q 뉴스 보도에 따르면 옳은 것은?
(a) 미국 민물송어는 수로를 손상시킨다.
(b) 미국산 달팽이가 뉴질랜드에서 발견되었다.
(c) 진흙 달팽이가 최초로 발견된 곳은 스네이크 강이었다.
(d) 발견한 진흙 달팽이를 어부들에게 채집하도록 요청했다.

🛜 공략법

외래종의 확산으로 발생하는 문제에 대한 내용이다. 두 번째 문장에서 진흙 달팽이가 스네이크 강에서 처음 발견되었다고 했으므로 (c)가 정답임을 쉽게 알 수 있다. (a)는 언급되지 않은 내용이며, (b)는 정반대 진술이다. 또한 어부들에게 달팽이의 확산을 막기 위해 노력해 달라고 했으므로 (d) 역시 오답이다.

C 고득점 핵심 비법

- 먼저 담화문의 전체 흐름을 파악한 뒤, 두 번째 듣기에서 질문과 연계된 부분에 집중하여 정확하게 듣는다.

- 질문 유형에 따라 맞춤식 메모를 한다. 특히 세부 사항 파악 유형 문제에 대비해서는 숫자, 연도, 물품 종류 등을 세세하게 메모해야 하고, 추론 능력은 대의 또는 세부 내용을 바탕으로 하기 때문에 세부 내용도 간과할 수 없다는 것을 기억한다.

- 질문 종류별로 오답일 확률이 높은 경우를 알아 두면 도움이 된다.
  - 대의 파악 오답 유형: 담화문 내용의 일부에 해당하는 세부 사항으로 만든 선택지, 주제와 관련은 있으나 너무 범위가 넓은 일반적인 내용의 선택지, 언급된 어휘로 구성된 점 외에는 내용과 전혀 관련이 없는 선택지 등이 오답일 확률이 높다.
  - 세부 내용 파악 오답 유형: 담화문에 언급된 어휘로 만들어진 선택지나 내용과 전혀 무관한 선택지, 일부만 사실인 선택지 등이 오답으로 제시될 가능성이 크다.
  - 추론 오답 유형: 상식적으로는 맞지만 내용과는 무관한 선택지, 담화문에서 언급된 어휘로 만들었지만 내용과는 무관한 선택지, 추론 가능한 내용과 정반대의 선택지 등이 종종 사용되는 오답 유형이다.

- 대의 파악이나 세부 내용 파악 유형의 문제를 대비하려면 paraphrasing 연습을 하는 것이 좋다. 언급된 어휘를 그대로 사용하면 오답일 확률이 높은 반면, 정답의 경우 언급된 어휘를 paraphrasing해서 만드는 경우가 많다.

PART I

A 유형 분석

두 줄의 대화문을 읽고 빈칸에 문법적으로 적절한 표현을 4개의 선택지 중에서 고르는 문제이다.

제시 방법   두 줄의 대화문이 주어진다.

문항수   20문항

측정 영역   실시간과 비슷한 시간 제약 속에서 문법적으로 정확한 영어를 대화 속에서 구사할 수 있는지 측정한다.

빈출 토픽   일상 생활 대화 중에 흔히 접할 수 있는 주제가 많이 사용되므로 청해나 어휘 영역의 대화 부분과 비슷한 내용이 나온다.

B 대표 기출문제

> A   Don't take that last cookie. It's for Dan.
>
> B   But he ___________________ all the cookies last time.

✔ (a) ate
 (b) eats
 (c) has eaten
 (d) had been eating

💬 **해석**

A   마지막 쿠키 먹지 마. 댄 줄 거니까.
B   하지만 댄은 지난번에 쿠키를 다 먹었잖아요.

📡 **공략법**

시제 문제는 함께 쓰이는 시간의 부사에서 힌트를 찾아야 한다. 이 문장에서는 last time이 시간의 부사 역할을 하고 있다. last는 지난 일을 나타내므로 항상 과거 시제와 함께 쓰인다. 따라서 (a)가 정답이다.

C 고득점 핵심 비법

- 정확한 영어를 적재적소에 사용하는 능력이 중요하므로 눈으로만 익히는 문법 지식을 배제한다. 대화체를 소리 내어 읽는 연습을 해서 문법이 내재화되어 상황에 맞게 즉각적으로 사용할 수 있는 수준까지 끌어올리도록 한다.

- 문법 네 가지 Part 중 비교적 평이한 수준이기 때문에 시간 안배 차원에서 신속하게 풀고 다음 Part로 넘어가도록 한다. 단, 첫 줄은 빈칸에 올 적절한 답을 찾는 데 단서가 되므로 생략하고 넘어가면 함정에 빠지는 경우가 종종 있다. 신속하게 문제를 읽어나가되 읽지 않고 건너뛰는 일은 없어야 한다.

- 문법 문제의 빈칸은 주로 두 번째 줄에 오지만 일부 문제는 첫 번째 줄에 빈칸이 오기도 한다. 이런 유형에서는 두 번째 줄을 제대로 읽어야 출제자의 함정에 걸려들지 않는다. 즉, 빈칸 위치에 상관없이 문제에 나오는 대화는 모두 다 읽고 정확한 내용을 파악해야 오답 함정을 피해 정답을 찾을 수 있다.

- 문법 문제라고 해서 대화의 문법적인 요소만 신경 쓰면 안 된다. 상황에 적절한 어법을 고른다는 자세로 문제를 풀도록 한다. 예를 들어 대화 내용에 현재 시제가 여러 개 나온다고 무조건 현재 시제를 답으로 고르면 오히려 오답일 경우가 많다.

- 일상 대화 구문의 어법을 묻는 Part이므로 대화체의 정확한 표현을 익히는 것이 도움이 된다. 즉, 문법책의 모든 문법 요소를 처음부터 공부하는 것보다는 일상 대화 구문 표현 위주로 외울 수 있는 수준까지 익혀 두면 짧은 시간 내에 정확하게 구사할 수 있는 표현들이 많아지고 이렇게 되면 문법 Part 1도 쉽게 정복할 수 있다.

PART II

A 유형 분석

하나의 문장을 읽고 빈칸에 문법적으로 가장 적절한 표현을 4개의 선택지 중에서 고른다.

제시 방법   하나의 문어체 문장이 주어진다.

문항수   20문항

측정 영역   문어체 영어의 정확한 어법 구사력을 측정한다.

빈출 토픽   학술문과 실용문 등 일상에서 접하는 문어체 문장에 언급되는 주제가 주로 사용된다.

B 대표 기출문제

> ___________________ the movie twice, Bob did not want to see it again.

    (a) He had seen
    (b) Had he seen
✔ (c) Having seen
    (d) To have seen

💬 **해석**

그 영화를 두 번 봤기 때문에 밥은 그것을 또 보고 싶지 않았다.

📶 **공략법**

접속사가 없으므로 (a)와 같은 완전한 절은 올 수 없다. (d)와 같은 to부정사는 문두에 오면 보통 목적의 의미를 가지므로 문맥상 어울리지 않는다. 따라서 빈칸에는 분사구문이 나와야 하는데 주절의 주어 Bob이 영화를 직접 본 것이므로 능동의 현재분사 (c)가 정답이다. 영화를 본 것이 먼저 일어난 일이므로 완료분사 Having seen을 썼다.

C 고득점 핵심 비법

- 구어체 문장보다 문어체 문장의 의미 파악이 까다로울 수 있으므로 평상시 문어체 문장의 직독직해 연습을 충분히 한다. 특히 관계사들로 연결된 문장, 절 안에 또 다른 절이 있는 문장 등 복잡한 문장을 평상시에 많이 접해 보도록 하자. 난해한 문장을 만났을 때 바로 의미를 파악할 수 있어야 문법 Part 2 문제를 신속하게 해결할 수 있다.

- 주어와 동사가 여러 개 나오는 긴 문장은 주절의 주어와 동사를 파악한 후, 다른 문법 사항들을 따져 보도록 한다. 특히 대표 빈출 유형이자 기본이 되는 주어–동사 수 일치 문제는 주절의 주어와 동사를 파악해야만 풀 수 있는 문제이다.

- TEPS 시험에서는 한국인이 특히 취약한 관사와 문장 구조 등에 대해 묻는 문제가 다수 출제된다. 이를 대비하기 위해서는 문장 내 쓰임새를 익혀 두는 것이 낱낱의 문법 지식을 알고 있는 것보다 신속하고 정확하게 문제를 푸는 데 많은 도움을 줄 것이다. 영어 활용 능력 수준 측정을 위해 TEPS가 고안된 점을 염두에 두고, 평소에 정확한 영어 구사 능력 함양에 집중하도록 한다.

- 문법 Part 1과 마찬가지로 정확한 어법을 익히려면 청해 Part 4 긴 담화문 속에 나오는 문장이나 어휘 Part 2 문장을 익혀 두는 것도 좋다. 각 분야별 어휘와 구문에 익숙해질수록 읽고 이해하는 속도가 자연히 빨라지게 되고, 아울러 문장 안에서 정확한 쓰임새도 익힐 수 있기 때문이다.

PART III

A 유형 분석

네 줄의 대화문을 읽고 문법적으로 이상한 부분이 있는 문장을 고르는 유형의 문제이다.

제시 방법　네 줄의 대화문이 주어진다.

문항수　5문항

측정 영역　길어진 대화에서 비문법적 요소를 가려내는 능력을 측정한다.

빈출 토픽　일상 생활에서 접하는 대화에 나오는 주제가 주로 사용된다.

B 대표 기출문제

> (a)　A　Let's go to an amusement park this weekend.
> ✔ (b)　B　Well, that's not what I had planned during the weekend.
> (c)　A　Oh, are you going to do anything special?
> (d)　B　Actually, I just want to stay home and relax.

💬 **해석**

(a)　**A**　이번 주말에 놀이공원에 가자.

(b)　**B**　음, 그건 내가 주말에 계획한 게 아닌데.

(c)　**A**　아, 뭐 특별한 거라도 하게?

(d)　**B**　실은 그냥 집에서 쉬고 싶어서.

📡 **공략법**

과거완료 had p.p.는 과거보다 더 앞선 시제를 나타낼 때 쓰므로 (b)에서처럼 현재 시제와 함께 쓸 수 없다. 다른 계획을 세운 것은 과거의 일이므로 had planned가 아니라 단순과거인 planned가 되어야 한다.

C 고득점 핵심 비법

- 주어진 선택지가 따로 없어서 어떤 문법에 관한 문제인지 전혀 알 수 없고 주어진 대화 내용을 읽으면서 틀린 부분을 골라야 하기 때문에 보다 적극적인 태도로 문제에 임해야 한다. 즉, 각 대화에서 어느 문법 요소가 틀렸는지 모르는 상태에서 틀린 부분을 찾아야 하기 때문에 대화 내용을 파악함과 동시에 모든 품사와 구문 요소가 정확한지도 일일이 확인하는 습관을 평소에 들여야 당황하지 않고 실전에서 실력 발휘를 할 수 있다.

- 주어진 시간 내에 틀린 문법 사항을 골라야 하기 때문에 즉각적으로 비문법적인 부분을 찾아내는 훈련이 평상시에 필요하다. 이렇게 하기 위해서는 다른 문법 Part의 문제 대비와 마찬가지로 일상 대화 및 학술문과 실용문을 많이 접해서 다양한 문장에 익숙해져야 한다.

- 모든 문법 학습 요소들이 다 출제되는 것이 아니라 단골로 출제되는 문법 사항이 있음을 알자. 문장 구조, 시제, 수 일치, 관사 등에 해당하는 문법 요소들을 집중해서 훈련하는 것도 단기간에 Part 3을 정복할 수 있는 길이다. 물론, Part 3 역시 제한된 문법 사항에만 국한해 다른 문법 요소를 무시했다가 낭패를 볼 수 있다는 것을 유의하자.

- Part 4에 비해 짧은 대화체라 약간 수월하게 보일 수 있겠지만 선택지가 주어진 Part 1과 2보다는 고난도인 경우가 많다. 특히 재빨리 읽으면서 틀린 문법 사항도 찾아내야 하므로 평상시 대화문의 정확도를 분석하는 것도 실전에서 틀린 부분을 파악히는 데 도움이 될 것이디. 즉, 정답을 찾는 데에만 급급하지 말고 힌 문제를 풀더라도 문법적으로 옳고 그른 부분들에 대한 분석을 자세히 하다 보면 실전에서 당황하지 않고 틀린 부분을 찾아낼 수 있다는 것이다.

PART IV

A 유형 분석

4개의 문어체 문장을 읽고 문법적으로 어색한 부분이 있는 문장을 고르는 유형의 문제이다.

제시 방법   4개의 문어체 문장이 하나의 지문으로 주어진다.

문항수   5문항

측정 영역   문어체 문장으로 구성된 지문에서 비문법적인 요소를 가려내는 능력을 측정한다.

빈출 토픽   신문, 잡지, 교재 등 일상 생활에서 문어체로 접하게 되는 주제가 등장한다.

B 대표 기출문제

> ✔ (a) In a study, separate groups of men was asked to run as hard and as long as possible on a treadmill. (b) Each group was cheered and encouraged, but at different intervals— either every 20, 60 or 180 seconds. (c) Researchers perceived no gains among those who were given verbal cues every 180 seconds. (d) It was found, however, that performance did improve for men cheered every 20 or 60 seconds.

💬 **해석**

(a) 한 연구에서 서로 다른 남성 집단에게 러닝머신 위에서 최대한 빨리 그리고 최대한 오래 달리도록 요구했다. (b) 각 집단은 각각 20초, 60초, 180초 간격으로 응원과 격려를 받았다. (c) 연구자들은 180초마다 응원을 받은 사람들에게는 이득이 없다는 것을 발견했다. (d) 그러나 20초, 혹은 60초마다 응원을 받은 남성들의 경우는 성과가 실제로 향상되었음이 밝혀졌다.

📶 **공략법**

A of B 형태에서 동사는 A와 일치시킨다. (a)에서 주어 separate groups of men의 동사는 groups와 일치시켜 복수 동사를 취해야 하므로 was를 were로 고친다.

C 고득점 핵심 비법

- Part 3 대화체에 비해 Part 4는 지문 길이도 더 길고 문어체라서 내용 파악이 훨씬 더 어렵고 시간도 가장 많이 걸린다. 그렇기 때문에 비문법적인 요소를 찾기가 특히 더 어려울 수 있으므로 신속하게 문어체 문장들을 읽고 직독직해를 통해 내용을 즉시 파악할 수 있는 능력을 평상시에 훈련하도록 한다.

- 지문 내용은 물론 문제에서 요구하는 문법 사항 예측이 어렵기 때문에 더욱 적극적인 문제 풀이 전략이 필요하다. 4개의 문장을 읽으면서 내용 파악을 하는 동시에 모든 가능성을 열어 두고 비문법적으로 보이는 부분을 찾아 나가야 하는데 이때 가능성이 있는 부분을 일단 밑줄 그어 놓은 뒤 신속하게 다시 그 부분들을 재확인하는 것도 정확도를 높이는 한 방법이 될 수 있다.

- 주어진 시간 내에 틀린 문법 사항을 골라야 하기 때문에 즉각적으로 비문법적인 부분을 찾아내는 훈련이 필요하다. 이를 위해서는 정확한 표현을 즉각적으로 사용할 수 있을 정도로 알고 있어야 한다. 즉, Part 3 대비를 위해서 대화체를 많이 익혀 둠으로써 신속하게 비문법적인 대화 부분을 알아차리는 훈련을 하듯이, Part 4 대비책으로 학술문과 실용문을 접하면서 거의 암기할 정도로 정독하는 것도 문법 내재화를 도울 것이며, 이런 훈련 과정을 거치고 나면 자연스럽게 틀린 부분이 눈에 잘 띌 것이다.

- Part 2에 나오는 문장 네 개가 한꺼번에 출제된다고 생각하면 좀 부담이 덜어질 것이고 Part 2 문장들에서 문법적 오류를 찾는다고 생각하면 이제 마음도 편해질 것이다.

  - 시제 문제: 각 문장마다 여러 시제가 혼합되어 있는 경우가 대부분이기 때문에 시제의 형태만 참고해서 틀린 시제를 찾는 것은 거의 불가능하다고 봐야 한다. 내용 파악이 선행되어야만 시제가 잘못 쓰인 곳을 찾을 수 있다.

  - 관사 문제: a와 the의 쓰임 여부는 4개 문장에서 어떤 명사가 이미 앞서 언급된 것이고 아닌지를 이해한 후에 결정되므로 내용 파악이 우선되어야 한다.

PART I

A 유형 분석

두 줄의 대화문을 읽고 빈칸에 가장 잘 어울리는 어휘를 고르는 문제이다.

제시 방법   두 줄의 대화문이 주어진다.

문항수   25문항

측정 영역   대화에서 사용하는 구어체 표현을 적절하게 활용할 수 있는지 측정한다.

빈출 토픽   일상 생활과 관련 있는 주제가 많이 출제된다.

B 대표 기출문제

> A   What took you so long to get here?
> B   Sorry, I was _________________ a meeting.

✔ (a) attending
  (b) including
  (c) reducing
  (d) skipping

💬 **해석**

A   여기 오는 데 왜 이렇게 오래 걸렸니?
B   미안. 회의에 참석했었어.

(a) 참석하다
(b) 포함하다
(c) 줄이다
(d) 건너뛰다

📶 **공략법**

시간이 오래 걸린 이유를 묻고 있으므로 회의에 '참석했다'는 문장이 되어야 한다. '참석하다'는 의미의 동사 (a) attend는 다음에 전치사를 쓰지 않는 타동사이므로 attend a meeting이 된다.

C 고득점 핵심 비법

- 짧은 시간 내에 문맥에 어울리는 어휘를 골라야 하기 때문에 많은 어휘를 알고 있는 것뿐만 아니라 문맥(context)에 적절한 어휘를 사용할 수 있는 능력을 키우는 것도 중요하다. 따라서 어휘를 처음 접할 때엔 참고 자료를 동원해서 문장 내에서 쓰이는 다양한 예문을 동시에 익혀 두어야 한다. 시간 내에 모든 어휘 문제를 잘 풀기 위해서는 특히 문맥 속에서 각 어휘의 쓰임을 거의 외우다시피 알고 있어야 시간 낭비 없이 즉각적으로 빈칸에 올 정답을 고를 수 있을 것이다.

- 해당 어휘의 우리말을 단순하게 암기하는 것은 별 도움이 안 된다. 우리말로는 그럴듯해도 쓰임이 어색한 어휘의 뉘앙스 차이를 구분할 줄 알아야 하므로 문장 전체로 어휘를 이해하는 것이 장기적으로 유리하다.

- 청해의 대화 파트뿐만 아니라 문법 Part 1과 3에 언급된 대화들도 어휘 실력 향상을 위해 활용될 수 있음을 기억하고 어휘 영역 이외의 빈출 표현도 문맥 속에서 익혀 두도록 한다.

- 대화를 신속히 읽고 즉각적으로 빈칸을 채워 넣어야 하기 때문에 실제 대화를 하면서 적절한 어휘를 사용할 수 있을 정도의 실력이 되도록 많은 표현을 통째로 익혀 두어야 한다.

- 일상적인 대화 속에서 자주 등장하는 어휘뿐만 아니라 이어동사, 이디엄 등도 출제되므로 숙지해 두도록 한다.

- 형태상·의미상 혼동되는 어휘, 의미 덩어리로 사용되는 연어 등의 정확한 활용법도 아울러 알아 둔다.

PART II

A 유형 분석

한 개의 문어체 문장을 읽고 빈칸에 가장 잘 어울리는 어휘를 고르는 문제이다.

제시 방법 한 개의 문어체 문장이 주어진다.

문항수 25문항

측정 영역 일상 생활에서 접할 수 있는 문어체 표현을 문맥에 맞게 사용할 수 있는지 측정한다.

빈출 토픽 학술문뿐만 아니라 실용문에 이르기까지 매우 다양한 주제를 다룬다.

B 대표 기출문제

> To ___________________ military messages over radio, a secret code based on a Native American language was used by the US in World War II.

   (a) infuse
   (b) conflict
✔ (c) transmit
   (d) intercept

💬 **해석**

무선으로 군사 메시지를 전송하기 위해, 제2차 세계대전 당시 미국은 인디언 언어를 기반으로 한 비밀 코드를 사용했다.

   (a) 불어넣다
   (b) 상충하다
   (c) 전송하다
   (d) 가로막다

📶 **공략법**

목적어가 메시지이기 때문에 '보내다, 전송하다'는 의미의 동사가 필요하다. 따라서 답은 (c)이다. 접두어 trans-에는 이동의 의미가 있다.

C 고득점 핵심 비법

- 학술문과 실용문의 주제별 빈출 어휘를 익혀 둔다. 빈출 어휘는 정답 선택지뿐만 아니라 오답 선택지에 나오는 어휘도 포함한다. 주제별로 자주 출제되는 어휘는 한정되어 있기 때문에 기출 어휘가 다시 출제될 확률이 높다.

- Part1과 마찬가지로 각 어휘의 쓰임새를 알아야 하기 때문에 전체 문장을 익히도록 한다. 그래야만 문법적으로도 정확한 어휘 활용 능력을 키울 수 있기 때문이다.

- 미묘한 뉘앙스 차이가 있는 쉬운 어휘의 용례 예문을 적극적으로 활용해야 한다. 의미가 비슷해 보이는 어휘들끼리 묶어서 따로 정리하면 도움이 될 것이다.

- 신문 기사, 잡지, 광고, 학술지, 비평 등의 실용문과 전문적인 학술문에서 다양하게 출제되므로 평상시 이런 종류의 글을 많이 접하는 것이 도움이 된다. 15분이라는 짧은 시간 내에 50문항이나 되는 문제를 무리 없이 풀기 위한 대비법 중 하나가 주제별로 다양한 문장을 평소에 자주 읽는 것이다. 이렇게 함으로써 필수 어휘를 자주 접할 수 있을 뿐만 아니라 문장 이해 속도도 향상될 수 있다.

- 대화체 문제와 마찬가지로 주제별 어휘뿐만 아니라 연어 및 형태상·의미상 혼동되는 어휘도 잘 알아 두도록 한다.

PART I

A   유형 분석

100단어 내외의 단일 지문을 읽고 빈칸에 들어갈 적절한 선택지를 고르는 문제이다. 14문항은 구나 절을 고르는 문제이고, 나머지 2문항은 문장과 문장 사이를 이어주는 연결어를 찾는 문제이다.

제시 방법   지문의 처음 문장이나 마지막 문장, 드물게 중간 문장에 빈칸이 있는 한 개의 글이 주어진다.

문항수   16문항

측정 영역   글의 전반적인 이해 능력 및 논리적인 흐름 파악 능력을 평가한다.

빈출 토픽   학술문과 실용문에서 골고루 출제된다.

B   대표 기출문제

> Deerbar's annual sale is now on! To make way for next year's new models, Deerbar is selling off its entire remaining inventory at wholesale prices! This week only, get heavily discounted refrigerators, washer-dryer combos, freezers and microwaves. We will even include free delivery anywhere within the city limits! Don't delay. If you want ________________________, come to Deerbar!

(a) this year's latest kitchen gear
(b) fashionable home furnishings
✔ (c) deals on major home appliances
(d) affordable equipment for the office

해석

디어바 연례 세일 중입니다! 내년도 신형 모델 입고를 위해 디어바에서는 남아 있는 전 재고 물량을 도매가에 처분하고 있습니다. 이번 주 단 한 주, 폭탄 세일가로 냉장고, 세탁기–건조기 콤보, 냉동고와 전자레인지를 들여가십시오. 시 경계 내라면 어디든 무료 배달까지 해 드립니다! 미루지 마십시오. 저렴한 가격의 주요 가전제품을 원하시면 디어바로 오십시오!

(a) 올해의 최신 부엌용품을
(b) 유행하는 가구를
(c) 저렴한 가격의 주요 가전제품을
(d) 적정한 가격의 사무용 장비를

디어바의 연례 세일 광고이다. 이 가게에서 취급하는 물건은 냉장고, 세탁기, 전자레인지 등이므로 가전제품을 구매하려고 하는 사람을 대상으로 하는 광고임을 알 수 있다. 가전제품은 home appliances라고 하며 정답은 (c)이다.

C 고득점 핵심 비법

- 모든 지문을 자세히 읽겠다는 생각을 접는다. 1분에 한 문제씩 풀어야 하기 때문에 정독을 하기에는 절대적으로 시간이 부족하므로 주요 어휘 위주로 대의 파악 및 흐름 파악에 주력해야 시간 내에 문제를 다 풀 수 있다.

- 주제별 어휘를 평소 많이 알아 둔다. 청해, 문법, 어휘 등 TEPS의 다른 영역과 마찬가지로 방대한 어휘 지식을 갖추고 있어야 독해 속도도 빨라지고 정확한 이해가 가능하다.

- 빈칸의 위치에 따라 독해의 목적이 달라져야 한다. 빈칸이 첫 문장에 있는 경우 대의 파악만 해도 되지만 마지막 문장에 올 때에는 대의 파악뿐만 아니라 논리적 흐름도 염두에 두면서 독해를 해야 한다.

- 오답 함정 선택시 유형을 연습해 둔다.

  – 지문에 나오는 어휘로 만들었지만 문맥과 전혀 상관없는 선택지

  – 너무 일반적인 내용으로 만든 선택지

  – 상식적으로는 괜찮아 보이지만 내용과는 무관한 선택지

  – 지문 내용의 일부처럼 보이기는 하지만 논리적인 흐름 면에서는 어울리지 않는 선택지

PART II

A 유형 분석

100단어 내외의 단일 지문을 읽고 주어진 질문에 적절한 답을 4개의 선택지에서 고르는 유형이다.

제시 방법 한 개의 지문에 한 개의 질문이 주어진다.

문항수 21문항

측정 영역 단일 지문에 대한 전체 및 세부 내용 이해 및 추론 능력을 측정한다.
대의 파악(6문항) → 세부 내용 파악(10문항) → 추론(5문항) 순으로 나온다.

빈출 토픽 학술문과 실용문에서 모두 골고루 출제된다.

B 대표 기출문제

> Sam Cantwell and Jack Hansen are two of America's best-loved motivational speakers. They have each delighted thousands of listeners with their wit and wisdom, and now—in a never-before-held event—they have teamed up to create a unique, doubly rewarding experience. Join them as they tell their favorite tales of inspiration at Chancellor Hall this Friday and Saturday only, from 8:00 pm. Tickets are available at the door, or you may purchase tickets in advance through www.ticketsite.com.

Q What can be inferred about Cantwell and Hansen from the passage?

(a) They will stay together for a national tour.

(b) They are not likely to attract high ticket sales.

✔ (c) They are appearing together for the first time.

(d) They will give talks advocating a religious doctrine.

💬 해석

샘 캔트웰과 잭 핸슨은 미국 내에서 가장 사랑받는 두 명의 동기부여 연사입니다. 이들은 각각 재치와 지혜로 수천 명의 청중들에게 기쁨을 주었으며, 이제 과거에 유례없던 한 행사를 통해 이들이 의기투합하여 독특하며 두 배로 보람 있는 경험을 만들고자 합니다. 이번 주 금요일과 토요일 단 이틀, 오후 8시부터 챈슬러 홀에서 이들이 가장 좋아하는 감동의 이야기를 들려주는 자리에 함께하십시오. 입장권은 행사장에서 구매 가능하며, www.ticketsite.com 을 통해 예매를 하실 수도 있습니다.

Q 캔트웰과 핸슨에 대해 유추할 수 있는 것은?

(a) 전국 투어를 함께 다닐 것이다.

(b) 높은 입장권 판매를 유치할 것 같지 않다.

(c) 처음으로 함께 출연한다.

(d) 종교적 교의를 옹호하는 이야기를 할 것이다.

두 번째 문장에서 언급한 과거에 유례없는 행사(a never-before-held event)라는 표현으로 보아 두 사람의 연사가 함께 출연하는 것이 처음임을 추론할 수 있다. 따라서 정답은 (c)이다. (a)와 (b)는 지문의 내용만으로는 알 수 없으며, 사람들에게 영감을 주고 동기를 부여해 주는 내용의 연설을 할 것으로 예상되므로 (d)도 오답이다.

C 고득점 핵심 비법

- 직독직해하는 습관을 들인다. 우리말로 해석부터 하려고 덤벼들지 말고 신속하게 영어 지문을 읽으면서 내용을 이해하는 습관을 들여야 한다.

- 지문을 다 읽겠다는 생각을 버려라. 대의 파악 문제의 경우 주요 내용어 중심으로 읽고, 세부 내용 파악 문제는 질문에 따라 선택지의 진위 여부를 한 개씩 확인해 가며 읽거나 육하원칙 문제는 질문 내용을 제대로 파악하고 해당 부분을 신속히 찾아서 그 부분을 자세히 읽는다. 추론 문제는 대의 파악 및 세부 내용 파악이 선행되어야 하기 때문에 좀 더 시간을 할애해야 할 것이다.

- 오답 함정을 각 문제 유형마다 미리 알아 두고 잘 피하도록 한다.
  - 대의 파악 오답 유형 : 세부 사실을 대의로 혼동하게 하는 오답이 자주 출제된다.

  - 세부 내용 파악 오답 유형 : 일부 내용만 사실인 경우, 지문에서 언급된 어휘로 만들었지만 내용과는 상관없는 선택지를 주의하자.

  - 추론 오답 유형 : 그럴듯해 보이지만 지문 내용과는 상관없는 오답, 정답과 정반대 진술이 선택지로 제시되기도 한다.

PART III

A 유형 분석

5개의 문장으로 구성된 100단어 내외의 단일 지문을 읽고 글의 흐름상 어색한 문장을 찾는 유형의 문제이다.

제시 방법	주제문에 이어 4개의 문장이 제시된다.
문항수	3문항
측정 영역	지문의 응집력 파악 능력을 측정한다.
빈출 지문 토픽	학술문과 실용문 모두 골고루 출제된다.

B 대표 기출문제

See the memorable sights of London with Black Taxi Tours! (a) Our tour is the only one where you can enjoy seeing the sites of London in genuine London taxi cabs. (b) A detailed commentary from a trained London cabbie is included in your comprehensive two-hour tour. ✓ (c) To become a cabbie in London, you must have an extensive knowledge of the city's roads. (d) You won't find a better guide than our cabbies, so call our office now to book your tour.

해석

블랙 택시 관광으로 기억에 남을 런던 명승지를 돌아보세요! (a) 저희 관광은 진짜 런던 택시를 타고 런던의 관광지를 즐길 수 있는 유일한 관광 상품입니다. (b) 숙련된 런던 택시 기사의 자세한 해설이 전체 2시간 관광에 포함되어 있습니다. (c) 런던에서 택시 기사가 되려면 런던의 도로에 대한 해박한 지식이 있어야 합니다. (d) 저희 기사들보다 더 나은 가이드는 찾을 수 없을 것입니다. 그러니 지금 저희 사무실로 전화하셔서 블랙 택시 관광을 예약하십시오.

공략법

런던 택시를 이용한 관광을 홍보하는 광고문으로, 택시 관광에 대한 간단한 안내와 함께 빨리 예약을 하라는 광고 문구가 나와 있는 글이다. 그러나 (c)에는 관광과는 관련없는, 택시 기사가 되기 위해 필요한 조건이 나와 있으므로 전체 문맥과 어울리지 않는다.

C 고득점 핵심 비법

- 처음 제시되는 주제문에서 벗어난 문장을 찾는 것이므로 4개의 선택지 문장을 읽을 때에 항상 주제문과의 연관성을 염두에 두고 읽도록 한다. 문법 Part 4의 경우 각 문장 간의 연관성까지 염두에 두고 내용을 파악할 필요는 없으나 독해 Part 3에서는 주제문과의 연관성이 문제 풀이의 핵심이다.

- 주제문과 연관성은 있으나 문장의 위치가 잘못되어 흐름을 깨는 유형도 있으니 흐름상 잘 어울리는지도 살피도록 한다.

- 글의 어조가 갑자기 바뀌는 경우도 어색한 문장에 해당하므로 어조의 변화도 주의하도록 한다.

- 주어진 주제문에 대한 문장이 3개 나온 뒤 새로운 주제문이 4번째 문장으로 나오게 되면 어색한 문장이 된다는 것도 기억한다.

서울대
최신기출

1

Listening Comprehension

Grammar

Vocabulary

Reading Comprehension

LISTENING COMPREHENSION

DIRECTIONS

1. In the Listening Comprehension section, all content will be presented orally rather than in written form.

2. This section contains four parts, each with fifteen individual items. For each part, you will receive separate instructions. Listen to the instructions carefully, and choose the best answer from the options for each item.

Part I   **Questions 1—15**

You will now hear fifteen individual spoken questions or statements, each followed by four spoken responses. Choose the most appropriate response for each item.

Part II   **Questions 16—30**

You will now hear fifteen short conversation fragments, followed by four spoken responses. Choose the most appropriate response to complete each conversation.

Part III   Questions 31—45

You will now hear fifteen complete conversations. For each conversation, you will be asked to answer a question. Each conversation and its corresponding question will be read twice. Then you will hear four options which will be read only once. Based on the given information, choose the option that best answers the question.

Part IV   Questions 46—60

You will now hear fifteen short talks. After each talk, you will be asked to answer a question. Each talk and its corresponding question will be read twice. Then you will hear four options which will be read only once. Based on the given information, choose the option that best answers the question.

GRAMMAR

DIRECTIONS

This section tests your grammar skills. You will have 25 minutes to complete the 50 questions. Be sure to follow the directions given by the proctor.

Part I Questions 1—20

Choose the option that best completes each gap.

---

1. A: Is it totally necessary to clean the kitchen now?

B: There won't be time later, so we ___________ do it right away.

(a) may
(b) could
(c) would
(d) have to

2. A: You're still in touch with your school friends?

B: Of course. I find that childhood friendships ___________ the longest.

(a) last
(b) lasts
(c) was lasting
(d) were lasting

3. A: Was that call from a telemarketer?

B: Yes, it was another salesperson ___________ to get me to buy something.

(a) tried
(b) to try
(c) trying
(d) is trying

4. A: Did it really take two extra hours to drive home yesterday?

B: Yeah, the traffic was ___________ bad!

(a) far
(b) that
(c) such
(d) much

5. A: Your garden gets plenty of attention.

B: I know. ___________ people pass it without admiring it.

(a) The
(b) Few
(c) Both
(d) Little

6. A: What kind of car will you get when you trade in your old one?

B: I ___________. Maybe an SUV.

(a) don't decide
(b) hadn't decided
(c) wasn't deciding
(d) haven't decided

7. A: Will Lucy be home when we get back?

B: No. She ___________ by the time we arrive.

(a) has left
(b) had left
(c) will have left
(d) will have been leaving

8. A: I'm going out for a stroll.

B: I'd rather you ___________ late at night.

(a) not walk around alone this
(b) not walk around alone when is
(c) do not walk around alone this is
(d) do not walk around alone when this

9. A: John, where are you planning to live after retirement?

    B: I long ____________ to my hometown of Sicily, but I'm not sure yet.

    (a) return
    (b) to return
    (c) returning
    (d) to have returned

10. A: Do we get marks for class participation?

    B: Yes. Your participation mark ____________ your general involvement in discussions.

    (a) reflects
    (b) reflected
    (c) is reflected
    (d) was reflected

11. A: How was the intern's work?

    B: Honestly ____________, I think it could be better.

    (a) spoken
    (b) to speak
    (c) speaking
    (d) to be speaking

12. A: What did the finance committee say?

    B: Well, they recommended that the company ____________ its funds from the more volatile investments.

    (a) withdraw
    (b) withdrew
    (c) will withdraw
    (d) has withdrawn

13. A: You finally finished your PhD!

    B: Yeah, it took me eight years, which ____________ my plan.

    (a) isn't
    (b) aren't
    (c) wasn't
    (d) weren't

14. A: Why are you selling your car?

    B: I can't afford the monthly payments. If only I ____________ a cheaper one!

    (a) will buy
    (b) would buy
    (c) had bought
    (d) have bought

15. A: Your grandmother seems kind, but she has high expectations.

    B: Yes. She's very loving, ____________ a bit demanding on occasion.

    (a) if
    (b) as
    (c) since
    (d) unless

16. A: Did you donate to charity this year?

    B: Yes. I don't have much, but I gave ____________.

    (a) that little what I spare
    (b) what I spare that a little
    (c) what little I had to spare
    (d) little what I had to spare

17. A: Mike, where did you go after class this morning?

    B: I was just in the library, reviewing _____________ I had learned.

    (a) that
    (b) who
    (c) what
    (d) which

18. A: Thank you for returning my lost wallet!

    B: Don't mention it. _____________ decent person would have done the same.

    (a) Any
    (b) Many
    (c) Any of
    (d) Many of

19. A: Did that coffee help you study?

    B: Not really. It only _____________ jittery.

    (a) succeeding to make me feeling
    (b) successfully made me feeling
    (c) succeeded in making me feel
    (d) successful to make me feel

20. A: It's too bad you had to call off the game.

    B: Well, with all the rain, I had no choice but _____________ .

    (a) to do
    (b) do so
    (c) doing
    (d) to do so

Part II   Questions 21—40

Choose the option that best completes each gap.

21. Thomas offered to pay his children's tuition fees _____________ they achieve consistently high grades.

    (a) in case
    (b) whether
    (c) whereas
    (d) provided

22. The girl _____________ book was stolen had to borrow the teacher's.

    (a) who
    (b) whose
    (c) of whom
    (d) of whose

23. The Trinity Mirror is by far _____________ publisher of national and regional newspaper titles in Britain.

    (a) large
    (b) larger
    (c) largely
    (d) the largest

24. The buildup of the German Army after World War I _____________ by the rise of Hitler's Third Reich in 1933.

    (a) is bolstered
    (b) was bolstered
    (c) has been bolstered
    (d) will have been bolstered

25. Cutting back on high-fat foods has helped many people achieve a sharp reduction __________ their cholesterol levels.

(a) in
(b) by
(c) on
(d) for

26. Laura considered the internship offer too good __________.

(a) to let slip an opportunity by
(b) an opportunity to let slip by
(c) by an opportunity to let slip
(d) to let slip by an opportunity

27. __________ a chef with lots of experience, the bistro owner hired one who had worked at many excellent restaurants.

(a) Needing
(b) To need
(c) Needed
(d) Need

28. Whether __________ punishments or rewards, Jesse will motivate his students to work harder.

(a) it be by means of
(b) the means it be of
(c) by his means were
(d) he was by means of

29. Despite having taken five years of lessons, Sylvia still __________ not play the piano, no matter how hard she tried.

(a) must
(b) could
(c) would
(d) should

30. Already having climbed __________ the ship, Martin realized that he had left his wallet in the tourist boutique.

(a) aboard
(b) beyond
(c) instead of
(d) aside from

31. William Faulkner and Virginia Woolf, __________, were leading exponents of literary modernism.

(a) but mention two names
(b) two names but mention
(c) to mention but two names
(d) names but two to mention

32. __________ when they set out that rain would cut their day short.

(a) Did the hikers know little
(b) Know little did the hikers
(c) Did the hikers little know
(d) Little did the hikers know

33. The budget for the following three years __________ when the financial crisis rendered its calculations obsolete.

(a) has already drawn up
(b) had already drawn up
(c) has already been drawn up
(d) had already been drawn up

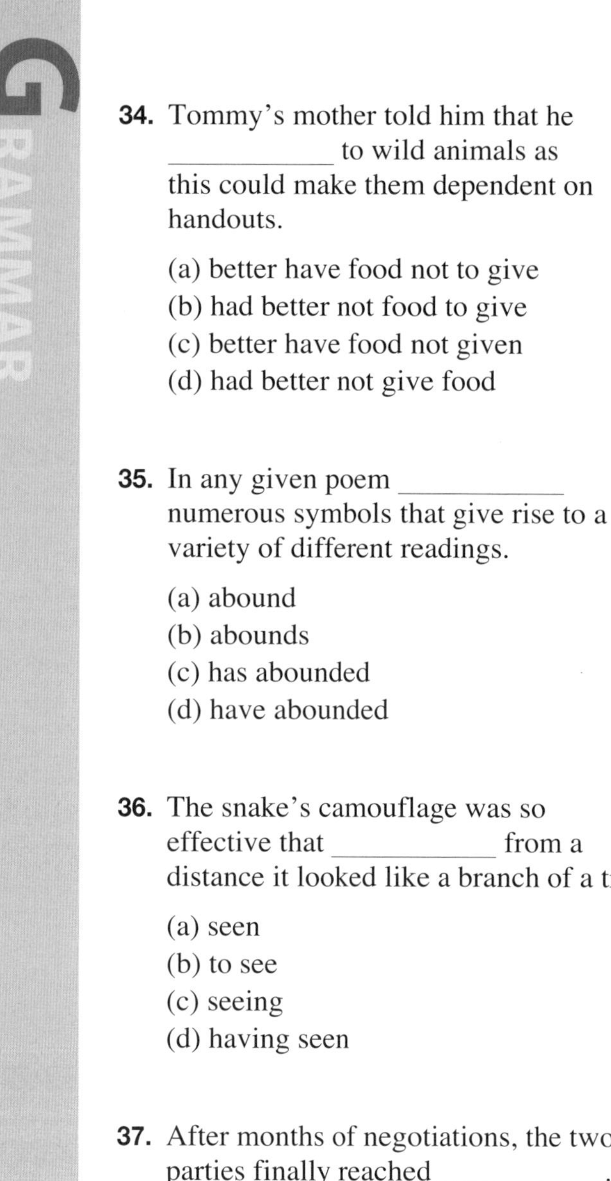

34. Tommy's mother told him that he ______________ to wild animals as this could make them dependent on handouts.

(a) better have food not to give
(b) had better not food to give
(c) better have food not given
(d) had better not give food

35. In any given poem ____________ numerous symbols that give rise to a variety of different readings.

(a) abound
(b) abounds
(c) has abounded
(d) have abounded

36. The snake's camouflage was so effective that ____________ from a distance it looked like a branch of a tree.

(a) seen
(b) to see
(c) seeing
(d) having seen

37. After months of negotiations, the two parties finally reached ____________ .

(a) compromise
(b) a compromise
(c) any compromise
(d) much compromise

38. After a failed attempt to climb a small mountain, Luke was wary ____________ .

(a) to try larger of anything
(b) to try anything of larger
(c) of trying anything larger
(d) of trying larger anything

39. Due to the store's limited quantities, only those customers who ____________ the display first were able to purchase the Curly Lovebears.

(a) have been reaching
(b) were reaching
(c) have reached
(d) had reached

40. If you and your spouse want to spend a holiday filled with ____________ , consider our five-day vacation package to Tahiti.

(a) romance
(b) romances
(c) a romance
(d) some romances

Part III **Questions 41—45**

Read each sentence carefully and identify the option that contains a grammatical error.

41. (a) A: I was going to spend Christmas at home, but I'm not sure so now.

(b) B: But I thought your plans were already set. What changed?

(c) A: The flights home are really expensive. I'm not sure I can afford to go.

(d) B: Keep looking. You may get lucky and find a cheap flight.

42. (a) A: I'm always late for my classes because of my commute is so long.

(b) B: You won't have that problem if you move into campus housing.

(c) A: Living on campus isn't for me. I like the privacy of an off-campus apartment.

(d) B: Then you're just going to have to accept getting up early.

43. (a) A: I heard you were sick in bed all weekend with a cold, Glenn.

(b) B: That's true. I'm still not totally well, but I'm feeling much better.

(c) A: That's good to hear. Ann told me she has brought you some soup on Sunday.

(d) B: Yes. It was a great relief because I was too weak to get out of bed.

44. (a) A: Did you take a shortcut on your way here, Lynn?

(b) B: No, why do you ask? Am I early or something?

(c) A: Oh, no. I just thought it would have taken it longer.

(d) B: Nope. I just followed the directions you suggested.

45. (a) A: Are we booking the same venue for this year's management conference?

(b) B: Yeah, we've decided to reserve the same hotel where we used last year.

(c) A: Really? I thought people were dissatisfied with the facilities last time around.

(d) B: Some people were, but it's still the most convenient venue overall.

Part IV **Questions 46—50**

Read each sentence carefully and identify the option that contains a grammatical error.

46. (a) Wind turbines are machines that convert the wind's energy into electricity. (b) These turbines have been in use from the late nineteenth century until the present. (c) As people switch to renewable energy, these devices are becoming increasing popular. (d) The use of such machines is not only trendy; it is also becoming a necessity.

47. (a) Giovanni Santoro, a native of Rome, is a phenomenon in the fashion world. (b) His clothes for both men and women are sold in countless stores worldwide. (c) His approach to clothing design emphasizes look smart while being comfortable. (d) This approach clearly has marketplace appeal: Santoro's annual sales top US $100 million.

48. (a) New areas of the Arctic have been opened up for drilling, greatly worrying environmentalists. (b) Oil companies state that they have extensive precautionary measures in place to prevent oil spills. (c) However, environmentalists are concerned about more than an oil spill, devastating though may be. (d) Oil drilling can release harmful amounts of methane and black carbon into the atmosphere.

49. (a) Antioxidants have been featured prominently in recent health and wellness studies. (b) Research has found that the more antioxidants one gets, the lower one's risk of cancer is. (c) It should be noted, however, that antioxidants work best when consuming in food rather than pill form. (d) It doesn't take much: eating a few pieces of fruit will do for one's daily intake of antioxidants.

50. (a) It is commonly said that dolphins are among the most intelligent creatures in the animal world. (b) They possess brains that are similar to those of humans in terms of size of theirs relative to body mass. (c) In studies, they have been shown to exhibit a capacity for mimicry unrivaled by other mammals. (d) They have also been found to communicate with each other with various sounds, such as whistles and clicks.

This is the end of the Grammar section. Do NOT move on to the next section until instructed to do so. You are NOT allowed to turn to any other section of the test.

VOCABULARY

Part I Questions 1—25

Choose the option that best completes each gap.

1. A: Where does this store stock sugar?

B: It's at the end of ___________ twelve.

(a) line
(b) aisle
(c) stripe
(d) hallway

2. A: Are you Craig? I'm Jan. We met in an online class.

B: Jan! It's great to ___________ meet you in person!

(a) lastly
(b) finally
(c) extremely
(d) continuously

3. A: Mary should've never started that fight with Paul, don't you think?

B: I don't want to ___________. I'd rather stay out of it.

(a) take sides
(b) make a play
(c) jump the gun
(d) pass the buck

4. A: Did Carl listen to you about not buying a guitar for lessons?

B: Yes, he took my ___________ to rent one instead.

(a) range
(b) advice
(c) appraisal
(d) resolution

5. A: Today's drive should be pretty, with the leaves turning colors.

B: Yes, I'm looking forward to the ___________ views.

(a) hefty
(b) scenic
(c) potent
(d) watchful

6. A: It's so frustrating going to airports these days.

B: Yeah, the security measures are a huge ___________.

(a) bother
(b) inquiry
(c) restraint
(d) prevention

7. A: Your daughters get along so well.

B: Yes, the ___________ they have for each other is clear.

(a) likelihood
(b) fondness
(c) relativity
(d) affliction

8. A: Aren't you going to ___________ your seat belt?

B: Oh, I forgot. I'll buckle up now.

(a) seal
(b) fasten
(c) unlock
(d) replace

9. A: I practice my violin every day, but
    I'm not improving.
    B: I'm sure your ____________
    impresses your teacher nonetheless.

    (a) cohesion
    (b) persistence
    (c) deliberation
    (d) constitution

10. A: Was everyone in agreement about
    implementing the new fee structure?
    B: No. Ed ____________ it on the
    grounds that the policy isn't fair to
    the clients.

    (a) attested
    (b) opposed
    (c) conceded
    (d) reconciled

11. A: Did the earthquake destroy many
    dwellings?
    B: Unfortunately, yes. It ____________
    whole villages.

    (a) bet on
    (b) took to
    (c) drove out
    (d) wiped out

12. A: There's no time to waste in getting
    our restaurant up and running.
    B: I agree. Everything needs to get done
    in a ____________ manner.

    (a) speedy
    (b) primary
    (c) transitory
    (d) momentary

13. A: Cedric's mom is very devout.
    B: Yeah. She's so ____________ that
    she attends church services daily.

    (a) pious
    (b) sacred
    (c) eternal
    (d) hallowed

14. A: The buffet had so many fancy dishes
    to choose from!
    B: Sounds like it was quite a
    ____________ meal then.

    (a) clement
    (b) succinct
    (c) sumptuous
    (d) clandestine

15. A: Have you decided who to vote for in
    this election?
    B: No, I'm still ____________ about it.

    (a) over the top
    (b) on the fence
    (c) crying over spilled milk
    (d) barking up the wrong tree

16. A: Excuse me. The TV in my hotel
    room isn't working.
    B: I can ____________ that right away.
    I'll switch you to a different room.

    (a) deter
    (b) assert
    (c) rectify
    (d) append

17. A: Have you recovered enough from the flu to return to work?

B: No. I think I should wait until all my symptoms ___________.

(a) abate
(b) detain
(c) refrain
(d) founder

18. A: My grandfather is still very active. He runs three miles every day!

B: Wow. He's fortunate to be so ___________ at his age.

(a) nebulous
(b) vigorous
(c) rampant
(d) acute

19. A: I feel drained after working so hard.

B: All the work on this project has really ___________ my strength, too.

(a) stoked
(b) sapped
(c) scoured
(d) succored

20. A: How did this coffee get spilled?

B: Sorry, I ___________ the table, knocking the coffee off balance.

(a) razed
(b) jostled
(c) colluded
(d) impaired

21. A: Diana has been very ___________ since her promotion.

B: I guess she can't be too friendly now that she's our boss.

(a) aloof
(b) riddled
(c) stubbed
(d) fortuitous

22. A: Sean can't stand the sight of blood. He almost passes out.

B: Yeah, he's quite ___________. That's why he's afraid of doctors.

(a) impish
(b) prudish
(c) mawkish
(d) squeamish

23. A: Harold was in such a rage when his paycheck was withheld.

B: I know. He was absolutely ___________ about it.

(a) precarious
(b) flanked
(c) fecund
(d) livid

24. A: I can't understand why Stan keeps insisting on his ideas.

B: He's quite ___________, so it can be pretty hard to persuade him.

(a) grievous
(b) tentative
(c) obdurate
(d) surreptitious

25. A: Edna should stop living through her children.

B: You're right. Instead of living ___________, she needs to have her own fun!

(a) exaltedly
(b) vicariously
(c) ineluctably
(d) prolifically

Choose the option that best completes each gap.

26. Once you try the Sparkle Mop, you'll see how fun it can be to ____________ the floor.

   (a) slide
   (b) erase
   (c) clean
   (d) bathe

27. Thousands of people were ____________ from their jobs during the recession and so were left without incomes.

   (a) fired
   (b) halted
   (c) declined
   (d) restricted

28. The researchers had hoped the study's outcome would prove their hypothesis, but the ____________ did not support their theory.

   (a) issues
   (b) pieces
   (c) results
   (d) notions

29. Theresa Perkins's latest book is being ____________ as a teen novel—an advertising tactic that is working, as teens are buying it in droves.

   (a) marketed
   (b) converted
   (c) bargained
   (d) exchanged

30. Coffeehouses were a(n) ____________ part of intellectual life in eighteenth-century Britain, since they served as hubs for discussions.

   (a) intact
   (b) integral
   (c) excessive
   (d) respective

31. To encourage athletes to train harder, coaches should ____________ them with success stories of previous champions.

   (a) inspire
   (b) imitate
   (c) perform
   (d) presume

32. Employees must sign a confidentiality contract agreeing not to ____________ company information.

   (a) relent
   (b) affirm
   (c) intrude
   (d) disclose

33. For a standard serving, one ____________ of meat should be about the size of a pack of playing cards.

   (a) factor
   (b) flavor
   (c) portion
   (d) posture

34. Traditionally "masculine" ___________ such as military service and construction work are now being pursued by women as well.

(a) vocations
(b) conditions
(c) promotions
(d) assumptions

35. Special tests that measure natural ability can reveal if a student has a(n) ___________ in a particular area, like math or art.

(a) priority
(b) aptitude
(c) sentiment
(d) achievement

36. Janet believed that the staff meetings had been a(n) ___________ use of time, as brainstorming intensively enabled them to solve urgent problems.

(a) plentiful
(b) intentional
(c) productive
(d) charismatic

37. The violent swings in the stock market made the year a(n) ___________ one in many investors' lives.

(a) astute
(b) flippant
(c) tumultuous
(d) autonomous

38. Trisha Jackson so ___________ the concept of a socialite that she has become synonymous with the term.

(a) qualifies
(b) drenches
(c) embodies
(d) segregates

39. To ___________ the one hundredth anniversary of independence, the country's post office issued a special postage stamp.

(a) design
(b) mediate
(c) ameliorate
(d) commemorate

40. The mounting ___________ between the two clans culminated in a declaration of war.

(a) velocity
(b) hostility
(c) mobility
(d) elasticity

41. Tammy put out the small fire that broke out in her home by ___________ the flames with a cloth.

(a) soothing
(b) tumbling
(c) mustering
(d) smothering

42. The car accident was minor, but it still left the street strewn with broken glass and other ___________.

(a) debris
(b) havoc
(c) rancor
(d) turmoil

43. The CEO confirmed that the company is not cancelling the staff bonus and hopes this assurance will ___________ any unfounded rumors of bankruptcy.

(a) dispel
(b) amend
(c) initiate
(d) wrangle

44. Veerman Bank's monthly fee of $3.99 is ___________ compared to the much larger banking fees charged by its competitors.

(a) clerical
(b) belittled
(c) nominal
(d) petulant

45. The Olympic medalists were ___________ by fans in their home nations for their excellent performance at the games.

(a) lauded
(b) taunted
(c) mollified
(d) procured

46. The price of coffee in some shops has become ___________, rising far beyond what is justified by the shops' expenses.

(a) oblique
(b) portentous
(c) impeccable
(d) extravagant

47. Both sides in the immigration debate have used language that can only be described as ___________, inciting passionate reactions.

(a) incendiary
(b) nonchalant
(c) phlegmatic
(d) unflappable

48. When the old museum could no longer pay for maintenance, it called for donations to ___________ the costs.

(a) avert
(b) defray
(c) salvage
(d) conciliate

49. Andrew's disrespect for his coworkers was so ___________ that it could hardly be missed by observers.

(a) blatant
(b) pudgy
(c) stingy
(d) tepid

50. While contaminants were found in the city's water supply, they were in such ___________ amounts that they posed no public health risk.

(a) dissolute
(b) ephemeral
(c) constrained
(d) infinitesimal

This is the end of the Vocabulary section. Do NOT move on to the Reading Comprehension section until instructed to do so. You are NOT allowed to turn to any other section of the test.

READING COMPREHENSION

DIRECTIONS

This section tests your ability to comprehend reading passages. You will have 45 minutes to complete the 40 questions. Be sure to follow the directions given by the proctor.

Part I **Questions 1—16**

Read the passage and choose the option that best completes the passage.

1. Here at Miller Furniture, we're ______________________________. After last year's tremendous response, we decided to make it an annual event. So come down this Saturday, when we'll once again be selling all our floor models at 75% off the retail price in order to make room for next season's stock. This special sale is first-come, first-served and only includes the furniture currently set up in our showroom. These items won't last long, so come early!

(a) selling incoming items at a discount
(b) starting a customer rewards program
(c) giving a sneak preview of our new stock
(d) holding another sale on display furniture

2. In March 2012, the people of Kiribati found that they would have to ______________________________. At that time, Anote Tong, the president of the island nation, entered talks with Fiji's government to buy 5,000 acres of Fijian land. Rising ocean levels linked to global warming had already inundated several Kiribati villages, and Tong declared that there was no choice but to relocate his 113,000 citizens. According to his plan, the citizens of Kiribati will gradually be evacuated to Fiji, making them the first people to lose their entire homeland to global climate change.

(a) cede a substantial amount of territory to neighboring Fiji
(b) redouble its efforts to reverse the effects of climate change
(c) abandon their land because of the effects of global warming
(d) create barriers to protect its territory from encroaching tides

3. When the bubonic plague was ravaging Europe during the sixteenth century, nutmeg, a common spice, was looked to as a form of protection. People began wearing satchels of nutmeg, a move contemporary society might deem superstitious. People at the time attributed the spread of the plague to "foul odors," and many believed nutmeg's pungent aroma would fend off tainted air. Indeed, the nutmeg was effective as a preventative measure, but for a different reason: it repelled the fleas whose bites actually spread the disease. It seems that nutmeg ______________________________.

(a) masked the odor given off by plague sufferers
(b) was used to soothe the pain of infected flea bites
(c) was never actually used to reduce the risk of infection
(d) had some value after all in preventing the plague's spread

4. Babyco would like to apologize to our customers for
_______________________________. Following complaints about our Strollercoaster
line of baby carriages, we have determined that the product contains defective
components. The problem is with the braking mechanism: the stroller may indicate
that it is locked when in fact it remains unlocked. We are happy to exchange any
malfunctioning strollers, or to provide a redesigned component free of charge to solve
this issue.

(a) discontinuing one of our most popular products
(b) a design flaw that makes our strollers lock abruptly
(c) failing to investigate complaints about our line of strollers
(d) a faulty mechanism that compromises our strollers' safety

5. Classic arcade games often have a "kill screen" that appears towards the end of the game
and is _______________________________. The kill screen for the classic game *Dig
Dug*, for example, has the level starting with the enemy directly on top of the *Dig Dug*
character: a position that leaves the player no way to win. This kind of glitch stems from
a particular bug in the game's programming. Basically, a kill screen is a coding blunder
that prevents the player from advancing once they have reached that point in the game.

(a) considered the most difficult level to beat
(b) the result of an error in the game's coding
(c) where the player accomplishes his mission
(d) accessible only by using a secret cheat code

6. In Nathaniel Hawthorne's *The Scarlet Letter*, the wilderness becomes a powerful symbol
of _______________________________. While most of the novel takes place in an
isolated outpost on the American frontier, a number of scenes occur in the surrounding
wilderness. These scenes show the characters escaping the strict rules of Puritan society
in order to explore their own thoughts and desires. Thus, the wilderness is associated
with a state of liberation which both allows people to develop their personal identities
and leads them into conflict with the town's authorities.

(a) humanity's utter powerlessness over nature
(b) the authority of the rulers of Puritan society
(c) the isolation that comes with social conformity
(d) emancipation from oppressive social conventions

7. The latest exhibition at the Bruin Gallery, "Early English Romantic Paintings," includes beautiful works from the late eighteenth and early nineteenth centuries. But it hardly does the period justice. An exhibition claiming to tell the story of a period ought to display works that show the period's stylistic and thematic development. The Bruin allowed this opportunity to slip through its fingers—showing only the best-known works, while leaving huge gaps in its representation of the period. Overall, the exhibition provides a glimpse into early English romantic paintings, but one that ______________________.

(a) includes too many unrelated works from other eras
(b) fails to present a complete picture of the movement
(c) blunts its impact by trying to showcase too many styles
(d) leaves out the works people are most likely to recognize

8.

To the Editor:

Your article on the inspirational athlete John Burns showed that he does not take health in body and mind for granted. However, it also continually referenced Burns's handicap. That he uses a wheelchair is incidental to his athleticism and should have been mentioned only once in your profile. Instead, nearly every paragraph mentions his impairment, and his courage and tenacity as an athlete are glossed over. Burns is a hero in every sense of the word, and your article ______________________.

Sincerely,
Jack Baxter

(a) gave too little attention to the injury that handicapped him
(b) marginalized him while focusing on able-bodied athletes
(c) should have focused less on his physical disability
(d) clearly identified what motivates him to succeed

9. Dieters are often advised to drink eight glasses of water per day to flush toxins from their bodies. Although I'd never felt so much was needed, I gave it a try when I decided to lose weight last year. Much to my surprise, about a week into my experiment, I began feeling fatigue and nausea. I visited my doctor and he told me I was washing too much sodium from my system and advised me to reduce my water intake. So while many do need to drink eight glasses of water a day, _______________________________.

(a) I needed much more than that to stay healthy
(b) I have never tried to implement the plan myself
(c) it is only advisable for those on a weight loss plan
(d) it is just a guideline and not universally applicable

10. Since Arthur Conan Doyle created the highly rational detective Sherlock Holmes, it would seem safe to assume that he was dedicated to a highly rational and scientific worldview. Yet this was not the case. In his later years, Doyle was enamored of spiritualism, or the belief that supernatural beings communicate with the living. These views led him to behave in ways not in keeping with his celebrated protagonist, such as defending the existence of fairies and gnomes. That Doyle was such a fervent adherent of the supernatural _______________________________.

(a) explains why his characters tended to embody those views
(b) was something he did not reveal to even his closest friends
(c) is surprising given the nature of his chief fictional protagonist
(d) undermined his ability to craft convincingly rational characters

11. The flow of ancient artifacts into the United States has been waning, and now many items are making their way back out of the US. For decades, collectors purchased these relics without concern for their provenance. However, a new emphasis on documenting how artifacts were acquired revealed that many objects owned by collectors had been obtained by looters and smuggled abroad. Recently, these items have begun to be returned to their countries of origin, with Italy and Greece, for instance, receiving approximately $1 billion worth of stolen goods. These countries have benefited from this trend in America to _______________________________.

(a) pay huge sums to purchase their historical artifacts
(b) prosecute its citizens for looting archaeological sites
(c) replace lost objects with items from their own collections
(d) scrutinize artifacts' provenance and repatriate stolen ones

12. Some countries have faced a tough choice between food and energy. As these countries cultivate crops such as corn and wheat to create biofuels, they sacrifice grains and farmland that can be used to feed their populations. To address this issue, researchers are attempting to develop a second-generation of biofuels using weeds that grow on infertile land or waste water—such as duckweed—as bioenergy sources. If successful, these second-generation biofuels will allow researchers to solve the problem of first-generation biofuels by ________________________________.

(a) using animal fats that are discarded by humans
(b) utilizing plants prized for yielding both food and fuel
(c) consuming less energy than their predecessors to create biofuels
(d) providing renewable energy without compromising food sources

13. The Bethlehem Hospital steering committee has concluded that the "tele-ICU" monitoring system for our intensive care unit ________________________________.
The system, which allows doctors to remotely monitor patients' conditions using cameras, computers, and microphones, was designed to increase standards of treatment during busy periods. However, doctors and nurses found the tele-ICU system intrusive: many complained that the cameras in patient rooms made them fearful they were constantly being watched. And our data show that critical errors actually increased during the period the tele-ICU was in use.

(a) will permit the hospital to reduce the number of staff on duty
(b) has failed to improve the quality of patient care in the hospital
(c) requires a review to tackle issues related to equipment coordination
(d) provides effective monitoring of hospital personnel during treatment

14. In a study of attack advertising in politics, psychologist Drew Westen demonstrated that viewers of these ads ________________________________. Seeking to understand why candidates rely so heavily on a type of advertising that American viewers profess to despise, Westen examined the effects of two classic examples of the genre on viewers. What he discovered was that, despite their objection to the vicious nature of the advertisements, viewers were nonetheless affected by them in the way advertisers desired: viewers absorbed the negative associations that biased them against the advertisements' targets.

(a) do not pay them the attention that advertisers want them to
(b) are subconsciously influenced by messages they find offensive
(c) bounce back quickly from the initial negative impact of these ads
(d) helped change advertising practices by voicing their objections to them

15. American universities have increasingly sought to participate in the free market. No longer is higher education dedicated solely to the ideals of learning and scholarship. Rather, it is driven by profits. Universities are preoccupied with ways of generating income, such as sports programs, commercial research, and partnerships with large corporations. _______________________________, the traditional goals of the university are now taking a backseat to more worldly concerns.

(a) Regardless
(b) Nonetheless
(c) In other words
(d) That being said

16. In a series of classic lectures, the English poet W. H. Auden explored what distinguishes major from minor writers. He argued that minor writers produce consistently capable work, often in a personal style, yet never risk failure by experimenting with different techniques or undertaking ambitious projects. _______________________________, he argued, major writers come in two forms: those who devote their lives to a single, large-scale work, such as Dante, author of the *Divine Comedy*, and those who pursue a lifelong path of experimentation, such as Shakespeare.

(a) Otherwise
(b) In contrast
(c) For instance
(d) Nevertheless

17. Due to unforeseen complications related to last week's lightning storm, Henderson Hall, the main building for the English department, is currently without power. Thus, all English classes have been moved to O'Brian Hall until further notice. A list of new room numbers for the classes has been posted on the entrances to Henderson and O'Brian Halls. Thank you for your patience.

Q: What is the main purpose of the announcement?
(a) To warn students about an upcoming storm
(b) To give directions to the English department
(c) To inform students of a change in class location
(d) To apologize for a last-minute class cancellation

18. Prior to colonization, men and women from the Native American nation known as the Iroquois had distinct parts to play in society. As the nation has adapted to modern life, many of the functions traditionally performed by either men or women are now being shared. While women were once barred from political leadership, for example, there are several tribes with female chiefs today. Similarly, many men are assuming greater responsibility for household finances, whereas economic control of the household used to be a solely female endeavor.

Q: What is the passage mainly about?
(a) How gender roles have changed in Iroquois society
(b) The types of relationships Iroquois men and women have
(c) The household responsibilities of Iroquois men and women
(d) How Iroquois tribes are returning to a traditional way of life

19. Forget needing cash, credit cards, or a special ticket for school lunchtime. Food Service Solutions is testing a computer program in a Mulberry Fields school district that deducts the cost of a meal from the student's bank account by reading a student's fingerprint. School officials are excited about the new system, saying that not only will it eliminate the need for students to carry cash, cards, or tickets, but it will also ensure faster-moving cafeteria lines.

Q: What is the best title for the passage?
(a) Lunchtime Theft Thwarted by Fingerprints
(b) Fingerprints Soon Will Be a Thing of the Past
(c) Fingerprints to Become the New Lunch Tickets
(d) Students to Buy Meal Tickets Using Fingerprints

20. Because of security issues, St. Joseph's Hospital would like to advise employees to avoid walking to the off-site employee parking lot. The hospital provides numerous alternatives. There is a shuttle bus to the parking lot every 20 minutes from 6 a.m. to 11 p.m. that leaves from the front entrance. Additionally, in the hours when the bus does not run, security is available to drive any employee to the lot. These services have been available over the last year, and employees are encouraged to make continued use of them.

Q: What is the main purpose of the announcement?
(a) To inform employees of extended hours for the shuttle bus
(b) To determine how many employees use transportation services
(c) To remind employees of transportation options to the parking lot
(d) To advise employees to avoid parking off-site due to security issues

21. In the novel *Ulysses*, James Joyce uses three central characters to present alternative versions of events. The initial description of an event from one character's point of view creates a strong impression of how events unfolded. Then a subsequent exploration of the same events from a different character's viewpoint challenges the original interpretation. This technique of revisiting episodes from different angles demonstrates the unreliability of individual perspectives. It shows that each attempt to make sense of an event is constrained by the person's standpoint.

Q: What is the writer's main point about *Ulysses*?
(a) It demonstrates how perspective affects interpretation.
(b) It explores the development of individual points of view.
(c) Its characters accuse each other of misinterpreting events.
(d) It describes diverse events because of its multiple characters.

22. Researchers have found an unexpected correlation between vitamin E and the common childhood ailment of asthma. Tracking the health of expectant mothers, the scientists discovered that those with high vitamin E intake are about five times less likely than those with low levels of the vitamin to give birth to a child who develops asthma. The study cautions that only vitamin E obtained from food sources provides this benefit, however, and that children of mothers who take supplements show normal risk for the disease.

Q: What is the main idea of the passage?
(a) Excessive use of vitamin E pills heightens the risk of developing asthma.
(b) Supplements provide inadequate levels of vitamin E for pregnant women.
(c) Childhood asthma can be treated with a diet with high levels of vitamin E.
(d) Mothers with low vitamin E diets risk having children who develop asthma.

23.

Dear Ms. Frost,

Thank you for meeting with me last week. I appreciated the chance to learn more about VisionTech. After our talk, I am confident that I would be a good fit with your company. The graduate degree I earned in the field has prepared me for this internship. As you requested during our meeting, I will be sending along two reference letters shortly. I will be waiting to hear back from you.

Sincerely,

Gerard Blue

Q: Which of the following is correct about Gerard Blue according to the letter?
(a) He has yet to meet Ms. Frost face to face.
(b) He is currently an intern for VisionTech.
(c) He does not have a graduate degree.
(d) He will submit reference letters to Ms. Frost.

24. John Milton received an exceptional education. His father had been disinherited by his family for converting from Catholicism to Protestantism but became prosperous enough to send young John to an elite private school, where he began learning Greek and Latin. Milton's strong academic performance secured him a spot in Cambridge, where he made a name as a writer of essays and poetry. These intellectual experiences equipped him for his greatest undertaking, writing the first epic poem in the English language, *Paradise Lost*.

Q: Which of the following is correct about John Milton according to the passage?
(a) His father was disinherited for embracing Catholicism.
(b) His father could not afford to send him to a private school.
(c) He first started learning Greek and Latin at Cambridge.
(d) He earned a reputation as writer while studying at university.

25. Welcome to Le Parisien Hotel. Checkout is at 11 a.m., but can be extended to 4 p.m., based on availability, if requests are made in advance. The entire room service menu, including breakfast, is available 24 hours a day. It may be viewed using the "Room Service" option on Channel 1 of your television and ordered by calling the restaurant. As a thank you for choosing Le Parisien, we have provided you with several coupons for discounts at local attractions. Please enjoy your stay.

Q: Which of the following is correct about Le Parisien Hotel according to the announcement?
(a) Late checkout is unavailable without exception.
(b) Room service can be ordered any time of the day.
(c) Room service can be ordered via the television.
(d) The coupons provide discounts for hotel facilities.

26.

> Dear Friends,
>
> As most of you know, I have accepted a position abroad and will be leaving CodePro this Friday. I'll stop by your desk tomorrow to say goodbye in person, but I just want to write to everyone to say what a wonderful three years I've had here. I've learned a lot, especially about web design, and am grateful for all your help. Thanks again to everyone.
>
> James Hutton

Q: Which of the following is correct about James Hutton according to the letter?
(a) He has a new job in a different country.
(b) He is writing on his final day at the company.
(c) He has no plans to bid farewell to his colleagues in person.
(d) He has worked for the company for a total of one year.

27. In order to book your campsite online, you must join Sapphire National Park's free online membership program. As a member, you will have access to the park's online booking system and will be eligible to receive optional updates on conditions at the park. In addition, you will be given exclusive online resources such as maps and guides. If you would prefer not to become a member, please call us to reserve your campsite.

Q: Which of the following is correct according to the announcement?
(a) Online reservations can be made without obtaining membership.
(b) The program has a membership fee that must be paid online.
(c) The park reserves special electronic materials solely for members.
(d) Membership is necessary to make reservations over the phone.

28. Tulip mania was a six-month episode in Dutch history that started in November 1636. Tulips had always been popular since their introduction to Europe in the mid-sixteenth century, but during the time of tulip mania, the price of tulip bulbs skyrocketed to the point that one could fetch ten times the average annual salary. The most expensive tulips were those with multicolored petals, caused by the mosaic virus. Flowers infected with this virus took longer to cultivate than those that were not infected, which further stoked bidding for these exotic-looking flowers.

Q: Which of the following is correct according to the passage?
(a) Tulips were introduced to Europe in the year 1636.
(b) Tulips were unpopular when first introduced to Europe.
(c) Mosaic tulips were worth more than other types of tulips.
(d) Mosaic tulips took less time to cultivate than other tulips.

29. In 1952, Michael Ventris deciphered an ancient Mediterranean script known as Linear B. For years, scholars' attempts to decipher the script were hampered by their belief that it could not have been used to represent a Greek language. Ventris originally hypothesized that the script was based on a variant of Etruscan, but after discovering that some symbols were names of cities on the Greek island of Crete, he countered academic consensus and proclaimed that it represented a version of Greek. Most scholars refused to budge and expressed skepticism about Ventris's findings even after he had deciphered Linear B entirely.

Q: Which of the following is correct according to the passage?
(a) Scholars had long believed that Linear B encoded a Greek language.
(b) Ventris originally thought that Linear B represented an Etruscan language.
(c) Ventris's final conclusions about Linear B matched the academic consensus.
(d) The scholarly community swiftly embraced Ventris's theory about Linear B.

30. Faced with increasing demand on their electrical supply, governments have begun turning to "smart" power grids. On standard grids, electricity flows in a single direction, from power plants to electricity consumers. The new systems enable consumers to add power generated locally using, for example, solar panels back into the grid. This also promises more stable energy distribution, as households can grab power from local networks when the grid is down. The new systems also facilitate two-way communication between power companies and consumers, allowing consumers to use power when it is plentiful, getting it at a discount, and power companies to be alerted immediately when outages occur.

Q: Which of the following is correct about "smart" grid systems according to the passage?
(a) They are being utilized in response to a decrease in demand for power.
(b) They ensure power flows in a single direction from companies to users.
(c) They restrict the distribution of power over community networks.
(d) They allow utilities to lower prices when energy is abundant.

31. The US Navy's oldest research vessel is the Floating Instrument Platform, called FLIP for short. The ship is shaped like a 108-meter-long spoon. It lacks an engine, so it must be towed from wherever it is docked to the next research location. Once in position, the "handle" of the spoon fills with water, causing it to sink and bring the ship to a vertical position. The "bowl," which is where the crew and scientists live, stays above water. Effectively, the ship "flips" into a buoy that reaches 91 meters below the ocean's surface.

Q: Which of the following is correct about the FLIP?
(a) It is the latest addition to the navy research fleet.
(b) It remains at sea permanently rather than docking.
(c) It has the ability to tow research equipment to sea.
(d) It submerges only partially to facilitate experiments.

32. The religious beliefs in modern Africa vary by region. In North Africa, the predominant belief system is Islam, which was established there during the seventh century. This is also the major religion of the nomadic peoples of the Sahara Desert to the south. Still farther south, traditional religious beliefs survive. These religions nearly always combine belief in a supreme being with worship of various minor deities and ancestors. For the vast majority of the area south of the Sahara, however, Christianity is the principal faith.

Q: Which of the following is correct according to the passage?
(a) Islam declined in North Africa in the seventh century.
(b) The primary religion of the Sahara is ancestor worship.
(c) Most traditional African religions have multiple deities.
(d) Christianity has yet to gain many adherents in Africa.

33. The Brownsville Teacher's Association (BTA) is proud to endorse Ms. Meredith Brooks
for mayor. Ms. Brooks brings a deep understanding of the issues faced by local teachers,
an understanding that comes only with first-hand experience. This knowledge will allow
Ms. Brooks to implement the tough policy changes needed to restore Brownsville's
public schools to the top spot in state rankings. Promising to stand up for public
education, Ms. Brooks is the only candidate who is firmly on the side of Brownsville's
teachers.

Q: What can be inferred from the passage?
(a) Meredith Brooks is running for reelection as mayor.
(b) Meredith Brooks has no experience as a school teacher.
(c) The BTA advocates upholding current education policies.
(d) Brownsville's schools used to be at the top of the state rankings.

34. Screenwriter Charlie Hurst is known for his unconventional scripts, but his directorial
debut, *Layers*, reaches a new level of inaccessible quirkiness, false profundity and art-
house pretentiousness. Previous films based on his screenplays, such as *The Perpetual
Quest* and *Allusions*, garnered critical acclaim and box office success because they had
seasoned directors who aimed for a coherent narrative. The lack of such a director's
steady hand is all too evident in *Layers*, which is a series of random personal grievances
masquerading as philosophical questioning.

Q: Which statement about *Layers* would the writer most likely agree with?
(a) It will fail at the box office despite its artistic merit.
(b) It does not contain a sufficiently coherent narrative.
(c) It offers filmgoers meaningful philosophical insights.
(d) It represents a departure from Hurst's typical content.

35. The great baseball player Hank Aaron went to a high school without a baseball team, so
he played on its softball and football teams instead. Although he received scholarship
offers for football, he quit the sport because he feared he would get injured playing it
and ruin his chance to play professional baseball. He got his first break while playing
in a recreational baseball league, which eventually led him to play in a segregated
professional baseball league. It was while playing there that he came to the attention of
major league scouts.

Q: What can be inferred about Hank Aaron from the passage?
(a) His priority in high school was playing professional football.
(b) He excelled at football while playing on his high school team.
(c) He was an amateur when major leagues scouts recruited him.
(d) His decision to play softball came after a serious football injury.

36. Archaeological and geological studies suggest that the downfall of civilizations can be explained by climate change. Despite mounting evidence, many people refuse to accept this theory because they equate it with environmental determinism, a theory that claims that climate determines character—for instance, that tropical climates foster indolence. The theory of environmental determinism, popular until the early twentieth century, has been dismissed as unscientific speculation used to justify racism. However, the climate change theory of civilizations' decline is fundamentally different from environmental determinism, as it focuses on the social, political, and technological adaptations to changing weather patterns.

Q: Which statement would the writer most likely agree with?
(a) Environmental determinism is applicable to the modern world.
(b) The climate change theory is another ruse to justify racist claims.
(c) Recent scientific findings provide support for environmental determinism.
(d) Climate change provides a valid explanation for the demise of civilizations.

37. The notion of survival of the fittest is often applied to social groups, where exceptional beauty or intelligence is assumed to provide individuals with an advantage. What we find more often, however, is that standing out limits an individual's chances of excelling in groups. It seems that those possessing unique qualities or talents are perceived by others as a threat. This is not to say that those of no more than average ability will scramble to the top. Successful individuals tend to enjoy definite strengths while being able to blend in with the majority.

Q: Which statement would the writer most likely agree with?
(a) Average people are often hostile to exceptional individuals.
(b) The weakest members of society will eventually rise to the top.
(c) Flaunting one's talent will increase one's chances of success in society.
(d) People are usually threatened by talent but not personal traits such as beauty.

Part III **Questions 38—40**

Read the passage and identify the option that does NOT belong.

38. I recently found an unusual way to cope with the stress in my daily life. (a) My tendency to work hard used to put a lot of stress on people around me. (b) I heard about a club that practices "laughter yoga," and on a whim, I went. (c) The group's theory is that laughter, even at nothing funny, releases stress. (d) I have found the classes to be so effective that now I attend every week.

39. Hundreds of dams have been built along the Mississippi River for a variety of purposes. (a) Many dams were constructed to make the channel deep enough for large barge traffic. (b) Arch dams are relatively thin because their curved shape allows them to easily hold back water. (c) Others were designed to create a permanent water supply for nearby towns and farms. (d) Most of the dams, however, were erected mainly to prevent damage caused by flooding.

40. Please be advised that SolarCom is ramping up solar-panel production to meet rising demand next year. (a) Many homeowners are seeing the long-term benefits of solar energy and are buying up solar panels. (b) Also, orders from emerging markets rose sharply last year, and this is predicted to continue. (c) In fact, several companies have set up their own solar-panel production facilities in developing countries. (d) The combination of demand from these sources means next year is likely to be lucrative for SolarCom.

This is the end of the Reading Comprehension section. Please remain seated until the proctor has instructed otherwise. You are NOT allowed to turn to any other section of the test.

서울대
최신기출
2

Listening *Comprehension*

Grammar

Vocabulary

Reading *Comprehension*

LISTENING COMPREHENSION

DIRECTIONS

1. In the Listening Comprehension section, all content will be presented orally rather than in written form.

2. This section contains four parts, each with fifteen individual items. For each part, you will receive separate instructions. Listen to the instructions carefully, and choose the best answer from the options for each item.

Part I Questions 1—15

You will now hear fifteen individual spoken questions or statements, each followed by four spoken responses. Choose the most appropriate response for each item.

Part II Questions 16—30

You will now hear fifteen short conversation fragments, followed by four spoken responses. Choose the most appropriate response to complete each conversation.

Part III — Questions 31—45

You will now hear fifteen complete conversations. For each conversation, you will be asked to answer a question. Each conversation and its corresponding question will be read twice. Then you will hear four options which will be read only once. Based on the given information, choose the option that best answers the question.

Part IV — Questions 46—60

You will now hear fifteen short talks. After each talk, you will be asked to answer a question. Each talk and its corresponding question will be read twice. Then you will hear four options which will be read only once. Based on the given information, choose the option that best answers the question.

GRAMMAR

DIRECTIONS

This section tests your grammar skills. You will have 25 minutes to complete the 50 questions. Be sure to follow the directions given by the proctor.

Part I Questions 1—20

Choose the option that best completes each gap.

1. A: The weather is so mild today!

B: Yes, I expected it to be much ___________.

(a) cold
(b) coldly
(c) colder
(d) coldest

2. A: Did you finish writing your essay?

B: No, I ___________ concentrate because of the noise in the hallway.

(a) mustn't
(b) couldn't
(c) wouldn't
(d) shouldn't

3. A: It seems like the only thing Tim does lately is study!

B: I know! He ___________ for nine hours every day this week.

(a) studies
(b) had studied
(c) has been studying
(d) had been studying

4. A: Is your laptop still working after you dropped it?

B: Yes. Fortunately, there wasn't ___________ harm done.

(a) a
(b) the
(c) any
(d) many

5. A: Have you and your wife gotten your tax refunds yet?

B: I got mine last week, but my wife is still waiting for ___________.

(a) its
(b) our
(c) hers
(d) their

6. A: The cookies that were in the oven burned.

B: Oh, no! We ___________ have kept a better eye on them.

(a) may
(b) must
(c) would
(d) should

7. A: How was the latest Fran Rivera book?

B: It is ___________ that I am reading it again.

(a) a novel written such beautiful
(b) written such a beautiful novel
(c) such a beautifully written novel
(d) such a novel beautifully written

8. A: Did the doctor tell you to take a pill three times a day?

B: Yes, he said to take it ___________ eight hours.

(a) each
(b) other
(c) every
(d) either

9. A: Where's Kurt's hometown?
    B: It's located 70 miles south
       ______________ Seattle.

    (a) of
    (b) to
    (c) than
    (d) along

10. A: Should I wear a sweater out today?
    B: Yes, I wouldn't want ______________
       cold.

    (a) to your catching
    (b) catching your
    (c) to catch you a
    (d) you to catch a

11. A: Where's Jonathan? I can't find him.
    B: I don't know. Last I saw him, he
       ______________ at the end of this row.

    (a) seated
    (b) is seated
    (c) was seated
    (d) was seating

12. A: Can I borrow one of your CDs?
    B: I don't listen to them anymore, so
       take ______________ you like.

    (a) where
    (b) which
    (c) wherever
    (d) whichever

13. A: How tall is Maria's brother?
    B: I'm not sure, but ______________ at
       least six feet.

    (a) I would guess he is being
    (b) he would guess as being
    (c) I would guess him to be
    (d) he would guess as to be

14. A: You should really try to get over
       your fear of insects.
    B: Impossible. The ______________
       thought of them makes me queasy.

    (a) right
    (b) such
    (c) even
    (d) very

15. A: Phil keeps making up reasons to
       explain why he can't help around the
       house.
    B: ______________ heard so many
       elaborate excuses to get out of doing
       chores.

    (a) Never have I
    (b) Never I have
    (c) Have I never
    (d) Have never I

16. A: Would you mind helping me move
       in a few weeks?
    B: I wish I could, but I ______________ in
       Europe then.

    (a) would travel
    (b) was traveling
    (c) will be traveling
    (d) would have traveled

17. A: Who's your favorite guitarist?
    B: Troy Franklin. He plays
       ______________ Robert Johnson.

    (a) calling of mind the style in
    (b) in a style that calls to mind
    (c) in my mind calling the style
    (d) a style that calls in the mind

18. A: Dave, do you want to get the package ___________?

    B: No, I will pick it up later.

    (a) deliver
    (b) delivers
    (c) delivered
    (d) delivering

19. A: Jim is always tending to his shrubs and flower beds.

    B: He really prides himself ___________ his gardening skills.

    (a) in
    (b) to
    (c) by
    (d) on

20. A: What happens to my deposit if I cancel my reservation?

    B: If you cancel within two days, your deposit ___________.

    (a) will not forfeit
    (b) does not forfeit
    (c) will not be forfeited
    (d) is not being forfeited

Part II **Questions 21—40**

Choose the option that best completes each gap.

21. Teams ___________ owners are fans of the sports club are often more successful.

    (a) who
    (b) which
    (c) whom
    (d) whose

22. In 1991, at age 11, Daisy Eagan became the youngest actress ___________ a Tony award.

    (a) won
    (b) to win
    (c) winning
    (d) having won

23. Intense solar storms produce waves of radiation that reach Earth, ___________ radio communication.

    (a) impede
    (b) impeded
    (c) impeding
    (d) having impeded

24. The director had the actors rehearse different versions of the scene until he found one ___________.

    (a) he was satisfied it
    (b) was satisfied with it
    (c) which was satisfied him
    (d) with which he was satisfied

25. The pool of home buyers ____________ with the economic recovery, making analysts optimistic about the housing market.

(a) is grown
(b) are grown
(c) is growing
(d) are growing

26. Jake is skilled with handling pets because he ____________ many in his lifetime.

(a) owns
(b) will own
(c) is owning
(d) has owned

27. ____________, Fred could not work with her because of their vastly differing working styles.

(a) Much respecting Amy as he had
(b) Respecting Amy as much he did
(c) Much respect that he had for Amy
(d) As much respect as he had for Amy

28. Laura's first job involved ____________ computers in a sales office.

(a) maintain
(b) maintained
(c) to maintain
(d) maintaining

29. Vegetarianism, the health benefits ____________ are well known, also helps to protect the environment.

(a) what
(b) which
(c) of what
(d) of which

30. Dr. Martin Luther King Jr. ____________ his "I Have a Dream" speech during a peaceful civil rights rally on August 28, 1963.

(a) presents
(b) presented
(c) has presented
(d) had presented

31. Aaron wanted to pursue a master's degree but felt it would not be feasible without ____________.

(a) financial assistance
(b) financial assistances
(c) a financial assistance
(d) any financial assistances

32. Although most news in the 1930s ____________ depressing, people still bought newspapers to stay informed about the situation.

(a) was
(b) were
(c) has been
(d) have been

33. Had Tom known that his secretary was suffering from so much stress, he ____________ her to work late on the project.

(a) will not ask
(b) had not asked
(c) would not ask
(d) would not have asked

34. ____________ presiding Supreme Court justices ruled in the plaintiff's favor.

(a) Seven of the all
(b) Of all the seven
(c) All seven of the
(d) All of seven the

35. Stock prices for oil companies showed a dramatic increase, ____________ those of most other companies plummeted.

(a) while
(b) so that
(c) whether
(d) except that

36. Despite repeated warnings about her poor grades, Terry showed ____________ effort to improve.

(a) few
(b) any
(c) little
(d) much

37. After Ian Lane's engrossing debut novel, many critics wondered how ____________ was capable of producing such a disappointing follow-up piece.

(a) a writer as he such
(b) he as a such writer
(c) a writer such as he
(d) he such as a writer

38. The fact that John failed his driver's test ____________.

(a) was to his embarrassing
(b) was embarrassed to him
(c) caused him embarrassment
(d) caused to him to be embarrassed

39. ____________ herself for misplacing such a crucial document, Frannie tore apart her room in search of her passport.

(a) Blamed
(b) Blaming
(c) To blame
(d) Had blamed

40. Although producing recycled paper requires less energy than producing regular paper ____________, the extent of energy savings is debatable.

(a) is
(b) does
(c) does it
(d) requires it

Read each sentence carefully and identify the option that contains a grammatical error.

41. (a) A: Do you mind if I ask how you injured your leg, Tom?
(b) B: Well, I'm ashamed to say I broke it while skiing.
(c) A: Were you able to have a doctor look at it right away?
(d) B: Yes. He said it was hurt seriously when I have fallen down.

42. (a) A: You look a little upset. Is anything the matter?
(b) B: I was reprimanded despite I haven't done anything wrong.
(c) A: Oh, no. So was the boss angry with you about something?
(d) B: He was, but he didn't have all the facts. The mistake wasn't my fault at all.

43. (a) A: Why did Jason look so annoyed after talking to his parents?
(b) B: They're forcing him to learn an instrument he doesn't like.
(c) A: Really? Well, what instrument do they want him to learn?
(d) B: They're insisting that he will start taking private trombone lessons.

44. (a) A: It's 11 pm, and we're not even close to finishing this project.
(b) B: Yeah. It wasn't the wisest idea to wait until the last minute to start.
(c) A: I know. We're very unlikely that we'll be able to finish it on time.
(d) B: Let's not be so pessimistic. If we work all night, we might pull it off.

45. (a) A: I was wondering if I could take you up on your offer of help.
(b) B: Absolutely. What's the problem? Is your car acting up again?
(c) A: It is, and I can't pay to a mechanic. Could you take a look at it?
(d) B: Sure. When I have time later, I'll come by and check it out.

Part IV Questions 46—50

Read each sentence carefully and identify the option that contains a grammatical error.

46. (a) Many consumers rush to acquire the latest technologies as soon as they are available. (b) Constantly replacing older gadgets can have unforeseen environmental impacts, though. (c) This is due to the fact that whereas people purchase newer gadgets, they usually throw their old ones away. (d) These discarded devices contain many toxic elements that can contaminate the ecosystem.

47. (a) Regular health checkups play an important role in maintaining our health. (b) What is more important, however, is examining the choices we make every day. (c) Healthy living consists of making well-informed decisions about diet, exercise, and habits. (d) In fact, research shows that making good choices every day improve our health significantly.

48. (a) Because they contain phytoestrogens, soy products are believed by some to increase the risk of breast cancer. (b) Indeed, in laboratory tests, phytoestrogens have been proven to induce breast cancer cells to proliferate. (c) However, diets high in soy have not been statistical linked to a greater risk of breast cancer in humans. (d) On the contrary, some studies have found that soy lowers the recurrence of and mortality from breast cancer.

49. (a) The gums are the soft tissue surrounded the base of the teeth. (b) Healthy gums are uniformly light pink in color with a firm texture. (c) Performing an important function, the gums anchor teeth and hold them in place. (d) They are not tightly wrapped around the teeth so as to avoid friction when chewing food.

50. (a) Before prescribing drugs, doctors ask patients if they are taking any other medications. (b) This is because certain drugs, when administering at the same time, react with each other. (c) Some drugs magnify the effects of other drugs, making them dangerously potent together. (d) Conversely, other drugs might cancel each other out when taken simultaneously.

This is the end of the Grammar section. Do NOT move on to the next section until instructed to do so. You are NOT allowed to turn to any other section of the test.

VOCABULARY

DIRECTIONS

This section tests your vocabulary skills. You will have 15 minutes to complete the 50 questions. Be sure to follow the directions given by the proctor.

Part I　Questions 1—25

Choose the option that best completes each gap.

1. A: Can we meet on Thursday?

B: I'm sorry, but my ___________ is full that day.

(a) chore
(b) record
(c) instance
(d) schedule

2. A: Is there a ___________ to the waterfall?

B: Yes, there's a small trail just ahead.

(a) land
(b) path
(c) wind
(d) branch

3. A: I've never seen anyone work as hard as Megan.

B: Right, no one is more ___________ than she is.

(a) permissive
(b) inclusive
(c) frequent
(d) diligent

4. A: Can the research project be done by one person?

B: No, the sheer size of the task ___________ at least two people being assigned to it.

(a) submits
(b) contains
(c) presents
(d) necessitates

5. A: Please transfer me to the director's office.

B: I'll need to know the ___________ you're calling about, please.

(a) core
(b) range
(c) matter
(d) ground

6. A: The travel packs we got are so handy.

B: Yes, they certainly are ___________.

(a) delicate
(b) intimate
(c) stubborn
(d) convenient

7. A: Would you like me to fix you a drink?

B: No, please don't go to any ___________.

(a) grant
(b) scope
(c) handle
(d) trouble

8. A: Would the company ever give me an advance on my paycheck?

B: Only under extreme ___________ would they consider such a thing.

(a) regards
(b) moments
(c) regulations
(d) circumstances

9. A: Do you believe Henry's fishing story?

B: Of course. He wouldn't ____________ something like that.

(a) pass out
(b) jump on
(c) make up
(d) knock off

10. A: Lyle keeps his vintage posters in airtight frames so they won't get damaged.

B: Oh, that explains why they've remained in ____________ condition after all these years.

(a) replete
(b) volatile
(c) pristine
(d) contrite

11. A: When does this restaurant close?

B: I noticed the staff starting to clean up, so it's ____________ to be soon.

(a) likely
(b) forced
(c) capable
(d) allowed

12. A: What happens if our computers fail?

B: Don't worry. We have ____________ measures in place for this eventuality.

(a) liability
(b) extremity
(c) contingency
(d) complacency

13. A: The presentation didn't go well, I take it.

B: That's putting it mildly. It was a complete ____________.

(a) semblance
(b) restraint
(c) limerick
(d) debacle

14. A: Did you hear about that guy who escaped from prison?

B: Yes, he's still ____________ around here somewhere.

(a) on the loose
(b) on the fence
(c) off thc hook
(d) off the mark

15. A: Mary is upset—has anyone reached out to her?

B: Yes, I've attempted to ____________ her several times.

(a) lather
(b) muster
(c) salvage
(d) console

16. A: How many boxes do you need to finish packing? Ten? Twenty?

B: I think five boxes would ____________.

(a) reconcile
(b) concede
(c) comply
(d) suffice

17. A: Can I pay with my credit card?

B: Sure, just ____________ your card through the reader.

(a) swat
(b) clasp
(c) swipe
(d) clump

18. A: So your asking me to run an errand was just a ___________?

B: Yes, I needed you out of the house so I could prepare your surprise party.

(a) ruse
(b) riddle
(c) sweep
(d) clutch

19. A: Susan was thrilled to be promoted to manager!

B: If I were in her position, I'd be ___________, too.

(a) elated
(b) incited
(c) illuminated
(d) confounded

20. A: It's difficult talking with someone who's so obstinate about their beliefs.

B: I agree. Being ___________ like that just brings the conversation to a standstill.

(a) pivotal
(b) esoteric
(c) dormant
(d) dogmatic

21. A: We should file a complaint against this hotel. The rooms are filthy!

B: I'm not sure ___________ a complaint would do any good, though.

(a) chafing
(b) lodging
(c) boarding
(d) embedding

22. A: Your manager still hasn't looked at your proposal?

B: She's so busy that I'm sure it's going to continue to ___________ on her desk.

(a) erode
(b) secede
(c) tamper
(d) languish

23. A: You look very relaxed, nestled in that hammock.

B: Yes, I've been happily ___________ in it all afternoon.

(a) emblazoned
(b) exonerated
(c) ensconced
(d) enlivened

24. A: Marcus eats so sparingly. It really concerns me.

B: Well, he's not forcing himself to starve. He's just naturally ___________.

(a) abstemious
(b) innocuous
(c) amenable
(d) inimical

25. A: Georgina is finally starting to excel in her studies.

B: It seems she has ___________ after months of struggling.

(a) hit her stride
(b) jumped the gun
(c) laid down the law
(d) gone out on a limb

Part II Questions 26—50

Choose the option that best completes each gap.

26. Employees must ___________ their IDs prominently on their work uniforms to identify themselves as authorized personnel.

(a) claim
(b) require
(c) display
(d) demand

27. The committee assesses each research proposal on an individual ___________ before making a decision.

(a) basis
(b) band
(c) trade
(d) trend

28. The construction workers were tired after ___________ in the sun to lay the foundations for the new building.

(a) striking
(b) laboring
(c) impacting
(d) motivating

29. The earthquake caused loose rocks to ___________ down the hillside and roll onto the road.

(a) tumble
(b) shrink
(c) droop
(d) falter

30. Josephine ___________ her son for not finishing his homework, reprimanding him for his irresponsibility.

(a) scolded
(b) startled
(c) angered
(d) cramped

31. Before washing your clothes, separate your ___________ into white and dark piles.

(a) dressers
(b) garments
(c) decorations
(d) fabrications

32. Pita bread dough should be put on a preheated pan before baking instead of being ___________ on a cold pan.

(a) placed
(b) scaled
(c) sealed
(d) paved

33. Don't suffer this allergy season— use UltraCure, which ___________ common allergy symptoms such as sneezing.

(a) spoils
(b) relieves
(c) restores
(d) satisfies

34. Although the basketball team had no hope of winning, the players refused to ______________ the game and gave their best effort until the end.

    (a) deny
    (b) expire
    (c) retrieve
    (d) surrender

35. The campers tried using matches to ______________ their campfire, but the wood was too damp to burn.

    (a) blast
    (b) spray
    (c) ignite
    (d) scorch

36. With most of the country's companies headquartered there, Pakistan's largest city, Karachi, is the country's economic ______________.

    (a) hub
    (b) flux
    (c) stint
    (d) curb

37. Prior to the late 1400s, printers used a slash rather than a comma to ______________ a pause in transcribed speech.

    (a) decry
    (b) intend
    (c) intone
    (d) denote

38. Research into DNA indicates that every human being is ______________ from a common ancestor in Africa.

    (a) deemed
    (b) destined
    (c) decimated
    (d) descended

39. The revolutionaries formed a new government after ______________ the dictator and sending him into exile.

    (a) overseeing
    (b) wringing
    (c) annexing
    (d) ousting

40. When the candidate won the election, the mood at his headquarters was one of ______________, with his supporters and staff cheering together.

    (a) deviation
    (b) jubilation
    (c) euphemism
    (d) incumbency

41. Several factors are ______________ the Kiwi bird, the greatest threat being habitat loss.

    (a) vilifying
    (b) unveiling
    (c) retracting
    (d) imperiling

42. Teachers cannot openly express their political beliefs, yet these beliefs are often ______________ in their lessons in the classroom.

    (a) implicit
    (b) illiterate
    (c) indigent
    (d) irascible

43. The governments of oppressive regimes ______________ their citizens' access to information by blocking websites and censoring the news.

    (a) intimidate
    (b) advocate
    (c) evacuate
    (d) obstruct

44. Irregular nouns such as "children" are __________ from an earlier method of forming plurals in English.

(a) holdovers
(b) rejoinders
(c) precursors
(d) testaments

45. Everyone at the music festival was invited to take home a program as a(n) __________ from the event.

(a) archive
(b) excerpt
(c) memoir
(d) keepsake

46. The __________ of a cow can be used to make various leather goods.

(a) hide
(b) shell
(c) fleece
(d) casing

47. The company offers a salary __________ with the employees' skills and experience to ensure that staff are fairly treated.

(a) juxtaposed
(b) extraneous
(c) commensurate
(d) commiserating

48. Ron made so many foolish decisions that his friends wondered if he was utterly __________ of common sense.

(a) akin
(b) bereft
(c) fraught
(d) debased

49. Wilhelm's __________ for classical music was evident in childhood, as he sat for hours listening to his mother's records.

(a) alacrity
(b) penchant
(c) expedience
(d) promptness

50. The crew of the overburdened ship __________ some cargo midway through their journey in order to lighten its load and complete its journey safely.

(a) deported
(b) abolished
(c) abdicated
(d) jettisoned

This is the end of the Vocabulary section. Do NOT move on to the Reading Comprehension section until instructed to do so. You are NOT allowed to turn to any other section of the test.

READING COMPREHENSION

DIRECTIONS

This section tests your ability to comprehend reading passages. You will have 45 minutes to complete the 40 questions. Be sure to follow the directions given by the proctor.

Part I Questions 1—16

Read the passage and choose the option that best completes the passage.

1. Travelers abroad are advised to ___________________________. This applies equally to men and women. When you are in a foreign country, strangers may approach you to strike up a conversation. This can be a nice way to make friends, but be aware that not everyone has innocent intentions. If a person bombards you with questions, proceed with caution. In particular, avoid giving details about where you are staying, which will protect you against potential theft.

   (a) be wary of overly friendly strangers
   (b) acquaint themselves with local customs
   (c) stay in populated areas to avoid danger
   (d) avoid displaying obvious signs of wealth

2. The mayor's New Year's Eve speech was a disappointment to many viewers. Mayor Traver spent the first few minutes reviewing the pages of his speech, as though he had never seen them before. And then he read it word for word, barely looking up from the paper. With the local economy in a dire situation, citizens were in need of a heartfelt speech. At a time when the mayor could have inspired the city, he only succeeded in damaging his image with his ___________________________.

   (a) refusal to stick to his party's platform
   (b) over-rehearsed and overblown rhetoric
   (c) last-minute cancellation of his appearance
   (d) unconvincing delivery that left listeners cold

3. Many people know that John Wilkes Booth assassinated American President Abraham Lincoln, but one lesser-known fact is that the assassination was ___________________________. Booth and two fellow Confederate sympathizers conspired to assassinate Lincoln, Vice President Andrew Johnson, and Secretary of State William Seward. This was supposed to be the first step in overthrowing the Union government and replacing it with a Confederate one. Only Booth succeeded, however, and the Confederate uprising was ultimately crushed by the Union.

   (a) almost prevented by Lincoln's top officials
   (b) backed by Union leaders eager to gain power
   (c) key to the Union's plan to infiltrate the Confederacy
   (d) part of a larger plot to seize control of the government

4. When an argument is inevitable, it is important to _________________________.
Statements that use "I" instead of "you" are effective to this end. For instance, if a
colleague is not contributing enough to a project, instead of saying, "You aren't helping
enough," try, "I feel stressed from all this work." This sounds less accusatory, so it
avoids making the other person defensive. The less people have their back up against the
wall, the better the chance they will be open to dialogue about problems.

(a) avoid putting others on the defensive
(b) consider several solutions beforehand
(c) rule out the possibility that you are to blame
(d) assess whether the problem is worth addressing

5. Investment in start-up companies is down across the country, by as much as 12%
from last year, with one notable exception: Silicon Valley. Entrepreneurs in Silicon
Valley's technology sector have continued to attract capital. Start-ups there have
raised billions of dollars from venture capitalists. Indeed, in the tech market,
investment is actually up 4% compared to last year. While this lukewarm economy
has made it difficult for most entrepreneurs to get their businesses off the ground,

_________________________.

(a) those in Silicon Valley continue to do well
(b) the technology market is suffering worst of all
(c) venture capitalists have no tech companies to invest in
(d) its impact on Silicon Valley has been exceptionally protracted

6. Surgeons have begun offering cataract patients a new eye implant that
_________________________. Until now, people suffering from cataracts, which
cloud vision, could receive bifocal implants. These improved vision for objects that were
either very close or very far away. However, patients had trouble with middle-distance
objects, which meant they still needed glasses for activities such as reading or computer
work. The latest implants are trifocals, giving patients superior vision for all three
distances, freeing them from the burden of having to use additional eyewear.

(a) eliminates the need for implant patients to wear glasses
(b) prevents the onset of an eye condition that clouds vision
(c) provides the best vision for all but middle-distance objects
(d) improves the clarity of very nearby objects for the first time

7. The "Myth of the Flat Earth" ___________________________. Washington Irving's 1828 biography of Christopher Columbus, which portrays Columbus trying to convince skeptical inquisitors that the Earth is round, has been identified as the source of this idea. Actually, Irving's account lacked a historical basis. Columbus did try to persuade a committee in 1491, but the issue was not Earth's shape but its size and the length of Columbus's proposed journey. In fact, from the third century BC onward, almost all educated Western scholars believed that the earth was spherical, and medieval scholars were no exception.

(a) persisted despite Columbus's persuasive rhetoric
(b) was a medieval theory disproved by Columbus's voyage
(c) is a modern misconception about the medieval cosmological view
(d) was posited by medieval scholars to challenge ancient views on Earth

8. A recent study found that social networking sites ___________________________. In the study, a panel looked at photos and comments users posted to an online social networking site. These postings were used to rate the users' conscientiousness, agreeability, and intellectual curiosity—characteristics that are believed to improve a person's work performance. When the panel compared their ratings to those of the participants' actual job supervisors, they found they matched closely. The study's authors concluded that people's online personas on social networking sites are reliable indicators of the type of employees they will prove to be.

(a) can be a useful resource for those looking for work
(b) are used more frequently by introverted employees
(c) contain data that can predict employee performance
(d) reduce employee productivity and overall work ethic

9. Local governments in Texas have explored the possibility of a system that would improve tornado warnings by ___________________________. Systems currently in use rely on radar information from a single antenna, which can only provide updates every five minutes. Because tornadoes can form and dissipate during time spans shorter than this, these systems can completely fail to detect twisters. By creating a decentralized network of smaller, miniature-sized radar devices, scientists believe they can detect tornadoes faster, track them more accurately, and deliver warnings up to four minutes sooner.

(a) increasing the number and size of radar devices
(b) replacing old sensors soon after tornado damage
(c) enhancing the strength of central radar antennae
(d) using a distributed web of relatively small sensors

10. With his book *Do It Yourself*, businessman and philanthropist Morris Turner recounts
    the lessons learned on his road to riches. Taking over a small family-owned shoe
    business, Turner built it into a major national chain. His insights into growing a business
    will be familiar to readers of other motivational books, but his singular blending of
    philanthropy with business is what makes him really interesting. Giving away footwear
    to those in need was one of the main reasons he earned the good will of customers.
    This book makes stimulating reading, especially for its unique emphasis on showing
    _______________________________.

    (a) that charity is a worthy pursuit after retirement
    (b) how altruism has played a beneficial role in success
    (c) how children often mismanage their parents' ventures
    (d) that increasing sales to society's needy is a path to riches

11. Unlike vertebrates, insects possess a nervous system which
    _______________________________. Vertebrates rely on a concentrated mass of
    neurons, the brain, to regulate bodily functions. Insects also have a brain, but it is
    separated into three pairs of lobes, which control the visual system, the antennae, and
    the internal organs respectively. They also have other collections of nerves that perform
    many of the same functions as a vertebrate's brain but are located throughout their
    bodies. These control observable behaviors such as locomotion and reproduction.

    (a) is focused on a smaller number of functions
    (b) is far more spread out throughout their bodies
    (c) controls reproduction using a set of three lobes
    (d) regulates bodily functions rather than perception

12. As a partner in a management consulting firm, I provide advice on improving the
    way businesses are run. When companies hire me, what they are looking for is a fresh
    perspective on the culture, organization, and practices in their business. They have
    plenty of competent managers who know how to analyze companies. What they lack is
    an outside insight, the ability to step back and look at the situation objectively. For our
    clients, what we bring to the table is _______________________________.

    (a) our familiarity with their unique culture and challenges
    (b) the finishing touches for a total business restructuring
    (c) detachment from the inner workings of their business
    (d) ample experience in training fledgling managers

13.

> To the Editor:
>
> The opinions expressed in the editorial "Rightful Owners" were oversimplified. I agree that cultural property misappropriated during colonial eras should eventually be repatriated. But with civil disorder breaking out and wars going on these days, some governments are not able to protect their museums. I think returning artifacts to these unstable countries would see them ending up on the black market or, what is worse, getting destroyed. The writer of the editorial
>
> _______________________________.
>
> Farhad Moazed

(a) slighted the fact that these artifacts had been stolen
(b) overestimated the social instability of these countries
(c) failed to account for the risk of returning these artifacts
(d) disregarded the sentiments of the artifacts' rightful owners

14. Literature has long been valued for its aesthetic merits, but a study has also demonstrated that reading fiction _______________________________. Researchers found that while reading novels, study participants showed neural activity in the same areas of the brain that process interpersonal interactions. They hypothesized that reading helps people understand the complex connections between themselves and those around them. This has been supported by later behavioral studies showing that when people increase the amount of fiction they read, they score higher on empathy tests.

(a) diverts people from relationships in the real world
(b) enhances understanding of human relationships
(c) holds less appeal for unemotional individuals
(d) teaches novelists better emotional control

15. Among scholars, there is a long-standing debate about how to classify Buddhism. There are those who emphasize its rational elements. For these people, it makes the most sense to categorize Buddhism as a philosophical system. _______________________________, there are those who believe that Buddhism's devotional elements, such as ritual and worship, place it in the tradition of other major world religions rather than philosophy.

(a) Therefore
(b) Otherwise
(c) Put another way
(d) On the other hand

16. When I became a teacher, I was intent on giving my students the support I lacked in school. Being a student who learned best working in groups and doing hands-on activities, I struggled during lecture-based lessons, and I resolved to make my classroom as interactive as possible. Not all of my colleagues were on board with my methods at first. _______________________________, not even I was totally convinced. I was charting new territory, after all. But after a few lessons, I saw my students becoming more engaged and that reassured me that I was on the right track.

(a) In fact
(b) Specifically
(c) To illustrate
(d) Nevertheless

Part II   **Questions 17—37**

Read the passage, question, and options. Then, based on the given information, choose the option that best answers the question.

17. Watching an Alfred Hitchcock movie is a unique experience. Hitchcock's films feature his expert framing of shots to play up certain emotions: anxiety, terror, empathy. Also, there are camera angles that simulate a person's gaze, making the viewer feel like a voyeur spying on the film's characters. All these elements were pioneered by Hitchcock and contribute to the inimitable feel of his movies.

Q: What is the passage mainly about?
(a) Hitchcock's films and their social impact
(b) The ways Hitchcock has influenced other films
(c) The genres that Hitchcock particularly excelled in
(d) Hitchcock's distinctive style and how it was achieved

18.

To the Editor:

The article "The Business of College Presidents" presented a one-sided view. Although college presidents have traditionally been distinguished scholars, there is another breed of person who is needed for these tough times. With schools struggling to manage their finances, leaders with corporate experience are needed. If people want thriving schools, they should recruit college presidents who can cut costs, forge private partnerships, and obtain major funding, not those who simply produce academic research.

Sincerely,

Eric Urie

Q: What is the writer's main point?
(a) Leaders of today's colleges need to have business acumen.
(b) Large companies are wielding undue influence in education.
(c) Business schools have become excessively focused on profits.
(d) College presidents need to be distinguished scholars of business.

19. Once a river down which Egypt's trade flowed, the Wadi Hammamat is now a dry riverbed prized for its ancient inscriptions. Archaeologists have painstakingly studied these markings, dating them from prehistoric times to specific Egyptian dynasties. These studies have revealed a wealth of information about the history of the region. Crude prehistoric drawings show the animals that inhabited the area 4,000 years ago, while inscriptions left by workers indicate the activities of Egypt's rulers over the ages.

Q: What is mainly being stated about the Wadi Hammamat?
(a) Its markings are considered primitive by archaeologists.
(b) It has become a trade route for ancient Egyptian artifacts.
(c) Its inscriptions hold valuable information for archaeologists.
(d) Its original purpose was to record the history of Egypt's kings.

20. When the Brandon Marseilles Quartet released its latest jazz recording, many music critics disparaged its traditionalism. But why is such a premium placed on innovation in jazz music? It is true that jazz was born of improvisation, but that does not mean every musician needs to find a wholly individual style of expression. Musical styles need to be practiced, not just advanced. The critics who sneer at musicians whose goal is to reveal the full potential of established styles hold an overly narrow view of musical greatness.

Q: What is the main purpose of the passage?
(a) To dispute the technical skill of the Brandon Marseilles Quartet
(b) To challenge the view that jazz musicians need to be innovative
(c) To praise the innovative style of the Brandon Marseilles Quartet
(d) To affirm the role of technique in producing innovative jazz music

21. The National Broadcasting Corporation provides licenses that allow senior citizens
to access television broadcasts free of charge. Those wishing to claim one of these
licenses must submit official proof of their age, such as a driver's license or passport, to
the Department for Seniors and Pensions. Those who lack official documentation may
request an in-person visit from a TV Licensing officer. This officer will decide whether
an applicant qualifies on a case-by-case basis.

Q: What is the main purpose of the report?
(a) To identify which television viewers are eligible for free services
(b) To describe ways applicants can contact the licensing department
(c) To notify applicants of services they receive with television licenses
(d) To explain how older viewers can show they qualify for free service

22. In social psychology, terror management theory has been used to account for some of the
world's deepest problems. The theory, which states that humans attempt to manage their
inborn fear of death by investing in cultural belief systems that give their lives meaning,
provides an explanation for the persistence of intercultural conflicts. By showing that
a challenge to a culture's core beliefs actually represents a terrifying attack on each
member's sense of personal significance, the theory provides a rationale for why people
so often respond to cultural outsiders with fear, mistrust, and even violence.

Q: What is the writer's main point about terror management theory?
(a) It has been used to mediate conflicts between hostile societies.
(b) It provides reasons why violent cultures show less fear of death.
(c) It posits that each culture has a distinct attitude toward mortality.
(d) It offers an explanation for the source of conflict between cultures.

23. Sign up to receive *Trendster*, the nation's leading health and nutrition magazine, and
take advantage of special promotional rates. Get six months for just $14.99 or a full year
for the low price of $25.99. Both deals represent discounts of over 50% off the cover
price. Plus, yearly subscriptions come with a free trial issue of the companion fashion
and beauty magazine, *Très Chic*! These deals are only good for the rest of the month, so
don't wait—order your subscription today!

Q: Which of the following is correct according to the advertisement?
(a) *Trendster* is the leading magazine for fashion and beauty.
(b) Discounts are not offered for subscriptions for under a year.
(c) Subscriptions for one year come with a trial issue of *Très Chic*.
(d) Promotional rates apply until the end of the following month.

24. Pearl S. Buck was an American author inspired by her experiences in China. Born in West Virginia, she was taken to China as an infant by her missionary parents. She remained there until she returned to the United States to attend university. Shortly after graduation, she returned to China and met her future husband. By the end of the decade, she had published a handful of short stories as well as her first novel. Her follow-up novel, *The Good Earth*, was a commercial success and earned her the Pulitzer Prize.

Q: Which of the following is correct about Pearl S. Buck according to the passage?
(a) She was born in China and lived there through childhood.
(b) She relocated to America after graduating from university.
(c) She became acquainted with her husband while in China.
(d) She was awarded the Pulitzer Prize for her debut novel.

25. The Carston University Library is introducing a new procedure for requesting books. If someone has borrowed a book that you need, you may recall it. Unlike holds, which are in place until the original borrower's due date, recalls require the original borrower to return the book within three days of the recall request. Users may only place two recall requests at a time, and once a recalled book has been picked up, it is not eligible for renewal.

Q: Which of the following is correct according to the announcement?
(a) Recalls are in place until the original borrower's due date.
(b) Users can request early return of books they need through recalls.
(c) There is no limit on how many recall requests users can make.
(d) Recalled books are eligible for renewal only once after pick-up.

26. In Medieval Europe, farm labor was supplied by a class of landless peasants known as serfs. These people were bound to the plot of land where they were born and barred from seeking employment elsewhere. They worked this land in exchange for part of their harvest and for the protection of their lords. They were also required to cultivate unoccupied fields upon their lords' request. What grain they were allowed to keep was never sufficient to improve their economic situation, so they remained among the poorest people of the time.

Q: Which of the following is correct about serfs according to the passage?
(a) They were allowed to look for work on various farms.
(b) They had no one to look to for protection.
(c) They could not refuse to farm unoccupied lands.
(d) They harvested enough to become prosperous.

27. Looking for accommodation during Mayfield's antique car convention? Avoid the overcrowded hotels downtown and choose the Plaza Hotel for peaceful nights at affordable rates. We are a mere 15-minute drive from the city and provide a complimentary shuttle to the convention center. For guests with a car, we will be waiving our usual parking fee during the convention. All this for just $90 a night! Plus, for just $10 extra per person, you can enjoy our sumptuous breakfast buffet. Make your reservation today!

Q: Which of the following is correct about the Plaza Hotel according to the advertisement?
(a) It is located right in the center of downtown.
(b) It offers transportation to the convention center.
(c) It charges a $10 parking fee during the convention.
(d) It provides a complimentary breakfast buffet.

28. Widely known in manufacturing, the "seven basic tools of quality" were developed in Japan following World War II. Japanese firms wanted to help lower-level workers understand statistical quality control, but realized that most people found the subject confusing. The seven tools, which depict information using visual aids such as flow charts, bar graphs, and scatter plots, were an effective way to explain quality control problems to people without extensive backgrounds in mathematics.

Q: Which of the following is correct about the "seven basic tools of quality" according to the passage?
(a) They were developed in Japan during World War II.
(b) They were created to teach managers quality control.
(c) They utilize visual representations of statistical information.
(d) They require detailed knowledge of mathematical concepts.

29. Astrid Ski Resort has opened 2 new ski runs this season. Both are designated black diamond, the most advanced category in terms of difficulty. We are proud to boast 8 advanced runs now, and 24 runs in all, and as always, we encourage skiers to exercise caution. Difficulty levels are posted on signs at the top of each slope and on maps next to each lift and at the lodge. Ski instructors are also available for individual and group lessons for all levels of skiers.

Q: Which of the following is correct according to the announcement?
(a) The newly opened runs are for skiers of all ability levels.
(b) There are more than 30 runs in total at Astrid Ski Resort.
(c) Difficulty levels for runs are posted at the top of the slopes.
(d) Ski lessons are being offered for beginner skiers only.

30. Work to reinforce the base of Brunsway County's renowned Ermine Bridge is slated to begin next month. Famed as one of the oldest of the county's wooden bridges, the structure is suffering from natural deterioration of its concrete foundations. The bridge is scheduled to close for three months to make way for workers. However, it will remain open until a temporary bypass to carry traffic over the river is complete.

Q: Which of the following is correct about Ermine Bridge according to the article?
(a) It is renowned as the sole wooden bridge in the county.
(b) It is suffering from deterioration of its wooden foundations.
(c) It is not set to close until an alternate route is complete.
(d) It is being replaced by a permanent bypass over the river.

31. A clown's made-up face is his or her trademark. To establish ownership of face-paint designs, the clown Stan Bult took to recording them on hollowed out eggs known as "clown eggs." This was the beginning of an international effort to register face-paint designs. Bult stored his collection at home and loaned them out for exhibitions. After his death, the practice continued until the collection was accidentally destroyed. Around twenty years later, the tradition was renewed by Clown Bluey, who commissioned professional artists to paint the faces on china-pot eggs.

Q: Which of the following is correct according to the passage?
(a) How the tradition of clown eggs got started is unknown.
(b) Stan Bult refused to exhibit his collection of painted eggs.
(c) Clown Bluey revived the clown egg tradition after Bult's death.
(d) Clown Bluey personally painted clown faces on china-pot eggs.

32. The ancient Greeks measured time by dividing day and night into ten sections each and then adding two more sections for both dawn and dusk. However, this system of 24 "temporal hours," originally devised by the Egyptians, was inconsistent. As the amount of time for daylight changed by season, with more hours of daylight in summer than winter, the length of the intervals varied. In the second century BC, Greek astronomer Hipparchos suggested a more consistent system that standardized time into sixty-minute intervals that would remain fixed year round. This proposal for "equinoctial hours" was ignored by his contemporaries.

Q: Which of the following is correct about the ancient Greeks according to the passage?
(a) They divided the day into 24 sections each for day and night.
(b) They created the measurement system used by Egyptians.
(c) They had a more consistent system than that of Hipparchos.
(d) They refused to adopt a system based on equinoctial hours.

33. Clarity is paramount when designing user interfaces for new computer applications. Many computer users lack the basic skills to navigate unfamiliar programs. This is the level of technological proficiency that designers should keep in mind when producing user interfaces. One example of how successful designers achieve clarity is breaking complex tasks down into a succession of separate screens. Although navigating more screens eats up users' time, doing so allows people to accomplish tasks with less confusion and fewer errors.

Q: Which statement would the writer most likely agree with?
(a) Users make more mistakes when navigating multiple screens.
(b) User interfaces should occupy fewer screens to prevent confusion.
(c) Interfaces should be navigable for people with basic computer skills.
(d) Complex user interfaces promote higher levels of computer proficiency.

34. As the owner of a company, I give out job titles more readily than pay raises to my employees. Some argue that titles should be used sparingly, but I can't see the harm in granting them, as long as they have been earned and they make the person feel appreciated. Elevated titles often boost employee morale and performance more than salary increases do. Furthermore, an official-sounding title can impress people and thereby allow employees to deal more effectively with partners and customers.

Q: Which statement would the writer most likely agree with?
(a) Elevated job titles bring psychological and business benefits.
(b) Inflating employee job titles jeopardizes company credibility.
(c) Job titles should be granted regardless of employee capability.
(d) An employee's salary should correspond to his or her job title.

35. After insisting for weeks that it was financially secure, Ryerson Bank has appealed to the federal government for a bailout. The bank claims it simply needs help "restructuring" its debt, but what it is essentially asking for is to avoid financial responsibility for its misjudgments. Under its proposal, Ryerson Bank will be accountable for a mere fraction of the bad loans it has dispensed. The public is opposed to the bailout, which would fall on the shoulders of taxpayers, yet the government sees no other option to prevent a systemic banking crisis.

Q: What can be inferred from the news article?
(a) The bank is in better financial condition than it was weeks ago.
(b) The bailout proposal has the reluctant support of the government.
(c) The government is downplaying the dangers of refusing a bailout.
(d) The government has pledged taxpayers will not pay for the bailout.

36.

> To the Editor:
>
> I was disgusted to read that apple growers can't find enough pickers! Pickers get $150 a day, but when our state employment agency sent 136 workers to an apple farm, only 6 stayed and worked. The others left, claiming it was too hard for them. As long as the unemployed can get welfare for 99 weeks, where is the motivation for them to seek work? Our politicians even want to increase welfare benefits to cover a full two years. I fail to see how this will help our economy.
>
> Antonio Grimaldi

Q: Which statement would the writer of the letter most likely agree with?
(a) Current welfare policies do not support the unemployed enough.
(b) Welfare can be a disincentive for unemployed people to find work.
(c) Too many farms are turning away potential employees to save on costs.
(d) Economic conditions have increased demand for jobs involving manual labor.

37. Officer Raymond Hoftbeck of the Shaneville Police Department pleaded not guilty today to fraud charges. Mr. Hoftbeck is accused of working for a private security firm while simultaneously collecting overtime pay with the police force, allowing him to earn twice his base salary as a police officer, according to his tax return. Mr. Hoftbeck's attorney asserts that his client did not violate any regulations because his overtime shifts never overlapped with his security work. However, the police department has suspended Hoftbeck and begun disciplinary hearings to seek his dismissal.

Q: What can be inferred about Officer Raymond Hoftbeck from the article?
(a) He is claiming that he never took a part-time security job.
(b) He failed to declare his overtime earnings to the government.
(c) He is not barred from holding a second job outside work hours.
(d) He was encouraged to plead not guilty by the police department.

38. Using a travel agent can be worthwhile for those wanting to stick to a tight budget for their vacation. (a) Even though they charge a fee, travel agents often offer discounts not available elsewhere. (b) They also have access to a network of partners that are willing to provide special travel deals. (c) Many young travelers realize after their first budget vacation that they want to work abroad. (d) With their years of experience, many travel agents can also point travelers to cheap areas to visit.

39. The minute chance that an asteroid could collide with earth has scientists seeking ways of changing the paths of such space objects. (a) Some scientists have proposed nudging asteroids off-course using solar-powered spacecraft. (b) Any rocket launched into space is at risk of sustaining damage from collisions with space debris. (c) A method of ramming objects using conventional shuttles has been tested by space agencies. (d) Meanwhile, astronauts have suggested using gravity tractors to drag objects onto new trajectories.

40. Companies have looked at innovative ways of helping their employees reduce their daily commuting time. (a) Most of these methods involve finding ways for employees to come to work outside the rush hour traffic times. (b) Workers have noted that they are most productive when working from home and have lobbied for no office hours. (c) Some companies have combined longer workdays with shorter work weeks so that employees can avoid congested roadways. (d) Other employers have experimented with staggering shifts, allowing their staff to start and end at times when travel is easier.

This is the end of the Reading Comprehension section. Please remain seated until the proctor has instructed otherwise. You are NOT allowed to turn to any other section of the test.

서울대
최신기출
3

Listening Comprehension

Grammar

Vocabulary

Reading Comprehension

LISTENING COMPREHENSION

DIRECTIONS

1. In the Listening Comprehension section, all content will be presented orally rather than in written form.

2. This section contains four parts, each with fifteen individual items. For each part, you will receive separate instructions. Listen to the instructions carefully, and choose the best answer from the options for each item.

Part I   **Questions 1—15**

You will now hear fifteen individual spoken questions or statements, each followed by four spoken responses. Choose the most appropriate response for each item.

Part II   **Questions 16—30**

You will now hear fifteen short conversation fragments, followed by four spoken responses. Choose the most appropriate response to complete each conversation.

Part III Questions 31—45

You will now hear fifteen complete conversations. For each conversation, you will be asked to answer a question. Each conversation and its corresponding question will be read twice. Then you will hear four options which will be read only once. Based on the given information, choose the option that best answers the question.

Part IV Questions 46—60

You will now hear fifteen short talks. After each talk, you will be asked to answer a question. Each talk and its corresponding question will be read twice. Then you will hear four options which will be read only once. Based on the given information, choose the option that best answers the question.

GRAMMAR

DIRECTIONS

This section tests your grammar skills. You will have 25 minutes to complete the 50 questions. Be sure to follow the directions given by the proctor.

Part I **Questions 1—20**

Choose the option that best completes each gap.

---

1. A: Do you prefer going out anywhere in particular tonight?

B: Wherever everyone else wants to go ___________ fine.

(a) is
(b) are
(c) is being
(d) are being

2. A: Are we canceling today's meeting? The boss can't come.

B: Yes, the meeting ___________ until tomorrow.

(a) postponed
(b) has postponed
(c) has been postponed
(d) will have been postponed

3. A: Did you finish your art project?

B: No, I didn't make ___________ progress.

(a) some
(b) much
(c) many
(d) several

4. A: When will dinner be ready?

B: By the time you return from the store, I ___________ making it.

(a) am finishing
(b) have finished
(c) will have finished
(d) will have been finishing

5. A: What's the best place you've ever traveled to?

B: I'd say Turkey is the most interesting place ___________ I've visited.

(a) that
(b) what
(c) where
(d) whose

6. A: How do you address your coworkers?

B: We call each other ___________ our first names.

(a) at
(b) of
(c) by
(d) on

7. A: Oh no! ___________ came off my coffee, so it spilled everywhere.

B: I'll grab a towel to help you clean it up.

(a) Lid
(b) A lid
(c) The lid
(d) Any lid

8. A: When is your essay due?

B: It has to ___________ by next Friday.

(a) complete
(b) be completed
(c) be completing
(d) have completed

9. A: Why haven't you come to choir
       practice this month?
    B: I've been too preoccupied
       ______________.

    (a) lately with plan my wedding
    (b) with plan my wedding lately
    (c) lately with planning wedding
    (d) with wedding planning lately

10. A: Congratulations on getting your
       doctorate!
    B: Thanks! It's always been my dream
       ______________ such a goal.

    (a) to reach
    (b) reaching
    (c) to be reaching
    (d) having reached

11. A: The coach shouldn't have blamed
       you in public.
    B: I know. It was inappropriate,
       ______________ the criticism was
       deserved.

    (a) just as
    (b) even if
    (c) as though
    (d) ever since

12. A: Should I accept this promotion? It'll
       be more work.
    B: Well, ______________, I'd take it.

    (a) were I in your position
    (b) I were in your position
    (c) your position were I in
    (d) in your position I were

13. A: How is the company's refinancing
       going?
    B: At this point it is unclear what
       ______________.

    (a) the optimal level of debt is
    (b) debt is the optimal of level
    (c) is the optimal of debt level
    (d) the level of debt is optimal

14. A: Why did you think the interview was
       so hard?
    B: They asked me about programming,
       ______________ I know nothing.

    (a) that
    (b) which
    (c) about what
    (d) about which

15. A: Why is the photocopier still broken?
    B: Someone was supposed to
       ______________, but no one did.

    (a) looking to repair it
    (b) looking to it to repair
    (c) look into it to get repaired
    (d) look into getting it repaired

16. A: Has the new cologne been selling
       well?
    B: I wish! Customers have shown
       almost ______________ interest in it.

    (a) no
    (b) few
    (c) any
    (d) some

17. A: How long do unrefrigerated eggs take to spoil?

B: __________ at room temperature, they're OK for several weeks.

(a) Stored
(b) Storing
(c) To store
(d) Having stored

18. A: James said you didn't enjoy your trip to Egypt.

B: I was tired because the hot weather __________ well.

(a) prevented me from sleeping
(b) prevented me from my sleep
(c) preventing me from sleeping
(d) preventing me from my sleep

19. A: Your French has improved a lot!

B: Thanks, but it'll still be a while before I can claim __________ in it.

(a) proficiency
(b) proficiencies
(c) the proficiency
(d) the proficiencies

20. A: Have you decided to travel home for Christmas?

B: It's an idea __________ .

(a) to be mulling over it
(b) mulling it over about
(c) I've been mulling over
(d) I've mulled over about it

Part II Questions 21—40

Choose the option that best completes each gap.

---

21. According to the course syllabus, students __________ attend all tutorials, or they will lose participation points.

(a) must
(b) could
(c) might
(d) would

22. Never has there been a better time for people __________ to explore financial opportunities in Asia.

(a) looked
(b) looking
(c) have looked?
(d) having looked

23. Jack was used to __________ to large groups, so he rarely got nervous when giving presentations.

(a) talk
(b) talking
(c) having talked
(d) have been talking

24. Mary was glad to find an empty seat in the subway because she __________ all day at her job at the supermarket.

(a) has stood
(b) is standing
(c) had been standing
(d) will have been standing

25. Because the suspect had clear evidence that he had been overseas, the detective concluded he ___________ not have been at the crime scene.

(a) will
(b) need
(c) could
(d) should

26. Although southern Europeans had begun using iron far earlier, it was ___________ in Scandinavia until around 500 BC.

(a) still common not to use
(b) still not in common use
(c) not commonly to use still
(d) not still commonly in using

27. The album quickly rose to the top of the charts, but received ___________ lackluster reviews from the critics.

(a) far
(b) too
(c) much
(d) rather

28. The newspaper printed an immediate retraction after it was proven that the journalist ___________ the truth.

(a) will embellish
(b) is embellishing
(c) has embellished
(d) had embellished

29. Many sportscasters believe that fighting between players, ___________ they feel happens too often, is ruining the sport of hockey.

(a) that
(b) who
(c) which
(d) whom

30. The family's plan to go sunbathing at the beach was contingent ___________ good weather.

(a) in
(b) to
(c) on
(d) from

31. Jonathan promised to bring back the ladder he had borrowed, but he never ___________.

(a) did
(b) brought
(c) had brought
(d) brought back

32. ___________ with new pop groups, The Spectaculars fell from stardom as quickly as they had risen to it.

(a) As often as it is the case
(b) Often as the case it is
(c) As is often the case
(d) The case is as often

33. Samples of bacteria from an underground cave network in New Mexico ___________ that antibiotic resistance is a primitive characteristic.

(a) suggest
(b) suggests
(c) is suggested
(d) are suggested

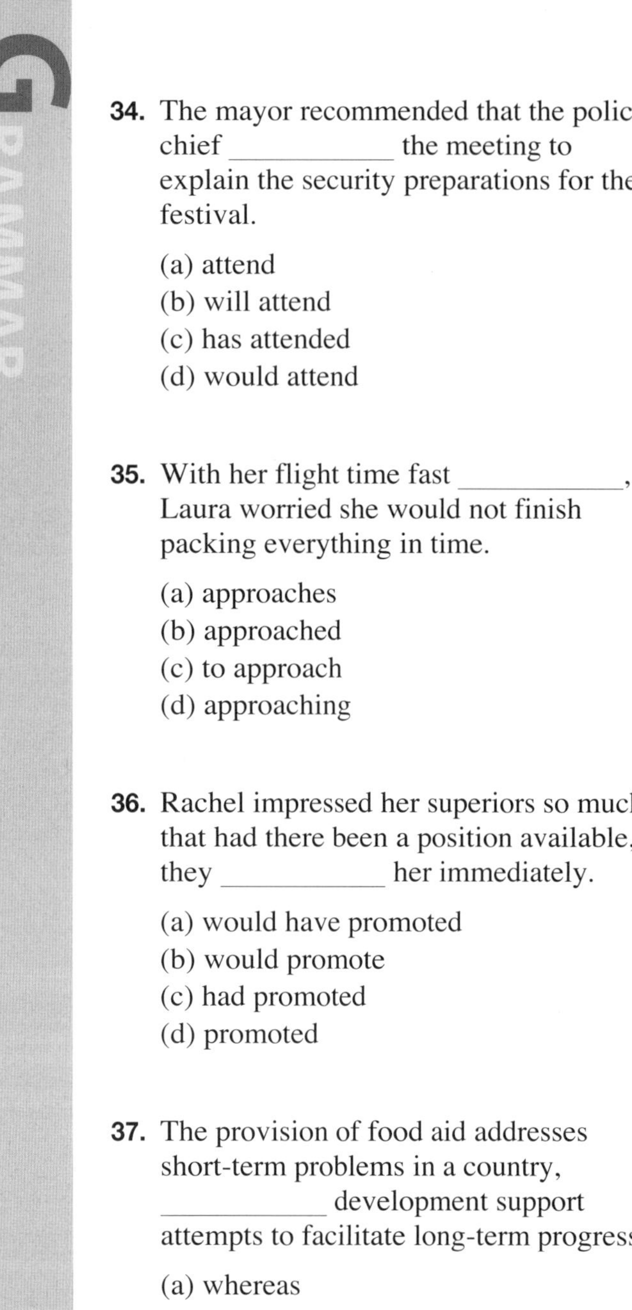

34. The mayor recommended that the police chief ____________ the meeting to explain the security preparations for the festival.

(a) attend
(b) will attend
(c) has attended
(d) would attend

35. With her flight time fast ____________, Laura worried she would not finish packing everything in time.

(a) approaches
(b) approached
(c) to approach
(d) approaching

36. Rachel impressed her superiors so much that had there been a position available, they ____________ her immediately.

(a) would have promoted
(b) would promote
(c) had promoted
(d) promoted

37. The provision of food aid addresses short-term problems in a country, ____________ development support attempts to facilitate long-term progress.

(a) whereas
(b) in case
(c) unless
(d) nor

38. ____________ to bring her notebook, Marissa was not able to take notes during the lecture.

(a) To forget
(b) Forgotten
(c) Having forgotten
(d) To have forgotten

39. Olive oil ____________ with herbs and spices can be used to add flavor to salads and pasta dishes.

(a) infuses
(b) infused
(c) infusing
(d) has infused

40. Despite majoring in literature, Arnold ____________ until after his graduation.

(a) read any poetry hardly
(b) read hardly any poetry
(c) did not read poetry hardly
(d) hardly did not read poetry

41. (a) A: I just learned the strangest thing about Terry, our coworker.
(b) B: Oh, Terry. You mean the shy, serious woman in accounting?
(c) A: Right. I just found out that she's the lead singer of a rock band.
(d) B: Really? I always pictured hers as being very conservative.

42. (a) A: It's almost time for us to go to the company dinner, isn't it?
(b) B: We're fine. The venue isn't far, and it won't take long to get there.
(c) A: I just want to arrive a bit early so we can get a table with friends.
(d) B: Don't worry. Even if we leave in an hour, we'll already get there in time.

43. (a) A: Do you think I'd be better off buying a used car as opposed to a new one?
(b) B: Used ones can be good. Just make sure to get one under warranty.
(c) A: That's smart. I'll bear it in mind when I'll start to look at different models.
(d) B: If you need any help, feel free to call me. I know a thing or two about cars.

44. (a) A: Hi, Tom. I heard you have some forthcoming public appearances.
(b) B: Yes. My publicist set them up to help promote me the new book I've written.
(c) A: Your readings are usually engaging, so I'm sure you'll draw a good crowd.
(d) B: Let's hope so. I think this is my best work to date, so I really want it to sell well.

45. (a) A: Your brother is one of the most experienced travelers that I know.
(b) B: Yes. He's been to regions none but the most intrepid travelers venture.
(c) A: He must have some fascinating stories about his experiences on the road then.
(d) B: Totally. He has a nearly inexhaustible supply of colorful anecdotes.

Part IV Questions 46—50

Read each sentence carefully and identify the option that contains a grammatical error.

46. (a) The age-old tradition of gift-giving is being transformed by modern technology. (b) People who used to spend hours shopping are now opting for electronic gift cards. (c) These cards are more convenience for givers and allow recipients to get what they want. (d) Plus, people can use these cards quickly and easily at many popular online retailers.

47. (a) Executives are under intense pressure from shareholders to deliver strong quarterly results. (b) Some have argued that this pressure can actually be detrimental to a company's long-term interests. (c) The emphasis placed on generating short-term profits often force executives to engage in risk-taking. (d) This behavior can lead to short-term gains that impress shareholders while setting the stage for disaster.

48. (a) Once, Chicago was thought mostly as a city corroded by racial tension and crime. (b) Today, it is known as a great cultural center with many theaters and art galleries. (c) Chicago is also famous for its modern architecture and impressive works of outdoor art. (d) In the city's downtown area, tourists can even see a famous sculpture by Pablo Picasso.

49. (a) People's idea of what constitutes a palatable dish varies greatly by geographical region. (b) Those inhabiting the Mediterranean, for instance, are considering octopus a delicacy. (c) Many people there would be shocked to discover that others find the dish repulsive. (d) On the other hand, their stomachs turn at the notion of frying potatoes in animal fat.

50. (a) Archaeological artifacts suggest that calendars have existed for approximately 6,000 years. (b) The calendars were used by advanced civilizations in the ancient world usually followed lunar cycles. (c) A more accurate system of sun-based measurement was introduced during the reign of Julius Caesar. (d) This Julian calendar was then replaced in 1582 AD by the even more accurate Gregorian calendar.

This is the end of the Grammar section. Do NOT move on to the next section until instructed to do so. You are NOT allowed to turn to any other section of the test.

VOCABULARY

Part I Questions 1—25

Choose the option that best completes each gap.

---

1. A: Hi, I'm Ed. I just started working here.

B: I didn't know we had any new ______________. Welcome!

(a) ranges
(b) requests
(c) nominees
(d) employees

2. A: You seem to like discussing political differences.

B: I do enjoy ______________ issues with people who have opposing views.

(a) debating
(b) speaking
(c) returning
(d) concealing

3. A: You got a gift certificate for winning the contest?

B: Yes, a ______________ worth $100.

(a) flier
(b) license
(c) voucher
(d) diploma

4. A: Is your flight to Toronto direct?

B: No, I have a(n) ______________ in Vancouver on the way.

(a) overlap
(b) layover
(c) takeover
(d) overhaul

5. A: Are those ants still a problem at your apartment?

B: No, I used a bug spray to ______________ them.

(a) release
(b) degrade
(c) suspend
(d) eradicate

6. A: How come Sharon wanted to meet after class?

B: She needed help ______________ with the work she missed.

(a) taking off
(b) catching up
(c) warming up
(d) coming forward

7. A: The doctor said my workout routine is too strenuous.

B: Then you'd better do more ______________ exercise.

(a) candid
(b) moderate
(c) repressive
(d) considerate

8. A: Can I schedule an eye exam next week?

B: Would Monday ______________ you? We have an opening then.

(a) suit
(b) spare
(c) check
(d) adapt

9. A: Thanks for all your help.

   B: You're welcome. I'm glad I could be of ___________.

   (a) necessity
   (b) assistance
   (c) recognition
   (d) indifference

10. A: This iced tea is so refreshing.

    B: It's great for ___________ your thirst.

    (a) wringing
    (b) maligning
    (c) quenching
    (d) prolonging

11. A: Your puppy seems like he's afraid of me.

    B: Yes, he's quite ___________ around strangers.

    (a) apt
    (b) timid
    (c) tolerable
    (d) impartial

12. A: Did you manage to talk your son out of majoring in art?

    B: I tried to ___________ him, but he chose it anyway.

    (a) elude
    (b) evade
    (c) deplore
    (d) dissuade

13. A: Are customers allowed through that door over there?

    B: No, it leads to a ___________ area only for staff.

    (a) resisted
    (b) dejected
    (c) restricted
    (d) prescribed

14. A: Why didn't Fred accept the transfer overseas?

    B: His enthusiasm ___________ when his wife didn't want to move.

    (a) ebbed away
    (b) scraped by
    (c) passed out
    (d) broke in

15. A: Did it rain the whole time you were at the beach?

    B: No, the showers were ___________.

    (a) mandatory
    (b) sporadic
    (c) succinct
    (d) oblique

16. A: More farm land is being developed into suburbs.

    B: Yes, cities are ___________ on rural areas.

    (a) insinuating
    (b) articulating
    (c) lampooning
    (d) encroaching

17. A: The boss congratulated us on our success!

    B: It's nice to be ___________ for working hard.

    (a) commended
    (b) authorized
    (c) sustained
    (d) beckoned

18. A: I've noticed Westerners don't stand very close to each other.

B: It's seen as an ___________ of personal space.

(a) invasion
(b) inception
(c) interruption
(d) intervention

19. A: I'll never finish my thesis.

B: But if you just keep working on it, your ___________ will pay off.

(a) perseverance
(b) complacency
(c) approbation
(d) affluence

20. A: Your article was very moving. Did you get a lot of responses?

B: Yes, I've been ___________ with hundreds of reader letters.

(a) inundated
(b) infiltrated
(c) deposed
(d) hurtled

21. A: My students played another prank on me today.

B: They really are a funny bunch, always making ___________.

(a) gall
(b) mischief
(c) profanity
(d) malevolence

22. A: Why was Allie's luggage inspected? Did she have something illegal?

B: No, nothing that could be considered ___________. Her laptop just set off the scanner.

(a) contraband
(b) tenacious
(c) statutory
(d) askew

23. A: Do you know why the police blocked this street?

B: The area is ___________ because of an accident.

(a) turned up
(b) hemmed in
(c) cordoned off
(d) brought back

24. A: Did Sheila really stop by just to borrow a hammer?

B: Well, that was her ___________ excuse. She actually wanted to see Dave.

(a) inexorable
(b) ostensible
(c) inclement
(d) transient

25. A: Theo argued really strongly for his proposal!

B: Yes, he's quite ___________ when defending issues he cares about.

(a) erratic
(b) vehement
(c) phlegmatic
(d) resplendent

26. Court witnesses have a ___________ to tell the truth, as they swear an oath to do so before testifying.

(a) trial
(b) case
(c) load
(d) duty

27. Skilled watchmakers can ___________ timepieces that have been damaged, restoring them to good working order.

(a) tie
(b) fix
(c) lay
(d) rip

28. State-of-the-art labs and government subsidies gave Almex Pharmaceuticals a(n) ___________ over their competitors in research and development.

(a) protest
(b) defense
(c) influence
(d) advantage

29. Alice was surprised but pleased when she was ___________ from among 73 women to be the beauty queen.

(a) selected
(b) received
(c) admitted
(d) projected

30. The Sphinx was buried up to its shoulders in sand until it was ___________ in the twentieth century and revealed to the world.

(a) deprived
(b) excavated
(c) depressed
(d) redistributed

31. Meeting in secret, the traders ___________ to manipulate stock prices in order to reap unlawful profits.

(a) kindled
(b) receded
(c) conspired
(d) vanquished

32. Because the military's spy plane was ___________, there were no crew members aboard to put at risk.

(a) inserted
(b) deceived
(c) detached
(d) unmanned

33. The earliest sculptures were quite ___________, but over time sculptures became more refined as artists' skills developed.

(a) fussy
(b) crude
(c) tender
(d) uptight

34. The bride ___________ the bouquet of flowers over her shoulder to the crowd waiting to catch it.

(a) tossed
(b) stroked
(c) hoarded
(d) surpassed

35. The unsafe conditions under which Medieval builders worked would be ___________ by the stricter health and safety laws of modern times.

(a) outraged
(b) provoked
(c) forbidden
(d) misdirected

36. When a fire broke out in the library, it took firefighters only minutes to ___________ it, preventing serious damage.

(a) reject
(b) extract
(c) relinquish
(d) extinguish

37. New rules to keep companies from overcharging customers will be ___________ on mobile phone companies by the government next month.

(a) implied
(b) relieved
(c) imposed
(d) diverted

38. Since few candidates applied, the company tried to make the job more ___________ by offering extra vacation time.

(a) capable
(b) extensive
(c) attractive
(d) receptive

39. The scholar, not content to make a small addition to knowledge, was determined to make a(n) ___________ research contribution.

(a) residual
(b) tentative
(c) intangible
(d) substantial

40. The military launched a(n) ___________ on the rebels in the country's western region, in an attempt to take back control of the area.

(a) pledge
(b) assault
(c) assertion
(d) platitude

41. A solution that kills bacteria can be sprayed to create a ___________ surface for safe food preparation.

(a) patchy
(b) sterile
(c) savvy
(d) virile

42. Medieval soldiers expected to get rich from foreign conquests by ___________ cities that they conquered and bringing the spoils home.

(a) forfeiting
(b) plundering
(c) postulating
(d) discharging

43. Frank had a feeling that something bad was going to happen, but no one would believe this ___________ of his.

   (a) foreclosure
   (b) forbearance
   (c) predilection
   (d) premonition

44. The use of public payphones has become obsolete now that mobile phones have largely ___________ them.

   (a) accrued
   (b) revoked
   (c) convened
   (d) supplanted

45. The Untouchables, the lowest caste, were ___________ under India's traditional caste system, shunned completely by all other classes.

   (a) adulated
   (b) salvaged
   (c) exempted
   (d) ostracized

46. Unemployed and unable to find a decent job, Chloe realized that quitting her previous job on a whim had been ___________.

   (a) arid
   (b) rash
   (c) bland
   (d) feeble

47. The relaxed and cheerful way the actors communicated with each other showed there was genuine ___________ between them.

   (a) radiation
   (b) animosity
   (c) chemistry
   (d) ascension

48. Going too long without eating can lead one to ___________ on a huge meal and feel bloated as a result.

   (a) hark
   (b) flout
   (c) quaff
   (d) binge

49. The restaurant guide gave Julio's Bistro its highest ___________ for exceptional food and service.

   (a) edifice
   (b) clamor
   (c) mandate
   (d) accolade

50. Even compared to the beauty of her sister, Jennifer was admired for her remarkably ___________ appearance.

   (a) garish
   (b) comely
   (c) feckless
   (d) piquant

This is the end of the Vocabulary section. Do **NOT** move on to the Reading Comprehension section until instructed to do so. You are **NOT** allowed to turn to any other section of the test.

READING COMPREHENSION

DIRECTIONS

This section tests your ability to comprehend reading passages. You will have 45 minutes to complete the 40 questions. Be sure to follow the directions given by the proctor.

Part I   Questions 1—16

Read the passage and choose the option that best completes the passage.

1. A recent study of science professors at major American research institutions has found that ___________________________. The results showed that the professors regarded female job applicants as less competent than males with the same credentials. This attitude held true regardless of the professors' age, sex, field, or tenure status. Perhaps this is not surprising in physics or engineering, which have proportionally more male students than females, but such was the case even in biology, where female students outnumber males. Overall, the likelihood of being hired was lower for women.

(a) there is a pervasive bias against women scientists
(b) the number of female biology students is shrinking
(c) gender bias in biology is generally directed against males
(d) more women are applying to work in physics and engineering

2. Are some languages faster than others? From a perceptual point of view, it appears that ___________________________. While there is a limit to how fast the muscles in the mouth can physically move, some languages pack more meaning into fewer syllables, and so information can be conveyed at a faster rate. For instance, to describe the field including biology, chemistry, and physics, English says "science"—two syllables—while German says "wissenschaft"—three syllables—and so listeners perceive English to be faster.

(a) distinctions are indiscernible to most listeners
(b) having native pronunciation is important
(c) English speakers are at a disadvantage
(d) differences in speed really do exist

3. A new study on adolescent behavior suggests that ___________________________. Researchers examined about 4,000 teenagers for one year, tracking the teens' friendship choices and their place in social circles. Their findings showed that teens that held a more central place in their network tended to pick on others more, possibly to solidify their position. Interestingly, the correlation between aggression and popularity in teens was nonexistent in the top 2% of popular students, who were drastically less aggressive.

(a) the desire for popularity prevents aggression
(b) aggression intensifies at the very peak of popularity
(c) social status affects the level of aggression teens display
(d) children are actually most aggressive before adolescence

4. The lasting love affair in Harvey Diaz's novel, *Daydreams of Fiction*, is not between the main character Julia and her apathetic boyfriend Manuel. Intrigue and romance scenes occur, but they are just temporary distractions. The great love of the protagonist of this novel is not a person but the literary canon. Julia simply lives for classic novels and finds more satisfaction from them than from any interpersonal relationship. The novel is a portrait of a woman who _______________________________.

(a) holds literature and reading closest to her heart
(b) discovers true love for the people surrounding her
(c) learns why real-life romance outweighs fictional love
(d) spends her troubled life searching for an ideal spouse

5. Since university students are easily accessible, many psychological researchers use them as subjects of experiments. However, students might not be representative of humanity as a whole. Now thanks to web technology, a new method of recruiting subjects is available: crowdsourcing. Several online companies offer services where researchers can set up experiments, and web users from many walks of life can participate for minimal compensation. In this way, crowdsourcing _______________________________.

(a) provides insight into students' psychology
(b) is influenced by the source of research funding
(c) is vulnerable to the prejudices of study subjects
(d) vastly broadens the diversity of research samples

6. High school teachers often focus on getting students to approach classical novels as literary scholars when instead they should be trying to _______________________________. Expecting students to pick up on every allusion and nuance of outdated language is not only unrealistic but alienating as well. Teachers should help students realize the importance of classics by showing how the themes of these classics apply to themselves. Supplementing the readings with popular modern movies or music that are loosely based on classics could help students see how certain themes span across various eras and cultures.

(a) stress the novels' historical background
(b) test students' comprehension of the content
(c) focus on appreciating the subtleties of language
(d) show how literature is relevant to students' lives

7. With its generous share of antioxidants, tea has long been said to improve cardiovascular health. It is customary, however, in many places to drink tea with milk, a practice that may nullify tea's salutary properties. Scientists speculate that this effect is a result of proteins in milk binding to and neutralizing antioxidants, and they have noted that even non-dairy soy milk has a similar antagonistic effect. So those who continue to add milk to their tea are _________________________________.

(a) amplifying its negative effects
(b) counteracting its health benefits
(c) introducing more antioxidants to it
(d) impeding digestion of milk proteins

8.

Dear Professor Grayson,

Thank you for providing a letter of recommendation for my graduate school application. I am writing because I _________________________________. In checking the status of my online application, I noticed that the site had some problem uploading your letter. Could you sign into the recommenders' portal and try entering it again? I would offer to do it myself, but confidentiality requirements prohibit me from handling the letter. Thanks again—I hope to be writing soon with news of my acceptance!

Sincerely,

Jessica Sanders

(a) need to ask you to submit the letter again
(b) have misplaced the letter that you sent me
(c) was not accepted to the school of my choice
(d) will require another copy for future applications

9. When the US Constitution emerged from the Constitutional Convention in Philadelphia in 1787, _______________________________. Its major opponents believed that it would enshrine a ruling aristocratic class—or even an actual monarchy—if it were ratified, and claimed that it was fundamentally flawed. Even its supporters were not completely satisfied with the results. They worried that the document was too weak and incoherent to preserve American republicanism from leaders bent on acquiring excessive power.

(a) its proponents had no misgivings at first
(b) its detractors criticized it in favor of a monarchy
(c) it effectively stripped the aristocracy of all power
(d) it was not immediately embraced without criticism

10. Looking at the period from 1861 to 1957, economist William Phillips observed that in years when unemployment in England was falling, the rate of inflation rose. On the other hand, when unemployment was rising, inflation tended to become lower. These observations led him to posit a pattern that was later dubbed the "Phillips curve," and in 1958, he published a work summarizing his finding that

_______________________________.

(a) low levels of unemployment effectively curbed inflation
(b) employers resist hiring workers when inflation starts increasing
(c) an inverse relationship exists between inflation and unemployment
(d) English workers' wages became overly inflated in the twentieth century

11. After decades of population decline, the city of Havermore is
__________________________________. While Mayor Margaret Dempsey has stated that
she opposes illegal immigration, she has also banned police from arbitrarily inquiring as
to an immigrant's status. Furthermore, the city has launched an initiative to help legal
immigrants start businesses and access educational opportunities. The city has seen a
10% increase in settlement by recent immigrants in the past year, so the measures seem
to be working.

(a) making more accommodations for immigrants
(b) granting all unauthorized immigrants legal status
(c) asking law enforcement to crack down on immigrants
(d) failing to make itself an attractive home for immigrants

12. As a music journalist I feel lucky to __________________________________. I'm far
from being a skilled musician myself, and sometimes I wish I could be more involved
in the creative process of music-making. However, my job gives me opportunities to
get to know music and the industry in a more intimate and wide-ranging way than most
musicians do themselves. Not only do I have the freedom to move across genres and
media, but I can also report on the artists' lives, their works, or the music business as a
whole.

(a) learn more about my own creative writing process
(b) get practical experience as a professional musician
(c) convince musicians to broaden their stylistic horizons
(d) be able to have a comprehensive view of a diverse field

13. A revolutionary technique which has recently been applied to old manuscripts promises
to __________________________________. By analyzing digital images of manuscripts,
researchers have succeeded in separating various layers of text and removing crossed-
out portions and corrections, thereby exposing earlier incarnations of various passages.
This development allows literary scholars to speculate about why authors made certain
revisions to their writing and also shows the true skill great authors had in crafting and
re-shaping their creations.

(a) replicate the first printed editions of famous works
(b) provide insights into authors' self-editing processes
(c) restore works to what authors originally wanted published
(d) help modern writers to better edit and organize their works

14. Do feelings of unfairness always lead to a desire for revenge? To explore the relationship between these emotions, researchers devised an experiment during which participants were paired and pitted against each other in a game involving monetary transactions. The game was designed so that participants were fined for taking money from their opponents and so that by the end, both suffered a net loss. While all participants felt the game was unfair, only those who lost more than their opponents felt a desire for revenge. Researchers concluded that by itself an unfair situation ___________________________________.

(a) pushes people to feel exploited unnecessarily
(b) unconsciously makes victims blame themselves
(c) actually prevents those who lost from fighting back
(d) is not cause enough to spur the wish for retribution

15. With fees that increase the longer one is a customer, auto insurers are sending a message to their long-time customers: it does not pay to stay. Instead of thanking customers for their business, insurers penalize them with higher premiums. _______________________________, they court new customers with discounted introductory prices, attempting to lure drivers away from other providers. Ultimately, this pricing system works strongly against customer loyalty, since drivers can switch insurers every few years to keep their premiums from creeping upward.

(a) Granted
(b) Otherwise
(c) For instance
(d) At the same time

16. Biofuels made of corn and soybeans have been touted as universally beneficial alternatives to oil. They have been hailed as both economically beneficial, in that they can serve as a buffer against oil price fluctuations, and as environmentally beneficial, since the growth of the crops they are based on sequesters atmospheric carbon dioxide. ____________________________, enthusiasm for biofuels may wane if they are widely adopted: their production demands large amounts of agricultural land, and they can potentially drive up the price of crops that are needed for food.

(a) Likewise
(b) Conversely
(c) Accordingly
(d) Nevertheless

Part II Questions 17—37

Read the passage, question, and options. Then, based on the given information, choose the option that best answers the question.

17. The board of directors has approved a new policy of awarding three days of leave, in addition to those granted in the normal contract, to one staff member from each department who has exhibited superior performance. Eligible workers will be evaluated and nominated by their respective department leaders, and finalists will be chosen by the board. Winners of this bonus leave will be announced at our December team meeting, and the days can be applied from the start of the new year.

Q: What is the announcement mainly about?
(a) A plan to calculate the amount of leave used by workers
(b) An initiative to compensate staff for unused vacation days
(c) A scheme to reward excellent workers with additional vacation
(d) An increase in the days of leave granted to workers in their contracts

18.

To the Editor:

As our town started developing two decades ago, residents were concerned with how urbanization might destroy the peace of our town. To assuage their concerns, ordinances limiting the amount of noise permitted were passed. However, certain residents are out in force, with their blaring stereos, and warnings are not even being issued. I'm not the only one who believes the noise regulation legislation should be enforced!

Sincerely,

Ann Jameson

Q: What is the writer's main point?
(a) Laws on noise need to be upheld more firmly.
(b) Urbanization has not intensified the noise problem.
(c) Residents should oppose the proposed noise legislation.
(d) Warnings have not been effective at lowering noise levels.

19. English author C. S. Lewis, famous for his magical kingdom of Narnia, was a prescient judge of literary works. He insightfully criticized many of his contemporaries and often independently arrived at opinions years in advance of the rest of his literary circle. For instance, he recognized the genius of P. G. Wodehouse before anyone else and championed the works of Trollope over those of Thackeray, a decision that recent critical history has borne out.

Q: What is the writer's main point about C. S. Lewis?
(a) He was regarded as a harsh critic of his literary peers.
(b) His literary precedents were adhered to by subsequent writers.
(c) He recognized talented writers before they were widely accepted.
(d) His Narnia novels have gained increasing acceptance in the literary circle.

20. It is important that those in the service industry do not categorically equate saying "yes" with customer satisfaction. If a customer makes a request that is not feasible, first apologize and explain clearly why the demand cannot be met. Next, consider the customer's original needs and try to recommend viable alternatives. Finally, by offering a free sample or gift, you can still show customers you care and keep them coming back.

Q: What are the instructions mainly about?
(a) The best way to handle impossible customer requests
(b) How to entice customers into buying different products
(c) The importance of carrying out customer requests precisely
(d) How to restore a business's reputation for inadequate service

21. The innovative work of Professor Clifford Mayes attempts to ground a pedagogical method in the psychoanalytical theories of Carl Jung. Following Jung's view that the human mind is endowed with archetypes, Mayes encourages teachers to learn about these timeless symbols—the Hero, Martyr, or Sage—and use them to enrich their classroom practices. For example, Mayes proposes that teaching can be understood as an archetypal heroic quest in which teachers and students ask serious questions together and work through their assumptions, beliefs, and doubts to transform themselves with self-understanding.

Q: What is the main topic of the passage?
(a) Mayes's contributions to Jung's theory of archetypes
(b) The role of Jungian archetypes in Mayes's teaching method
(c) Mayes's theory that teachers should undergo psychoanalysis
(d) The ways Jung incorporated Mayes's pedagogy into his theories

22. In 843, the Treaty of Verdun ended years of civil war and divided the Carolingian Empire into three sections—the East, Middle, and West Frankish Kingdoms. However, this division was done without considering the empire's geographical features or the cultural and linguistic differences of its people. Consequently, the Middle Frankish Kingdom quickly disintegrated, and the East and West Kingdoms fought for centuries to gain control of it. Thus, though the treaty was intended to resolve a conflict, it ultimately laid the groundwork for disputes that would persist well into the twentieth century.

Q: What is the writer's main point about the Treaty of Verdun?
(a) It distributed land unevenly among three kingdoms.
(b) Its ineffective division of territories led to centuries of conflict.
(c) It established territorial boundaries that remain intact in modern times.
(d) Its design served to unite disparate groups of people in a single empire.

23. Van Gogh painted two series entitled *Sunflowers*. The first, created in Paris, shows the flowers strewn on the ground, while the second, created in Arles, shows them arranged in vases. The first series was admired by fellow artist Paul Gauguin, whom Van Gogh hoped to impress with the second. Gauguin even acquired two works from the Paris series. Although the *Sunflowers* series were Van Gogh's first works that depicted only sunflowers, he had included sunflowers in some of his earlier still life and landscape paintings.

Q: Which of the following is correct about Van Gogh's *Sunflowers* series according to the passage?
(a) Both were created in Paris before Van Gogh moved to Arles.
(b) The flowers in the second series are contained in vases.
(c) Gauguin initially purchased a painting from the second series.
(d) They were Van Gogh's first attempt to paint sunflowers.

24. Several lots of methylprednisolone acetate shipped from Everhart Pharmaceuticals were found to be contaminated with a fungus which could cause meningitis. The contaminated drug, which is typically injected near the spine to treat pain, has resulted in eight deaths, and almost one hundred have fallen ill. Although not contagious like its bacterial counterpart, fungal meningitis poses severe health risks. If you received spinal injections after May 21, please consult your physician at the first sign of illness. Anti-fungal drugs will be administered only to patients already displaying symptoms.

Q: Which of the following is correct according to the announcement?
(a) The contaminated drug is used as a treatment for fungal meningitis.
(b) Nearly one hundred fatalities have been linked to the contaminated drug.
(c) Fungal meningitis is not contracted from others who are infected.
(d) Anti-fungal drugs are being distributed as a preventive measure.

25. Starista Coffee is making some changes to our Rewards program. We are now offering a free drink for every 10 drinks you buy instead of every 12 — and you can now substitute that free drink for any food item priced at $5 or less! Also, we are replacing the paper card and stamp system with plastic Rewards cards. Finally, Rewards members can now receive complimentary flavor syrups and soy milk substitutions with any drink. Thanks for being a member!

Q: Which of the following is correct about Starista's Rewards program according to the announcement?
(a) The number of purchases required for a free drink has increased.
(b) Its free reward drink cannot be redeemed for food costing over $5.
(c) It will continue to issue rewards using paper cards and stamps.
(d) Members now get syrup and soy milk substitutions for half-price.

26. Cellular senescence, or the inability of cells to divide, is a cause of age-related physical degeneration. Aging cells produce a protein called p16 that arrests cell division—a kind of self-destruct protocol. But in experiments on mice, researchers have found a way to use drugs to stop the production of this protein, thus preventing cellular senescence. Administering a certain drug to newborn mice profoundly delayed their aging over their life span. And even more interestingly, the drug successfully reversed signs of physical deterioration in mature mice.

Q: Which of the following is correct about the p16 protein according to the passage?
(a) Cellular senescence occurs because cells become unable to produce it.
(b) It is used by aging cells as a way to prevent their own destruction.
(c) Scientists improved the health of mice by giving them a dose of it.
(d) Drugs that blocked it were beneficial to both baby and mature mice.

27. A recent study has demonstrated that perceiving cuteness affects task performance. Researchers at a Japanese university asked participants to rate the cuteness and pleasantness of different images, and then split participants into groups to test their accuracy and speed in a game of manual dexterity. The first group saw images of puppies and kittens before the game, while the second saw images of older animals. The first group was 12% slower but 44% more accurate than the second group. And it seems cuteness really is the key factor: in subsequent tasks, researchers found that images of enticing food—which participants had rated as more pleasant than kittens—did not have the same effect.

Q: Which of the following is correct according to the passage?
(a) Researchers themselves rated how cute the images were.
(b) Participants who looked at older animals performed faster.
(c) Perceiving cuteness improves both accuracy and speed.
(d) Food images were rated as less pleasant than animal images.

28. Russian formalism refers to the theoretical approach of a group of scholars who transformed literary criticism from the 1910s to the 1930s by systematically analyzing the underlying forms that constitute literature. The label of "formalism," coined by the movement's detractors, was rejected by the formalists themselves as a distorted representation of their scholarly objective. After the 1930s, Stalin used the term to denounce elitist art. However, modern literary historians have revived it, since it manages to encompass all of the movement's diverse thinkers.

Q: Which of the following is correct about the term "formalism" according to the passage?
(a) It was created by ardent supporters of the movement.
(b) It was deemed a misnomer by those to whom it was applied.
(c) It was used by Stalin to praise the group's systematic analyses.
(d) It has been revived despite being unable to represent diverse theorists.

29. Because of the chemical similarities between hormones and neurotransmitters, many people believe they are the same thing. However, each substance is released and delivered differently. Hormones are released by the endocrine system: they are produced in specialized glands and must travel long distances through blood vessels to activate receptors on their target cells. Neurotransmitters, on the other hand, are released from the vesicles of a nerve cell and cross only a small space between cells to reach their destination.

Q: Which of the following is correct according to the article?
(a) Hormones and neurotransmitters share no chemical characteristics.
(b) Neurotransmitters are the transmitting medium of the endocrine system.
(c) Hormones are conveyed to their target cells through the bloodstream.
(d) Neurotransmitters must travel long distances to reach their target cells.

30. From about 1000 BC until the sixteenth century AD, the Mesoamerican peoples built huge pyramids. The oldest pyramid constructed by the Olmecs, known as La Venta, stands in Tabasco, Mexico, and was built somewhere between 1000 and 400 BC. Made of earth and stone, with a temple on top, it is believed to have been built for the worship and burial of dignitaries. Unlike at other Mesoamerican pyramids—for instance, the later pyramids of the Mayans—no tombs have been explored at La Venta, since the region's humid climate has made archaeologists cautious about disturbing the site and its contents.

Q: Which of the following is correct according to the passage?
(a) La Venta was built before 400 BC by the Olmecs.
(b) The Olmecs' oldest existing pyramid is called Tabasco.
(c) Olmec pyramids are thought to have been used solely for burial.
(d) No tombs have been explored in any Mesoamerican pyramids.

31. It has recently been found that high-cocoa mass chocolate has many nutritive properties. It provides daily doses of essential minerals such as magnesium and iron. Chocolate also contains flavonoids, which reduce the risk of blood clots, lowering the risk of heart attacks and strokes. Psychologically, it is said to have a calming effect, as it induces the brain to release endorphins. And surprisingly enough, a compound found in the cocoa bean husk coats the teeth, preventing plaque formation.

Q: Which of the following is correct according to the passage?
(a) Flavonoids reduce heart attacks by facilitating blood clotting.
(b) Chocolate has been linked to improved cardiovascular health.
(c) Chocolate calms people by suppressing endorphin release.
(d) A cocoa bean husk compound exacerbates dental plaque.

32. The newest cosmetic fad is snail slime, a complex mix of proteins that functions both as a protective layer against desiccation and damage as well as an adhesive that allows snails to stick to various surfaces. Its cosmetic properties were recently rediscovered by Chilean snail farmers who recognized its healing effects on their hands. However, its first recorded use dates back to Ancient Greece, with Hippocrates allegedly recommending it as a treatment for skin inflammation. Though scientifically unproven, the mucus is hailed as the latest skincare innovation to increase cell regeneration and replenish moisture.

Q: Which of the following is correct about snail slime according to the article?
(a) Snails use it as an adhesive as well as a means to maintain desiccation.
(b) Chilean farmers were the first ever to discover its healing properties.
(c) The ancient Greeks used it to treat inflammation but not on the skin.
(d) There is no scientific evidence supporting its regenerative properties.

33. The exorbitant prices that movie theaters charge for candy, popcorn, and soda are frustrating for moviegoers. But if you examine most theaters' operating budgets, the rationale for these prices becomes evident. A large portion of the cost of every ticket actually goes to paying film distributors, and another portion goes to the theaters' staffing and overhead costs. In the end, theater owners' profits are limited—with the exception of proceeds from the snack bar.

Q: What can be inferred about food costs in movie theaters from the passage?
(a) They directly pay for the costs of film distribution.
(b) They actually result in theater owners taking a loss.
(c) They constitute the main source of profit to the theater.
(d) They are set by food suppliers independent of the theater.

34.

Dear Mindy,

Thank you for the lovely flowers you sent me on my birthday! You've always been a pleasure to work with, and I've been more than happy to help you out after your surgery. Your recovery has been going well, and I'm sure you'll be out and about in no time. We can't wait to have you back on the team! Anyhow, I'll see you when I stop by around noon on Thursday to drop off your groceries. Call me if you need anything else!

Thanks again,

Sarah

Q: What can be inferred from the letter?
(a) Sarah found out about Mindy's surgery via letter.
(b) Mindy personally delivered the flowers to Sarah.
(c) Sarah is the doctor overseeing Mindy's recovery.
(d) Mindy is housebound from her recent surgery.

35. In the corporate world, executive compensation has ballooned because of peer benchmarking. This involves assigning pay that equals or exceeds the industry's median pay for a position. When executives earning less than the median renegotiate their contracts, they typically argue that they are underpaid, and boards of directors give them raises. Peer benchmarking leads to an overall increase in average executive pay, while neglecting more valid measures of executives' value.

Q: Which statement would the writer most likely agree with?
(a) Peer benchmarking limits executive compensation unfairly.
(b) Boards of directors are accurately assessing the value of executives.
(c) Executives are too wary of the cost increases driven by peer benchmarking.
(d) Peer benchmarking is a problematic way to assign executive compensation.

36. English explorer Sir Walter Raleigh (1554-1618) is best remembered for his journeys to the New World, but he was also a notable romantic. While in Queen Elizabeth I's court, Raleigh fell in love with one of the queen's ladies-in-waiting. The two secretly married without formally requesting the queen's permission, which earned them several months of imprisonment in the Tower of London. Following their release, Raleigh remained involved in politics, eventually being reelected to Parliament and leading two expeditions to the Americas in search of the gold of the legendary city of El Dorado.

Q: What can be inferred from the passage?
(a) Ladies-in-waiting could only marry with the queen's permission.
(b) Raleigh discovered the gold of El Dorado on his second expedition.
(c) Imprisonment in the Tower of London was reserved for violent criminals.
(d) Raleigh's first election to Parliament came after his release from incarceration.

37. The Dunmar Symphony Orchestra and Choir's most recent recording of Handel's *Messiah* has been released this week, to much fanfare. And this time, under the baton of conductor Daniel Runeberg, the piece has taken on a new spirit. Compared to his predecessor, Ivan Singer, Runeberg's conducting is more emotionally charged: the slow pieces are slower and more mournful, and the joyful pieces are more exuberant. Despite their different styles, even the staunchest lover of Singer's recording will not be disappointed, and fans can rest assured that this prestigious orchestra is in good hands with Runeberg.

Q: What can be inferred from the review?
(a) The orchestra has previously released a recording of Handel's *Messiah*.
(b) The recent recording was a collaboration between Runeberg and Singer.
(c) The orchestra earned its prestigious reputation under Runeberg's guidance.
(d) The reviewer thinks the recording is spoiled by overly emotional conducting.

38. While I sometimes regret not having children, as I grow older, I increasingly appreciate the freedom that it has allowed me. (a) It was not a conscious decision; rather my husband and I had busy careers that left us no time to consider having children. (b) But I believe that my marriage has benefited from it, as my child-rearing friends often suffer in their relationships. (c) Moreover, I have been able to explore other passions, like traveling, that would not have been possible with children. (d) This just shows that instead of viewing childbearing as a biological imperative, we should view it as an ethical choice.

39. Scented household products have become more pervasive in recent years, but they may pose a health risk. (a) Many of the most popular air freshening and laundry products contain chemicals that the government has deemed toxic or hazardous. (b) Generally, the products contain minimal amounts of the chemicals and thus do not have a negative effect on healthy adults. (c) Additionally, manufacturers have been forced to answer to conflicting consumer demands for both scented and scent-free products. (d) However, children are naturally more vulnerable, as are adults who have allergies or sensitivities to certain chemicals.

40. To the ancient Greeks, food was endowed with religious and philosophical significance. (a) As such, they only ate animals hunted in the wild or domesticated ones whose meat had first been sacrificed to the gods. (b) The wealthy were able to afford the luxury of varied foods, while the poor consumed a much less interesting diet. (c) Many ancient Greeks even distinguished between vegetables, deeming certain ones cleaner than others. (d) They also associated certain foods with various gods, such as Dionysus with wine and Persephone with bread.

This is the end of the Reading Comprehension section. Please remain seated until the proctor has instructed otherwise. You are NOT allowed to turn to any other section of the test.

서울대
최신기출

4

Listening Comprehension

Grammar

Vocabulary

Reading Comprehension

LISTENING COMPREHENSION

DIRECTIONS

1. In the Listening Comprehension section, all content will be presented orally rather than in written form.

2. This section contains four parts, each with fifteen individual items. For each part, you will receive separate instructions. Listen to the instructions carefully, and choose the best answer from the options for each item.

Part I Questions 1—15

You will now hear fifteen individual spoken questions or statements, each followed by four spoken responses. Choose the most appropriate response for each item.

Part II Questions 16—30

You will now hear fifteen short conversation fragments, followed by four spoken responses. Choose the most appropriate response to complete each conversation.

Part III **Questions 31—45**

You will now hear fifteen complete conversations. For each conversation, you will be asked to answer a question. Each conversation and its corresponding question will be read twice. Then you will hear four options which will be read only once. Based on the given information, choose the option that best answers the question.

Part IV **Questions 46—60**

You will now hear fifteen short talks. After each talk, you will be asked to answer a question. Each talk and its corresponding question will be read twice. Then you will hear four options which will be read only once. Based on the given information, choose the option that best answers the question.

GRAMMAR

Part I Questions 1—20

Choose the option that best completes each gap.

---

1. A: Have you bought Roland Dupont's latest novel?

B: No. All the copies at the bookstore _____________ sold out already.

(a) was
(b) were
(c) is being
(d) are being

2. A: How do I know if this fruit is good?

B: Just examine it very _____________ for bruises.

(a) careful
(b) carefully
(c) more careful
(d) more carefully

3. A: Why is Bob never able to pay his share of the rent?

B: Because he _____________ spending his money on frivolous things.

(a) keeps
(b) had kept
(c) will keep
(d) will have kept

4. A: Do you like Beethoven's early works?

B: Yes, they evoke _____________ of Mozart, whom I love.

(a) they
(b) them
(c) those
(d) theirs

5. A: Was that Cindy's new house we just drove by?

B: I'm not sure _____________, to be honest.

(a) where her new house is
(b) where is her new house
(c) of her new house is where
(d) of where is her new house

6. A: Was Jack injured in that car accident?

B: _____________ a few scrapes, he was unharmed.

(a) Excluded
(b) Excluding
(c) To exclude
(d) To have excluded

7. A: What kind of chocolate do you like best?

B: I like the varieties from Switzerland _____________ you brought back last time, the ones with a chewy center.

(a) that
(b) where
(c) of what
(d) of which

8. A: Have you picked a vacation spot yet?

B: Yes, I _____________ Thailand at the start of May.

(a) am visiting
(b) have visited
(c) have been visiting
(d) will have been visiting

9. A: I can't believe the Sharks lost
       tonight!
    B: Yeah, if they'd been better prepared,
       they ___________ the game.

    (a) will win
    (b) would win
    (c) will be winning
    (d) would have won

10. A: How was your second meeting with
       your future in-laws?
    B: Great! I found ___________ and
       friendly this time.

    (a) them even more approachable
    (b) their being even more approachable
    (c) their even being more approachably
    (d) them to be even more approachably

11. A: Any plans for the weekend?
    B: I was contemplating ___________ at
       the mall.

    (a) on getting done some shopping
    (b) some shopping getting it done
    (c) to get to doing some shopping
    (d) getting some shopping done

12. A: Was Beth too busy to come today?
    B: She ___________ on her essay when
       I called her this morning.

    (a) concentrates
    (b) is concentrating
    (c) has concentrated
    (d) was concentrating

13. A: I'm hungry. Is there any food in the
       fridge?
    B: Yes, there's ___________ ice cream
       left over from yesterday.

    (a) few
    (b) any
    (c) little
    (d) some

14. A: Do we really need outside sources
       for our presentation?
    B: Without ___________, we can't
       support our thesis.

    (a) research
    (b) a research
    (c) researches
    (d) the researches

15. A: Doesn't this house have any heating?
    B: ___________ in the eighteenth
       century, it only has heat in some
       rooms.

    (a) Building
    (b) To be built
    (c) Having built
    (d) Having been built

16. A: Can I offer you a slice of cake?
    B: No, thanks. I don't care much
       ___________ sweets.

    (a) of
    (b) on
    (c) for
    (d) with

17. A: I got Sam a bike for his birthday.

    B: Good choice. That's the
_______________ thing he asked for.

(a) so
(b) very
(c) such
(d) quite

18. A: How did you do in the spelling
contest?

    B: The judges declared _____________ in
the competition.

(a) my best spelling
(b) me the best speller
(c) to me as the best speller
(d) to my spelling as the best

19. A: Is Roger late to work again?

    B: He comes late almost every day,
_____________ I asked him to be
more punctual.

(a) in that
(b) as though
(c) even though
(d) provided that

20. A: What is the president's priority for
his second term?

    B: My guess is that he'll opt
_____________.

(a) to cut to public spending first
(b) first to cut to public spending
(c) cutting first public spending
(d) to cut public spending first

Part II   Questions 21—40

Choose the option that best completes each gap.

---

21. Customers who complete the survey
_____________ a coupon for a free latte.

(a) will award
(b) has awarded
(c) was awarded
(d) will be awarded

22. _____________ candidate's position on
education seemed the same, so Susan
could not decide which one deserved her
vote.

(a) All
(b) Few
(c) Every
(d) Other

23. Psychologist Abraham Maslow's paper
"A Theory of Human Motivation,"
_____________ he proposed his theory of
the hierarchy of needs, was published in
1943.

(a) that
(b) when
(c) in what
(d) in which

24. Despite _____________, Frank could not
solve the math problem before it was
due.

(a) he got help from his study group
(b) his study group was helping
(c) his study group helped him
(d) help from his study group

25. Cloudy weather ____________ until this coming Friday, but the weekend should be clear.

(a) will continue
(b) has continued
(c) will be continued
(d) is being continued

26. Savoring his mother's famous apple pie, Mike agreed that it was as good as ____________.

(a) ever
(b) it ever
(c) was ever
(d) it was ever

27. Somewhat of a rebel, Donna ____________ often skip class and go to the movies in her younger days.

(a) may
(b) must
(c) would
(d) should

28. Seventy percent of those who graduated from high school last year ____________ in a college or university as of this semester.

(a) enroll
(b) enrolls
(c) is enrolled
(d) are enrolled

29. Knowing that it was a public holiday, Jenny ____________ traffic to be light, which is why she was surprised by the traffic jam.

(a) expects
(b) is expecting
(c) has expected
(d) had expected

30. Carrie was not very tall, but with her high heels on, she had no difficulty ____________ the top shelf of the bookcase.

(a) reaching
(b) to reach
(c) reached
(d) reaches

31. Reginald discovered that getting a mortgage was the only way he ____________ afford to buy a home.

(a) can
(b) may
(c) must
(d) could

32. This year, ____________ of students with perfect attendance is at its highest level ever.

(a) percentage
(b) a percentage
(c) the percentage
(d) some percentage

33. ____________ develop an interest in poetry and begin writing his own verse.

(a) Jon did not until turned thirty
(b) Not until turned thirty did Jon
(c) Jon turned thirty not until did he
(d) Not until Jon turned thirty did he

34. The school board members expressed their concern about the superintendent's intention ____________ budget cuts.

(a) instituted
(b) instituting
(c) to institute
(d) having instituted

35. Robert was in no position ___________ line in salary negotiations with his employer because he had only joined the company the year before.

(a) taking a too hard
(b) taking too hard a
(c) to take a too hard
(d) to take too hard a

36. With Trevor ___________ money from the company, it was only a matter of time before he was caught.

(a) continuously embezzled
(b) continuously embezzling
(c) had continuously embezzled
(d) was continuously embezzling

37. After their weekend trip, the campers were so dirty that it looked as though they ___________ in weeks.

(a) have not showered
(b) are not showering
(c) had not showered
(d) do not shower

38. Parents were glad to see that the rapport between the teacher and the students in the classroom ___________ every day.

(a) has improved
(b) was improving
(c) have improved
(d) were improving

39. A new company policy ___________ all employees to turn off their computers when they leave for the day will be implemented next week.

(a) requires
(b) required
(c) requiring
(d) will require

40. The more closely nature is studied, the more widely ___________.

(a) is order to prevail found
(b) found to prevail order is
(c) order is found to prevail
(d) to prevail is order found

Part III   Questions 41—45

Read each sentence carefully and identify the option that contains a grammatical error.

41. (a) A: It's about time I went for a long ride to try it out my new bike.

(b) B: Oh, really? I'd love to come along to get some fresh air and exercise.

(c) A: Great. Where shall we go, then? I was thinking of the countryside.

(d) B: How about biking around Lake Carol? That would be more exciting.

42. (a) A: I'm worried my daughter Sarah has become anxious and withdrawn lately.

(b) B: That's not unusually for girls her age, but have you tried talking to her about it?

(c) A: Yes. She claims there's nothing the matter, but what if she's hiding something?

(d) B: Don't worry. With the two of you being so close, she'd tell you if there were.

43. (a) A: Amy, you've traveled quite a lot, right? Are you knowing much about Eastern Europe?

(b) B: I wouldn't say I know that much about the area, but I've visited a few countries there.

(c) A: Well, I was thinking of going to Poland next month and wondered if you had any advice.

(d) B: Oh, I had a great time there! The food was excellent and the architecture amazing!

44. (a) A: I can't believe Tina sank her entire life savings into opening a coffee shop downtown.

(b) B: Well, I applaud her of pursuing her dream! I wish I had the courage to take such a big risk.

(c) A: That's the problem. Since so many of these businesses fail, it seems the odds are stacked against her.

(d) B: With her skill in business and the investors she has behind her, I'm sure she'll be successful.

45. (a) A: Don't tell me you're still working on that proposal for Mr. Jones. You look totally exhausted!

(b) B: I've been working on it for straight nine hours today. It needs to be finished by tonight.

(c) A: Well, I'm going home in an hour, but if there's anything I can do before then, let me know.

(d) B: Thanks. Now that you mention it, I could really use your feedback on a couple of sections.

Part IV **Questions 46–50**

Read each sentence carefully and identify the option that contains a grammatical error.

46. (a) In response to an outbreak of West Nile Virus, Dallas's mayor has declared a state of emergency. (b) A $3 million campaign has also been launched to distribute pesticides via trucks and low-flying planes. (c) As a result, poison control centers have been flooded with calls from people concerning about the sprays. (d) However, the mayor insists that the pesticides, which imitate natural chemicals, are safe for people.

47. (a) After Russia's Crimean War, Tsar Alexander II wanted to sell Alaska, which he saw as a financial drain. (b) Initially, he offered the region to both the United States and Britain in an attempt to start a bidding war. (c) When the British expressed no interest in the offer, the US Secretary of State proposed a bargain price. (d) Later, Alaska proved to be rich in resources, making it worth much more than that the US had paid.

48. (a) Numerous studies have suggested that eating fish high omega-3 fatty acids can prevent strokes. (b) One study showed that eating two to four servings of fish per week cut the risk of strokes by up to 6%. (c) Furthermore, people who ate five servings per week were 12% less likely than others to suffer a stroke. (d) Taking omega-3 supplements, however, did not substantially reduce the chances of suffering a stroke.

49. (a) New research into fairy-wrens, a bird species living in Australia, shows that they have an interesting way of recognizing their offspring. (b) When a fairy-wren mother is incubating her eggs, she sings a unique tune, which her chicks learn while still inside their eggs. (c) After they hatch, the chicks sing the song to their mother, letting her know that they are not the offspring of another bird. (d) This type of signal is useful in case it helps members of the same family identify each other, allowing them to stick together.

50. (a) Investigators routinely use databases to match DNA found at crime scenes with samples taken from convicts. (b) Until recently, forensics experts were left with nowhere to turn when these searches failed to turn up matches. (c) Today, however, police can search samples just not from convicted criminals but also from ordinary people. (d) While the process is controversial, experts claim it can yield new leads in otherwise dead-end investigations.

This is the end of the Grammar section. Do NOT move on to the next section until instructed to do so. You are NOT allowed to turn to any other section of the test.

VOCABULARY

Part I   Questions 1—25

Choose the option that best completes each gap.

1. A: Hello, can you ___________ me to Ms. James, please?

B: Certainly. I'll transfer your call now.

(a) connect
(b) account
(c) network
(d) associate

2. A: When did you notice the security breach?

B: I only ___________ it a few minutes ago, sir.

(a) recalled
(b) detected
(c) remained
(d) supported

3. A: What time does the airport shuttle stop running?

B: I'm not sure. Try ___________ at the information desk.

(a) inquiring
(b) allowing
(c) claiming
(d) serving

4. A: Someone needs to update the training manual.

B: I know. I'm going to start ___________ it tomorrow.

(a) revising
(b) retailing
(c) conveying
(d) competing

5. A: Do you ever cheat on your diet?

B: No, I've ___________ it for a year.

(a) stuck to
(b) held out on
(c) gotten around
(d) done away with

6. A: Were you born here in Toronto?

B: No, I'm an Ottawa ___________. I moved to Toronto for university.

(a) origin
(b) native
(c) source
(d) inmate

7. A: Did Jamie ask you for a loan, too?

B: Yes, he ___________ me for money, but I didn't have any.

(a) aspired
(b) retreated
(c) implored
(d) consumed

8. A: Could you cover my morning ___________ on Friday?

B: Sorry, I'm already scheduled to work the afternoon one.

(a) shift
(b) pass
(c) term
(d) switch

9. A: Why is the train so late today?

   B: Service has been ___________ by ice on the tracks.

   (a) declined
   (b) deflected
   (c) disrupted
   (d) discarded

10. A: I need to take this DVD player apart to fix the problem.

    B: OK, go ahead and ___________ it, then.

    (a) eradicate
    (b) delineate
    (c) undermine
    (d) disassemble

11. A: The stock market seems steady lately.

    B: Yes, I'm glad there hasn't been much ___________ in a while.

    (a) instability
    (b) altercation
    (c) prevalence
    (d) reformation

12. A: Are you going shopping alone?

    B: I was going to, but if you want to come, I'd love having a(n) ___________.

    (a) amenity
    (b) affiliation
    (c) companion
    (d) commonality

13. A: Have the police caught the thief?

    B: Yes. Officers ___________ her this morning.

    (a) apprehended
    (b) sanctioned
    (c) explicated
    (d) confessed

14. A: Could you follow the teacher's explanation?

    B: Not at all. I was totally ___________ by it.

    (a) abstained
    (b) eschewed
    (c) denounced
    (d) bewildered

15. A: Why was Ben so angry when he went home?

    B: I don't know, but he sure left ___________.

    (a) to a tee
    (b) in a huff
    (c) on his toes
    (d) over the top

16. A: I'm going to paint my entire living room tomorrow.

    B: That's an ambitious ___________. Good luck!

    (a) outfitting
    (b) upbringing
    (c) undertaking
    (d) overbooking

17. A: I'm thinking about seeing a doctor about my chest pain.

    B: Good. Best to ___________ before it becomes serious.

    (a) go against the grain
    (b) take it or leave it
    (c) nip it in the bud
    (d) kick the bucket

18. A: Ray and I are going to the movies. Want to join us?

B: Thanks, but I'm more _____________ to watch videos at home.

(a) inclined
(b) consoled
(c) slandered
(d) protruded

19. A: Kay called Tom's report worthless.

B: She shouldn't have _____________ his work that way.

(a) truncated
(b) inculcated
(c) denigrated
(d) augmented

20. A: The critics were hard on your play.

B: That's putting it lightly—their reviews were _____________.

(a) sultry
(b) scathing
(c) desultory
(d) discerning

21. A: My bags are so big and heavy that they're really difficult to carry.

B: If they're that _____________, let's ask for some help.

(a) stalwart
(b) lugubrious
(c) expeditious
(d) cumbersome

22. A: Stacy was looking through the files quite _____________.

B: She must not have wanted anyone to see her doing it.

(a) infallibly
(b) boorishly
(c) ostentatiously
(d) surreptitiously

23. A: Do many scientists support string theory?

B: Yes, it has been _____________ by a lot of physicists.

(a) espoused
(b) apprised
(c) recanted
(d) divested

24. A: Andy has been flattering the boss a lot lately.

B: Yes, he's trying to _____________ himself with management.

(a) baffle
(b) rejoice
(c) intercede
(d) ingratiate

25. A: I wish the coach wouldn't shout at his players that way.

B: Me, too. He's practically _____________ orders at them.

(a) pampering
(b) bellowing
(c) scorching
(d) dousing

Part II   **Questions 26—50**

Choose the option that best completes each gap.

26. Dust & Shine offers a full refund to customers not totally ____________ with its cleaning service.

(a) included
(b) obtained
(c) required
(d) satisfied

27. Java Jake's Coffee ____________ 5% of its profits to charities that support the homeless.

(a) donates
(b) compels
(c) removes
(d) performs

28. Patients with diabetes should not take too much vitamin B, as high ____________ of the vitamin can complicate the disease.

(a) vents
(b) doses
(c) spans
(d) scales

29. The company changed its advertisements in an attempt to ____________ more consumers to buy its products.

(a) present
(b) arrange
(c) convince
(d) subscribe

30. The Wall Street Crash of 1929 saw financial markets ____________, with stocks losing a quarter of their value in just two days.

(a) tackle
(b) divert
(c) plunge
(d) detract

31. As Tom got an invitation to Jane's dinner, he ate a light lunch in ____________ of a good dinner.

(a) devotion
(b) departure
(c) anticipation
(d) supplement

32. The subject's gaze in the photograph is not straight but ____________ toward an object to the left of the camera.

(a) joined
(b) angled
(c) inhibited
(d) loosened

33. The ancient city of Rome was ____________ within a thick wall to protect it from invaders.

(a) enclosed
(b) reckoned
(c) implicated
(d) circumvented

34. Banished from his home in France, Napoleon was forced to live in _____________ on the remote island of Saint Helena.

    (a) exile
    (b) mandate
    (c) emulation
    (d) ordination

35. During the 1960s, many American college students _____________ against the Vietnam War by participating in anti-war rallies.

    (a) hesitated
    (b) backfired
    (c) surrendered
    (d) demonstrated

36. Golden Retrievers are such _____________ dogs that they put up almost no resistance to commands from humans.

    (a) docile
    (b) scanty
    (c) restive
    (d) feasible

37. Carl trusted Molly with his secrets because he knew she would never _____________ them to other people.

    (a) decry
    (b) repeal
    (c) divulge
    (d) bemoan

38. The defense lawyer stated that the _____________ against his client were completely false.

    (a) allegations
    (b) epidemics
    (c) vagaries
    (d) culprits

39. The drought lasted for several months, leaving the area's waterways severely depleted and its fields _____________.

    (a) rankled
    (b) decreed
    (c) parched
    (d) rectified

40. While it is true that some Romans enjoyed combat sports, many were so _____________ by the violence that they refused to attend these events.

    (a) inverted
    (b) appalled
    (c) fathomed
    (d) exonerated

41. A tightly focused report has no _____________ details—all information is relevant to the topic at hand.

    (a) retaliatory
    (b) superfluous
    (c) expropriated
    (d) consummate

42. ABC Company was fined for _____________ toxic chemicals from its factory into the local river.

    (a) liberating
    (b) executing
    (c) acquitting
    (d) discharging

43. Animal rights activists _____________ the mistreatment of animals and especially detest those who traffic in endangered species.

    (a) impel
    (b) abhor
    (c) exhume
    (d) emanate

44. Some hockey players are so
______________ that they will start a fight
for the most minor offenses.

(a) bellicose
(b) stringent
(c) receptive
(d) condensed

45. Becoming a novelist was the one
thing Gerry desired, the thing he
______________ most to achieve.

(a) eluded
(b) yearned
(c) solicited
(d) surmised

46. After lying ______________ for over a
hundred years, the Mount Tongariro
volcano suddenly became active again
and erupted in August 2012.

(a) reticent
(b) dormant
(c) diffident
(d) compliant

47. It was a(n) ______________ of several
problems rather than any one of them
individually that drove the company into
bankruptcy.

(a) invocation
(b) confluence
(c) admonition
(d) propinquity

48. The word "amateur" often carries
negative ______________ because it
is associated with a lack of skill or
dedication.

(a) cravings
(b) pinnacles
(c) deformities
(d) connotations

49. Roger was such a(n) ______________
worker that he could toil late into the
night without showing any signs of
exhaustion.

(a) corroded
(b) operative
(c) demeaning
(d) indefatigable

50. Many people ______________ at the
prospect of nuclear disarmament
because they deem it a high-minded
impossibility.

(a) scoff
(b) fawn
(c) wield
(d) merge

This is the end of the Vocabulary section. Do **NOT** move on to the Reading
Comprehension section until instructed to do so. You are **NOT** allowed to turn
to any other section of the test.

READING COMPREHENSION

DIRECTIONS

This section tests your ability to comprehend reading passages. You will have 45 minutes to complete the 40 questions. Be sure to follow the directions given by the proctor.

Part I **Questions 1—16**

Read the passage and choose the option that best completes the passage.

---

1. The City of Brunsway is holding a ceremony on June 21 to unveil a monument erected to ________________________. When the first settlers arrived in the area three centuries ago, they faced daunting challenges simply to obtain the necessities of life. But through sheer industriousness and determination, they built a town that would grow into a thriving city. This granite sculpture will serve as a lasting reminder to younger generations of the qualities of these great people.

(a) recognize the city's historical debt to its neighbors
(b) commemorate the hard work of the city's founders
(c) honor the creations of the city's artistic community
(d) celebrate the prosperity of the city's young workers

2. Last year, I went to Ukraine to photograph the Black Sea area. Along the way, I visited the historical city of Yalta, which I had known mainly as the site of political negotiations following World War II, and discovered a place quite unlike the one I had imagined. While there was no shortage of beautiful old buildings to photograph, the city was also a popular destination for vacationers from all over Europe thanks to its bustling beaches and seaside cafés. The journey showed me that Yalta ________________________.

(a) lacked the historical attractions I had envisioned
(b) had lost its charm as a resort because of the war
(c) held appeal both as a resort and for its history
(d) had changed drastically since I last visited it

3. Some three million shipwrecks sit on the ocean floor. The reason so many of them have not been explored is not lack of technology. Underwater robots make it possible to access even those at great depths. The issue is that this equipment is very expensive, and using it is feasible for exploring a small percentage of shipwrecks only, as the findings in most cases would not even pay for the exploration mission. In essence, the exploration of the world's sunken wrecks ________________________.

(a) is on hold until robots are able to probe greater depths
(b) is hindered by financial more than technological issues
(c) has slowed as discoveries of new wrecks have declined
(d) has become very profitable with the use of new methods

4. With its latest amendments to the city's transportation plan, Knoxville City Council has taken a major step toward _________________________________. After public hearings, the council voted to adopt amendments to its long-term plan to construct new pedestrian and cycling lanes throughout the city. These new routes, slated to be completed in stages over the next five years, will now include improved signage, lighting, medians, and curbs. These extra features are expected to help realize the project's goal of providing a safe way for residents to pursue healthy, active lifestyles.

(a) expanding public parking areas for the city's commuters
(b) repairing the city's aging paths for walkers and cyclists
(c) making walking and cycling in the city safer and easier
(d) increasing enforcement of safe driving regulations

5. The first six months of this year have seen record numbers of collisions between automobiles and animals on rural highways in Bloomview. Why the surge? Insurers blame the unseasonably warm weather, which has encouraged more people to visit their cottages and go camping. This has meant higher than average volumes of traffic on rural highways, where the bulk of the collisions have been recorded. Though hard to know for sure, it does seem that the number of accidents _________________________________.

(a) indicates that animal populations are out of control
(b) is simply the result of more drivers using roadways
(c) shows more animals are wandering into urban areas
(d) has resulted from the harsh weather on rural highways

6. In his celebrated essay "What Is Enlightenment?," the German philosopher Immanuel Kant argues that the _________________________________. At the start of his essay, he defines enlightenment as the ability to think independently rather than submit to the dogma of church or state. The only way he sees for people to achieve this level of intellectual maturity is through participation in public debate. Thus, he asserts that only a society that tolerates the free expression of differing viewpoints can foster enlightened individuals.

(a) religious authorities were keen to promote intellectual debate
(b) public debate over freedom of speech would destabilize society
(c) precondition for intellectual independence is freedom of speech
(d) participation in religious or political debates dulled the intellect

7. Having debuted at number one on the bestseller lists, the book *Future Dreams* attempts to bring the natural sciences to a wider audience. There is clearly a need for books that break down complex findings and present them in everyday language. Where the book's writers and editors go wrong is in taking the necessary task of simplification too far. So much is left out of the picture presented in this book that the reader is left with more questions than answers. Ultimately, *Future Dreams* is a work that _______________________.

    (a) places scientific rigor above commercial success
    (b) shows the public has no appetite for science writing
    (c) refuses to break down the scientific discoveries it covers
    (d) sacrifices too much complexity to make its subject accessible

8. The ancient Greek philosopher Plato wrote dialogues in which the main speaker is his teacher, Socrates. Scholars have wondered whether Plato's depiction of his teacher is historically accurate. Most believe that while the early dialogues are mostly faithful depictions of the master, many of the later dialogues, especially those in which Socrates expounds complex metaphysical theories, are probably creations of Plato's imagination. In essence, these scholars think that Plato _______________________.

    (a) confined himself to answering Socrates's questions in his later years
    (b) derived his metaphysical views from conversations with Socrates
    (c) sought new characters to replace Socrates as his views developed
    (d) utilized these dialogues to explicate his own philosophical views

9. Today the mayor announced that the City Public Library will be _______________________. The move comes in response to a deficit in revenues, which will require budgetary restraint in the coming years. Starting next January, the library will be closing thirty minutes earlier on weekdays, and weekend services, which have been popular with residents, will be eliminated. The city expects to save $250,000 compared to last year. These savings will come from the lower operation costs resulting from the library's reduced hours of service.

    (a) freezing the wages paid to its hourly employees
    (b) reversing its previous decision to extend its hours
    (c) eliminating unpopular services to help the state budget
    (d) shortening its operating hours to address budget issues

10. Alexander Pope was the first writer in English literature to
_________________________________. In the early modern period, writers in England
relied on the patronage of wealthy people to support their work. However, Pope's
popular translations of the ancient Greek epics *The Iliad* and *The Odyssey* enabled him to
earn sufficient income to concentrate full-time on producing his own poetry. This was a
luxury unavailable to any of his contemporaries in the literary world.

(a) focus on his poetic ambitions without help from patrons
(b) earn more money from his poetry than from his translations
(c) use his wealth to support the works of other struggling artists
(d) direct his attention to gathering donations for translation work

11. Responding to criticism that teachers' colleges overemphasize abstract pedagogical
theory, the Ministry of Education has decided to _________________________________.
Typically, aspiring teachers are required to pass three multiple-choice tests to obtain
initial certification. However, in the new system, instead of paper-based tests of
theoretical knowledge, teacher trainees will be required to submit lesson plans,
homework assignments, and videos of their teaching for certification. These materials
will demonstrate actual classroom skills such as the ability to engage students and to
account for different learning styles.

(a) adopt more practical criteria in certifying prospective teachers
(b) lower the passing grade for aspiring teachers' certification exams
(c) require teachers to devise more lessons with real-life applications
(d) implement stricter requirements for teachers to maintain certification

12. When villagers in Naluvedapathy, India, took on a project to get into the
Guinness World Records in 2002, they had no idea their efforts would
_________________________________. In planting more than 80,000 saplings along
their coastline within 24 hours, they set a world record, but they also did more. When
the 2004 Indian Ocean tsunami struck two years later, the new coastal forest acted as a
shield. While other villages were crushed, causing thousands of casualties, the people of
Naluvedapathy were largely unharmed, though some of their homes were flooded.

(a) warn villagers about an approaching tsunami
(b) help them rebuild from the damage of a flood
(c) spare them from the worst of a natural disaster
(d) cause massive flooding in the area two years later

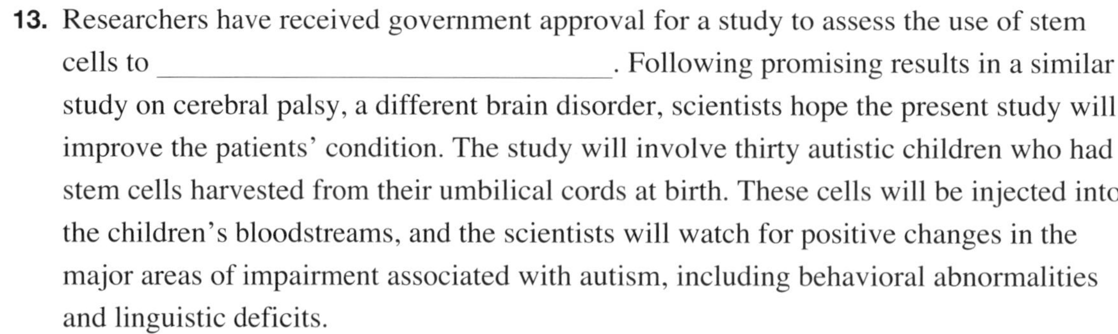

13. Researchers have received government approval for a study to assess the use of stem cells to _________________________________. Following promising results in a similar study on cerebral palsy, a different brain disorder, scientists hope the present study will improve the patients' condition. The study will involve thirty autistic children who had stem cells harvested from their umbilical cords at birth. These cells will be injected into the children's bloodstreams, and the scientists will watch for positive changes in the major areas of impairment associated with autism, including behavioral abnormalities and linguistic deficits.

(a) prevent the early onset of cerebral palsy in participants
(b) produce improvements in children suffering from autism
(c) provide language and behavior training to autistic children
(d) determine genetic factors contributing to a childhood illness

14. At the end of the seventeenth century, a number of prominent figures _________________________________. These figures, including Isaac Newton and Jonathan Swift, acknowledged the immense intellectual accomplishments of the modern world. However, believing that dismissing the works of ancient Greece and Rome, as some people were doing, was an act of arrogance, they refused to concede that the modern world had surpassed the ancient world in terms of learning. For these prominent figures, there was no substitute for an education in the classics.

(a) tried to recover sources of learning lost since antiquity
(b) sought to establish new foundations for modern learning
(c) spoke out in support of the enduring value of ancient works
(d) criticized the failure of modern thinkers to surpass the ancients

15.

> To Bingham Electronics:
>
> I am sending you a defective toaster, which a customer service representative assured me would be replaced free of charge. When I plugged it in for the first time, I saw a large spark and heard a loud popping noise. I was completely shocked that your product contained such a dangerous defect. _______________________________, I have used many of your products in the past without incident, so I remain hopeful that this was simply a chance misfortune. I look forward to receiving a replacement promptly.
>
> Sincerely,
>
> Pam Budgins

(a) Likewise
(b) As a result
(c) Nevertheless
(d) Put another way

16. In the 1980s, Soviet leader Mikhail Gorbachev began loosening censorship of the media. He hoped that this policy would reduce government corruption and strengthen people's trust in their leaders. However, the policy brought about unintended consequences. With greater freedom of information, people became increasingly disillusioned with their leaders, and soon they began demanding a complete change of government. _______________________________, the policy of freeing the press led to the Soviet Union's demise.

(a) Granted
(b) Ultimately
(c) By contrast
(d) To illustrate

Part II **Questions 17—37**

Read the passage, question, and options. Then, based on the given information, choose the option that best answers the question.

17. While some tech start-ups have what it takes to be successful, the vast majority will fail. What those in the former category have are products that enable customers to save time or produce superior work. Their products are also easier to use than the competition, such as being easy to install and having intuitive interfaces. Not to be forgotten is the enjoyment their products give users through sleek and attractive designs.

Q: What is the main topic of the passage?
(a) How start-ups attract investment in their work
(b) Why most new tech start-ups will ultimately fail
(c) The way tech start-ups foster innovative products
(d) The qualities of products from successful start-ups

18. The English Teaching Association is hosting its annual conference this coming November 13-15 on the topic of English in a globalized world. Those wishing to present their papers at the conference should submit their proposals no later than February 15 for consideration. Papers with either a theoretical or practical focus are welcome, but all submissions should be relevant to the main topic of the conference.

Q: What is the main purpose of the announcement?
(a) To propose topics for conference research papers
(b) To recruit volunteers for an upcoming conference
(c) To seek people to review submitted research papers
(d) To provide guidelines for submissions to a conference

19.

> To the Editor:
>
> The article entitled "Blaming the Obese" was correct that shaming obese people into changing their lifestyles is ineffective. What we need instead is a comprehensive approach that shows people the importance of making healthy choices. A good place to start would be a nationwide campaign to raise awareness of the illnesses associated with obesity, combined with specific recommendations for effective dieting. Providing information is key to helping people make positive choices.
>
> Jacqueline Baxter

Q: What is the writer's main point about obesity?
(a) It should be thought of as an illness.
(b) It is responsible for a rise in health care costs.
(c) It needs to be tackled by better public education.
(d) It cannot be overcome simply with lifestyle changes.

20. The so-called "Radium Girls" were a tragic but influential group of women in the history of industrial relations. Working at a paint factory in the early twentieth century, they were exposed to chemicals that their employer knew were toxic. They decided to launch a legal case against their employer, accusing the company of failing to protect its workers. Although their lives were cut short, the women's actions resulted in stronger laws to protect factory workers from dangerous chemicals and to hold companies responsible for negligence.

Q: What is the main topic of the passage?
(a) The Radium Girls' positive impact on workers' rights
(b) The discovery of radium's risks through the Radium Girls
(c) Why the US radium company hid its abusive labor practices
(d) How the Radium Girls never received compensation for their suffering

21. Studies have shown that the neurotransmitter dopamine, which facilitates communication between nerve cells, plays an important role in people's ability to store and recall past experiences. In tests where subjects were asked to identify photographs they had been shown six hours earlier, those given a chemical that is converted into dopamine in the brain performed 20% better than those in a placebo group. The findings provide strong evidence that the natural decline of dopamine levels over time is one reason why the elderly have trouble storing and retrieving memories.

Q: What is the passage mainly about?
(a) The impact of dopamine levels on memory
(b) The interaction of dopamine with other chemicals
(c) The rate at which dopamine decreases as people age
(d) The influence of recall tests on dopamine production

22. The tone of the works by American novelist Mark Twain underwent a profound change during his career. His most famous works, composed during the middle of his life, are full of humorous satire. These include the classics *Tom Sawyer* and *The Adventures of Huckleberry Finn*. However, toward the end of his life, Twain endured financial hardship as well as the deaths of his wife and daughters. These experiences filled him with bitterness over the perceived injustice of the world, an attitude that found expression in his less commonly read later works.

Q: What is the writer's main point about Mark Twain?
(a) He used humor to cope with his financial struggles.
(b) He earned sympathy for writing about his life's tragedies.
(c) His later works were popular despite their growing bitterness.
(d) His work became darker in tone in response to personal misfortunes.

23. The crowd at the protest over the Rothshire Transportation Authority's decision to hike fares grew for the third consecutive day. The authority claims that the price increase, the first in five years, is necessary to keep up with rising costs. However, local groups had begun protests before the hike was even implemented in an attempt to kill the move. Now that the price hike has come into effect, the groups are urging protesters to boycott city buses, which has resulted in a 10% drop in ridership citywide.

Q: Which of the following is correct according to the news report?
(a) The number of people attending protests has been in decline.
(b) Bus fares have been raised every year for the past five years.
(c) Protests started after the new fare hike was implemented.
(d) Ridership of buses has been reduced by calls for a boycott.

24. Come to Walker's Office Supply for our annual back-to-school sale! This weekend only, items in the store will be offered at discounts of up to 50%. Show your student ID at checkout and receive an additional 5% off all items except for electronics. And for all purchases over $20, you'll be entered into a lucky draw. Three runners-up will receive mobile phones, and the grand prize winner will take home a new laptop. Don't miss out!

Q: Which of the following is correct about Walker's Office Supply according to the advertisement?
(a) Its annual back-to-school sale is on for one week.
(b) Its special discount for students does not apply to all items.
(c) No purchase is required for customers to enter its lucky draw.
(d) The winner of its lucky draw will receive both a phone and a laptop.

25.

Dear Diana,

I meant to write you my first week in Beijing, but it's taken a few weeks to get settled. The apartment provided by the school is a furnished studio, close to work but not quite within walking distance. I assumed I'd be teaching middle school students, but they're actually in preschool. As for the food, it's growing on me, which says a lot considering my reluctance to try new things. Anyway, expect an update from me every other week!

Love,

Georgina

Q: Which of the following is correct about the writer according to the letter?
(a) She has already been in Beijing for over a week.
(b) She lives within walking distance of the school.
(c) She teaches classes of middle school students.
(d) She promises to contact her friend once a week.

26. The Republic of Ireland was long seen as an economic powerhouse in Europe. Driven by a comparatively modest corporate tax rate of 12.5%, it had the highest levels of growth in Europe from 1995 to 2007. Then things started to go wrong. The country's real estate bubble burst in 2007, leading to six months of recession in the middle of the year. Then the global financial crisis struck in 2008, and Ireland descended into a two-year recession. And it has never recovered from that shock, alternating since then between recession and anemic growth.

Q: Which of the following is correct about Ireland according to the passage?
(a) It led Europe with the highest corporate tax up to 2007.
(b) Its recession in 2007 was caused by a housing collapse.
(c) It experienced a two-year recession leading up to 2008.
(d) Its economy after 2010 has continued to expand steadily.

27. The first elephant proven to be capable of producing human speech lives at a zoo in South Korea. The creature, named Koshik, can "speak" five words by inserting his trunk into his mouth and whistling. Although Koshik does not seem to know what the words signify, he apparently learned them from his trainers. Separated from other elephants at the age of five, Koshik spent seven consecutive years without contact with his own kind. This isolation reportedly prompted him to try to bond with his human trainers by imitating their sounds.

Q: Which of the following is correct about Koshik according to the passage?
(a) He is the latest of several elephants to make human words.
(b) He produces human sounds by using his trunk to whistle.
(c) He is able to comprehend the meaning of his five words.
(d) He has spent his entire life in isolation from other elephants.

28. Tenants not renewing their leases must vacate their apartments by noon the day after the end of their lease period. Vacated rooms must be clean and contain all furniture in its original condition. Any costs related to cleaning or replacing items will be deducted from the tenant's security deposit. This deposit minus any charges will be transferred directly to tenants' bank account within ten days of vacating. Those wishing to receive a check must make arrangements with the building manager.

Q: Which of the following is correct according to the passage?
(a) Apartments must be vacated on the final day of the lease period.
(b) The cost of cleaning the room is the responsibility of the tenant.
(c) Tenants receive security deposits back on their move-out day.
(d) Bank transfer is the sole means of receiving the security deposit.

29. The love interests of the famous spy movie character James Bond are known as the Bond Girls. The actress Ursula Andress is usually credited as the first of these women for her role as Honey Ryder in the film *Dr. No*. However, an actress much less famous today, Linda Christian, had appeared more than a decade earlier as James Bond's lover. The reason she is not remembered as the first Bond Girl is that her role as Valerie Mathis in *Casino Royale* was in a television show rather than a feature film.

Q: Which of the following is correct according to the passage?
(a) The film *Dr. No* starred Linda Christian as Honey Ryder.
(b) Ursula Andress is now less famous than Linda Christian.
(c) Linda Christian became a Bond Girl after Ursula Andress.
(d) The first Bond Girl appeared on television rather than film.

30. The creator of the first commercially successful typewriter was an American named Christopher Sholes. Intent on improving earlier typewriter models, he created one with two rows of letters arranged alphabetically, but the keys had a tendency to get stuck. To solve this problem, he redesigned the keyboard so that the most commonly used letter combinations were separated, giving birth to the first QWERTY keyboard layout. Eventually, he sold the rights to this creation to a large company, which made further modifications to his keyboard layout and began large-scale manufacturing of the typewriter.

Q: Which of the following is correct about Christopher Sholes according to the passage?
(a) He is credited with inventing the very first typewriter.
(b) His first typewriter model featured a QWERTY keyboard.
(c) He altered his first keyboard design to stop jamming.
(d) His QWERTY keyboard design has remained unchanged.

31. An international team of scientists has discovered a new planet that could support life. The planet has been dubbed HD 40307g. It is one of six planets orbiting the same star, three of which were newly discovered by the team. The others are all too close to the star to support life, but HD 40307g, the most distant one, orbits at the same distance as Earth from the Sun. This would give it an Earth-like climate. Scientists also say the planet is relatively close to Earth—a mere 42 light years away, compared with Kepler-22b, another Earth-like planet, which is 600 light years away.

Q: Which of the following is correct about HD 40307g according to the passage?
(a) It belongs to a solar system that has three planets in all.
(b) It is further from its star than the other planets in its system.
(c) It orbits too far from its star to have an Earth-like climate.
(d) It is located 42 light years closer to Earth than Kepler-22b.

32. Brooksville is still recovering from last Wednesday's hurricane, which caused well over $25 million in damage. Residents continue to rely on gas-powered generators, as the city's electrical grid has yet to be restored. At the same time, residents are struggling to obtain fuel because only two-thirds of gas stations are operating due to a lack of supply. Meanwhile, only a fraction of the city's buses are running, so many people have been unable to return to work.

Q: Which of the following is correct about Brooksville according to the article?
(a) It has sustained no more than $25 million worth of damage.
(b) It has restored electricity to only a small number of homes.
(c) Two-thirds of its gas stations are closed due to lack of supply.
(d) Public transportation has resumed in a few of its neighborhoods.

33. In 1987, when the Joffrey Ballet decided to stage the ballet *The Rite of Spring* as originally choreographed by Vaslav Nijinsky, they faced a conundrum: the ballet's original choreography, first created in 1913, had only been performed eight times before being lost. While subsequent ballet companies had created new dance sequences, the Joffrey Ballet decided to hire Millicent Hodson to reconstruct the original Nijinsky version. Using photographs, reviews, and eyewitness interviews, Hodson essentially pieced together the original choreography while filling in any gaps with her own original ideas.

Q: What can be inferred from the passage?
(a) The Joffrey Ballet created a partial reconstruction of Nijinsky's work.
(b) Millicent Hodson discovered a copy of Vaslav Nijinsky's choreography.
(c) No audience members from Nijinsky's performances were alive in 1987.
(d) Nijinsky devised eight versions of the choreography for *The Rite of Spring*.

34. Within a week of getting my degree in business administration, I landed a job as an intern at a major company. I was excited about the opportunity to learn how a business worked from real executives. On my first day, my supervisor had me sort files and make copies. It didn't take long before I became disillusioned. I hadn't signed up for a job that had nothing to teach me. Three months later, still doing menial chores, I left in search of an employer that I could learn from.

Q: What can be inferred about the writer?
(a) He was let go after a three-month probation period.
(b) He was not able to meet the demands of the position.
(c) He wanted to have more challenging responsibilities.
(d) He left the company in order to start his own business.

35. Anne Moore built her following with novels that satisfy the reader's sense of justice. Her heroes are always rewarded and her villains punished. This has led critics to take issue with her for her supposedly one-sided worldview—and her latest novel, *Eventualities*, seems like her effort to prove them wrong. This novel demonstrates life's injustice, or the tendency for bad things to happen to good people. Unfortunately, her loyal fans will not find the same satisfaction they enjoyed in her previous works in this monument to cynicism.

Q: What can be inferred from the review?
(a) Anne Moore wrote her latest book to satisfy her followers.
(b) The critics praised Anne Moore for showing justice served.
(c) The villain of *Eventualities* is punished at the book's conclusion.
(d) *Eventualities* is less uplifting than Anne Moore's previous works.

36. With only modest advertising, the rapid growth of clothing company Rathberger has taken the fashion world by surprise. The company owes its success to an innovative business strategy. Rather than following its competitors and sending its manufacturing overseas, where labor costs are lower, the company manufactures its products domestically. This allows it to monitor quality more closely and keep the cost of transporting its goods to stores at a minimum. Most importantly, it appeals to its customers' sense of national pride in products made right at home.

Q: What can be inferred about Rathberger from the article?
(a) Its labor costs are higher than those of its competitors.
(b) Its clothes are sold mostly on the international market.
(c) Its strategy is to sacrifice quality to keep costs at a minimum.
(d) Its success stems mainly from extensive advertising methods.

37. The so-called relative age effect is the correlation observed between a child's date of birth and level of achievement. When children are born just after cut-off dates for school and sports teams, they are somewhat older than their peers. For example, children born at the start of the school year selection period can be almost a year older than their classmates. This head start appears to give children an enduring physical and intellectual edge on average, as many studies confirm that those born just after major cut-off dates predominate in elite sports, higher education, and even business.

Q: What can be inferred from the passage?
(a) Birth rates are higher near the end of school selection periods.
(b) Having older peers tends to improve people's athletic abilities.
(c) The influence of a person's birth month can persist into adulthood.
(d) Longer selection periods tend to reduce disparities in performance.

Part III   **Questions 38—40**

Read the passage and identify the option that does NOT belong.

38. One simple precaution can reduce the risk of electrical fires in the home. (a) Homeowners should never plug more than a few devices into a single electrical outlet. (b) When sockets are overloaded, they can cause fires that spread rapidly throughout the home. (c) Generating electricity from various alternative sources can contribute to protecting the earth's environment. (d) By spreading devices throughout the home, people decrease the risk of overloading sockets.

39. The introduction of a new gender-neutral pronoun into Sweden's national encyclopedia has some critics fuming. (a) They view the new word as an unwelcome attempt to meddle with their native language. (b) Those who live in Sweden are said to enjoy the highest levels of gender equality in the world. (c) In their view, the word represents an attempt by feminists to force their politics on society at large. (d) These critics claim that the language's two traditional gendered pronouns are perfectly adequate.

40. A.K. Ramanujan was a twentieth-century scholar noted for his controversial ideas about Indian literature. (a) The greatest uproar he caused originated from an essay interpreting various depictions of the Hindu gods Sita and Rama. (b) In this essay, Ramanujan noted that some ancient sources present the pair as siblings rather than as husband and wife. (c) The ancient works of Indian literature describing the gods contain not only stories but also philosophical reflections. (d) This seriously offended Hindu students who had grown up with the more traditional image of the gods as wedded.

This is the end of the Reading Comprehension section. Please remain seated until the proctor has instructed otherwise. You are NOT allowed to turn to any other section of the test.

서울대
최신기출

5

Listening Comprehension

Grammar

Vocabulary

Reading Comprehension

LISTENING COMPREHENSION

DIRECTIONS

1. In the Listening Comprehension section, all content will be presented orally rather than in written form.

2. This section contains four parts, each with fifteen individual items. For each part, you will receive separate instructions. Listen to the instructions carefully, and choose the best answer from the options for each item.

Part I **Questions 1—15**

You will now hear fifteen individual spoken questions or statements, each followed by four spoken responses. Choose the most appropriate response for each item.

Part II **Questions 16—30**

You will now hear fifteen short conversation fragments, followed by four spoken responses. Choose the most appropriate response to complete each conversation.

Part III   Questions 31—45

You will now hear fifteen complete conversations. For each conversation, you will be asked to answer a question. Each conversation and its corresponding question will be read twice. Then you will hear four options which will be read only once. Based on the given information, choose the option that best answers the question.

Part IV   Questions 46—60

You will now hear fifteen short talks. After each talk, you will be asked to answer a question. Each talk and its corresponding question will be read twice. Then you will hear four options which will be read only once. Based on the given information, choose the option that best answers the question.

GRAMMAR

DIRECTIONS

This section tests your grammar skills. You will have 25 minutes to complete the 50 questions. Be sure to follow the directions given by the proctor.

Part I Questions 1—20

Choose the option that best completes each gap.

1. A: Do I have to give a speech at the ceremony?

 B: Yes, all award winners __________ an acceptance speech.

 (a) preparing to require
 (b) require preparation to
 (c) are required to prepare
 (d) are prepared to be required

2. A: Have you read John Aldrin's latest novel?

 B: I have. I __________ it right after its release.

 (a) buy
 (b) bought
 (c) was buying
 (d) have bought

3. A: What are you doing tonight?

 B: I'm going to see some friends of __________.

 (a) me
 (b) my
 (c) mine
 (d) myself

4. A: We haven't seen Marcie much lately.

 B: She __________ really busy with her classes these days.

 (a) is being
 (b) has been
 (c) was being
 (d) will have been

5. A: Is the zoo close enough to walk to?

 B: No, it's __________ across town. We should take the subway.

 (a) much
 (b) way
 (c) that
 (d) so

6. A: Grace is so good at swimming.

 B: I know. I __________ like to learn how to swim like her.

 (a) can
 (b) must
 (c) could
 (d) would

7. A: Did you stay long after I left the library last night?

 B: Not __________ much work left, I went home shortly after.

 (a) having
 (b) to have
 (c) having had
 (d) to have had

8. A: What's the company getting us for Christmas?

 B: I think we __________ a gift card, like last year.

 (a) give
 (b) will give
 (c) are given
 (d) will be given

9. A: How's your job search going?

   B: OK. I've really realized

   ______________.

   (a) to value of the networking
   (b) of the networking value
   (c) the value of networking
   (d) valuing of networking

10. A: Can I take the morning off
       tomorrow?

    B: We have a meeting at 10 a.m., so
       ______________ to the office.

    (a) rather you would come
    (b) I would rather you come
    (c) you would rather coming
    (d) I rather would you coming

11. A: Where are you traveling this
       summer?

    B: Right now, Hawaii is ______________.

    (a) my choosing destination
    (b) choice of the destination
    (c) my destination of choice
    (d) the destination of choosing

12. A: When do you get up on Sundays?

    B: ______________ alone, I'd probably
       sleep till noon, but my roommate
       wakes me up around 9 a.m.

    (a) Left
    (b) Leaving
    (c) Having left
    (d) To be leaving

13. A: Who's helping with the charity
       drive?

    B: Well, it's ______________ given that
       Fran will volunteer.

    (a) a
    (b) the
    (c) any
    (d) every

14. A: Derek's leading another project?
       He's already so busy!

    B: Well, the boss personally requested
       that he ______________ it.

    (a) oversee
    (b) will oversee
    (c) has overseen
    (d) is overseeing

15. A: We just missed the bus again! This is
       the third time that happened today.

    B: I know. ______________ such bad luck
       before!

    (a) Have never had we
    (b) Never have we had
    (c) Have we had never
    (d) Never we have had

16. A: Are there any leftovers from dinner?

    B: Yes, we have ______________ leftover
       spaghetti in the fridge.

    (a) some
    (b) a few
    (c) many
    (d) several

17. A: People say Ted's quite well off.

    B: Really? His simple lifestyle shows no signs of his ___________ wealth.

(a) purport
(b) purported
(c) purporting
(d) being purported

18. A: It's warmer than I expected.

    B: Yes, we ___________ have brought our sweaters.

(a) couldn't
(b) mustn't
(c) needn't
(d) won't

19. A: I feel sorry for Cindy. She's been unemployed for a year!

    B: It must be hard ___________ her, both financially and socially.

(a) of
(b) on
(c) among
(d) against

20. A: Medical dramas make it seem like doctors have lots of free time.

    B: Yeah, doctors have far less time than they're ___________ .

(a) having portrayed
(b) portrayed as having
(c) having been portrayed
(d) portrayed as having been

Part II   **Questions 21–40**

Choose the option that best completes each gap.

21. As a caregiver in a daycare center, Cecilia was accustomed to ___________ the emotional outbursts of young children.

(a) handle
(b) handled
(c) handling
(d) have handled

22. Julia does not suffer from stage fright, ___________ years performing on stage when she was young.

(a) spent
(b) spending
(c) having spent
(d) to have spent

23. The man's friends, many ___________ he had known since childhood, gathered at his home for his sixtieth birthday party.

(a) whom
(b) whose
(c) of whom
(d) of whose

24. Following extensive pilot testing, the software was redesigned ___________ the needs of its users.

(a) to better accommodate
(b) as a better accommodation
(c) as better to accommodate of
(d) to a better accommodation of

25. The president could not persuade legislators ____________ the kinds of laws he had promised to voters during his campaign.

(a) enact
(b) to enact
(c) enacting
(d) are enacting

26. Over a third of the books in the library ____________ when a fire broke out there last weekend.

(a) was burned
(b) were burned
(c) has been burned
(d) have been burned

27. The number of members in the soccer club ____________ over the last several years.

(a) have not changed
(b) are not changing
(c) has not changed
(d) is not changing

28. Audiences said that Joey Caltone's new movie was the best they ____________ all year, though most critics disagreed.

(a) had seen
(b) were seeing
(c) will have seen
(d) had been seeing

29. The contractor's estimates, which were acceptable last week, ____________ too expensive now in light of upcoming budget cutbacks.

(a) are
(b) had been
(c) have been
(d) were being

30. ____________, persistent rain delays put the tennis tournament two hours behind schedule.

(a) Much disappointment of fans
(b) Much to fans' disappointment
(c) Fans' much to disappointment
(d) Fans' disappointment of much

31. After teaching himself the basics of writing poems, Jerome decided to take a class in ____________.

(a) poetry
(b) poetries
(c) the poetry
(d) some poetries

32. Tucked away in a remote northwestern county ____________ the state's most popular hiking trails.

(a) is
(b) are
(c) is being
(d) are being

33. If the warranty ____________ before its expiration date, the computer's repairs would have cost Erica nothing.

(a) is being renewed
(b) has been renewed
(c) had been renewed
(d) was being renewed

34. Phuket, Thailand, is a good honeymoon vacation spot, ____________ some people claim that it is overrun with tourists.

(a) although
(b) in case
(c) unless
(d) as if

35. Everyone was surprised when the Gray Jays won the game, since ___________ odds were so strongly against them.

(a) the
(b) little
(c) much
(d) every

36. Patrick was humble about his success, saying that he would never have made it so far if not ___________ him.

(a) the opportunities afforded for
(b) for the opportunities afforded
(c) the opportunities were afforded for
(d) for the opportunities were afforded

37. The coaching staff offers guidance and support for all students, ___________ age or ability.

(a) up to
(b) far from
(c) rather than
(d) regardless of

38. Getting eight hours of sleep every night is of course desirable but, for most working adults, ___________.

(a) unfeasible
(b) unfeasible to
(c) is unfeasible to
(d) is unfeasible to get

39. Parents were already protesting funding cuts, rumors ___________ had reached them weeks before.

(a) that
(b) which
(c) of that
(d) of which

40. The brain injuries of athletes ___________ to those of soldiers, since they frequently present in similar ways.

(a) often liken
(b) often likens
(c) is often likened
(d) are often likened

Part III   Questions 41—45

Read each sentence carefully and identify the option that contains a grammatical error.

41. (a) A: I heard that you've just come back from Lake Baikal. How was it?
(b) B: Great! I'd recommend going to anyone wanting a nice vacation.
(c) A: Was it easy to find accommodation at a hotel there? I heard it's quite remote.
(d) B: Actually, I stayed in a cabin where one of my Russian friends owns.

42. (a) A: Are you going to be doing the marathon for cancer research next month?
(b) B: Of course I do. I've already started collecting donations for it.
(c) A: Great! You should join me and my friends in our training sessions.
(d) B: OK! I'd love to, since I've been pretty bored training by myself.

43. (a) A: Did Sam mention how he did on his math final?
(b) B: He hasn't told me already. It seems like he's upset about his score.
(c) A: Really? That's a shame. He studied so hard for it, too.
(d) B: I know! Plus, it was one of his favorite classes this semester.

44. (a) A: Did you see the huge crowd of people outside the stadium while you were driving home?
(b) B: Yeah, but I didn't pay attention what was happening. What was all the commotion about?
(c) A: There's apparently some kind of free concert by a heartthrob pop star that teen girls love.
(d) B: Oh, I heard about that on the radio. I didn't know it was happening tonight, though.

45. (a) A: Timothy Sawyer's lead in the race for governor seems to be slipping as of late.
(b) B: Yeah, but the polls show he has still been able to maintain a slight advantage.
(c) A: I suppose. But do you think he has held onto all of those votes until election day?
(d) B: Definitely. He just needs to make it through the final few days of the campaign.

Part IV   Questions 46—50

Read each sentence carefully and identify the option that contains a grammatical error.

46. (a) Even the most educated Europeans knew little about the world outside Europe in the early 1400s. (b) To the south, the deserts of northern Africa were mysterious lands for most people. (c) To the east, Asia was rarely visited, and stories about life there were so incredible that few believed them. (d) And to the west of Europe lay the Atlantic Ocean, but at the time nobody knew how widely it was.

47. (a) Somewhat unusually, Bach did not end his secular cantata BWV34a in a chorale. (b) To do so would have been customary in Bach's time in this type of work. (c) Yet neither in this cantata or in its non-secular adaptation does Bach do so. (d) Instead, he ends the piece with a chorus for voices, strings, and continuo.

48. (a) Plantera Mosquito Spray alleviates the discomfort resulted from mosquito and insect bites. (b) This pleasant-smelling spray is also effective at keeping insects at bay during outdoor activities. (c) Those seeking added protection can put our spray directly onto their clothing and shoes. (d) And with its all-natural menthol-based formula, Plantera is safe for use even on young children.

49. (a) Recently, the United States space agency, NASA, which renamed two of its orbiting satellites. (b) These were given new names to honor James Van Allen, a magnetospheric scientist. (c) The Van Allen Probes, as they are now called, are intended to observe radiation belts around Earth. (d) Their mission is to help scientists understand how these belts respond to incoming solar radiation.

50. (a) A rod-wielding character called Krampus is part of the Christmas tradition in regions of Austria and Germany. (b) This likely began as part of a pagan tradition to ward off the harsh winter weather and was later incorporated into the holiday. (c) Clad in a shaggy fur costume and a hideous mask, Krampus appears on the streets in early December with Santa Claus. (d) While the saint gives sweet treats to good children, and Krampus threatens bad children with lashes from his rod.

This is the end of the Grammar section. Do NOT move on to the next section until instructed to do so. You are NOT allowed to turn to any other section of the test.

VOCABULARY

DIRECTIONS

This section tests your vocabulary skills. You will have 15 minutes to complete the 50 questions. Be sure to follow the directions given by the proctor.

Part I — Questions 1—25

Choose the option that best completes each gap.

1. A: Excuse me, where's the post office?

B: Sorry, I'm new here and not ____________ with the area.

(a) curious
(b) familiar
(c) adequate
(d) acceptable

2. A: What do the rings on the Olympic flag represent?

B: Each one ____________ one of the five continents.

(a) signs in
(b) bears on
(c) shows up
(d) stands for

3. A: Would using visual aids help my students concentrate?

B: Sure, that'll make them ____________.

(a) vivid
(b) vague
(c) audible
(d) attentive

4. A: What are the airline's rules on cancellations?

B: I'll call them to find out their ____________.

(a) settings
(b) features
(c) regulations
(d) conclusions

5. A: I'd like to see that documentary about bullying.

B: Let's go to the ____________ being held at the community center, then.

(a) outlook
(b) highlight
(c) watching
(d) screening

6. A: Was the project proposal you gave me the final version?

B: No, it was only the first ____________.

(a) sort
(b) raise
(c) draft
(d) sight

7. A: Do you have any ____________ into why Paula and Drew broke up?

B: They've been reticent about it, so I have no clue.

(a) prospect
(b) scheme
(c) insight
(d) notice

8. A: I gained weight during the holidays.

B: Me, too. I always get a bit ____________ from all the sweet treats.

(a) bushy
(b) chubby
(c) tangled
(d) bundled

9. A: Do you think the mayor will actually cut taxes?

   B: I doubt it. That promise should be regarded with ___________.

   (a) suspicion
   (b) obscurity
   (c) conjecture
   (d) imagination

10. A: I should have thought more carefully before opening my mouth.

    B: Well, from now on, consider the ___________ before each statement.

    (a) consequences
    (b) supplements
    (c) terminations
    (d) remainders

11. A: Our production process is too complex. We should fix it.

    B: I agree. A complete ___________ is needed.

    (a) upstart
    (b) markup
    (c) shortfall
    (d) overhaul

12. A: Did you see the soccer game last weekend?

    B: No. I've been too ___________ in my studies to follow sports lately.

    (a) wrested
    (b) splurged
    (c) immersed
    (d) relinquished

13. A: Can you keep a secret?

    B: You bet. I'm always ___________ when it comes to private information.

    (a) uncovered
    (b) secluded
    (c) arduous
    (d) discreet

14. A: Ed told me we're getting a new director.

    B: That's just ___________. Nothing's been officially announced yet.

    (a) speculation
    (b) summation
    (c) captivation
    (d) provision

15. A: Did Jane save her lottery winnings?

    B: No, she ___________ them all on useless things.

    (a) begrudged
    (b) dismantled
    (c) squandered
    (d) circumvented

16. A: The doorbell keeps ringing, but there's nobody there.

    B: Maybe some kids are playing a ___________.

    (a) skid
    (b) feud
    (c) treat
    (d) prank

17. A: Our stocks have lost so much value!

B: Don't worry. Things will improve, and we'll ___________ our losses.

(a) recoup
(b) realign
(c) reassure
(d) reanimate

18. A: Has the jury reached its verdict yet?

B: No. They are still in ___________ over the case.

(a) intention
(b) justification
(c) deliberation
(d) consolidation

19. A: Max failed his driver's license test, but he doesn't seem discouraged.

B: Yeah, he isn't ___________ by such small setbacks.

(a) daunted
(b) tolerated
(c) proffered
(d) condoned

20. A: I saw you sleeping at your desk earlier today!

B: I sometimes ___________ for a few minutes while studying.

(a) doze
(b) slant
(c) wither
(d) dwindle

21. A: Do you buy generic drugs or branded ones?

B: Being somewhat ___________, I usually try to get the cheaper generic ones.

(a) frugal
(b) monetary
(c) superfluous
(d) magnanimous

22. A: Will your old car make it through this winter?

B: It had better ___________! I can't afford a new one now.

(a) take in
(b) pass on
(c) hold up
(d) play off

23. A: Allie can't decide whether to go to her best friend's wedding or her cousin's.

B: She's in a tough spot. That's quite a ___________.

(a) quibble
(b) malady
(c) detriment
(d) conundrum

24. A: Kevin really dressed up for the party. His outfit is fabulous!

B: He certainly looks ___________ in his tuxedo.

(a) tepid
(b) dapper
(c) salutary
(d) intractable

25. A: You're really working hard on your dissertation, Elaine.

   B: Yeah, I'm ____________ it so I can submit it early.

   (a) chalking up to
   (b) limbering up for
   (c) plugging away at
   (d) casting around for

26. Although the condo is outside the city, it is near the subway, making it easy for residents to ____________ to work downtown.

   (a) capture
   (b) progress
   (c) commute
   (d) approach

27. The babysitter gave the children ____________ amounts of cake so that no child could complain another had received more.

   (a) eager
   (b) equal
   (c) literal
   (d) smooth

28. Two rival parties formed a(n) ____________ before the election, agreeing to support each other against the ruling party.

   (a) alliance
   (b) rupture
   (c) expedition
   (d) precedence

29. Many people eat garlic for its ____________ properties, believing that it will cure them of various ailments.

   (a) prescriptive
   (b) imminent
   (c) medicinal
   (d) stubborn

30. The revelation that cave paintings in Spain were created by Neanderthals ____________ archaeologists who had believed Neanderthals incapable of symbolic artwork.

   (a) conceded
   (b) excavated
   (c) astonished
   (d) surmounted

31. Bacteria are so resistant to extreme conditions that they can survive in harsh climates where other organisms would ____________.

   (a) perish
   (b) herald
   (c) invoke
   (d) broach

32. Holman's Cough Syrup provides ____________ from cold and flu symptoms so you can get the rest you need.

   (a) relief
   (b) merit
   (c) virtue
   (d) regard

33. Runners build up their ___________ by running increasingly greater distances until they can go for hours without stopping.

    (a) breadth
    (b) stamina
    (c) extension
    (d) hindrance

34. Employees need to understand a company's policies, so staff handbooks should use language that is ___________ and unambiguous.

    (a) perceptive
    (b) susceptible
    (c) comprehensible
    (d) commemorative

35. Religious believers sometimes show their ___________ by undertaking pilgrimages to distant shrines.

    (a) divinity
    (b) exertion
    (c) devotion
    (d) symmetry

36. Keeping a spare tire is important in case a sudden ___________ should cause one of your tires to become flat.

    (a) exposure
    (b) puncture
    (c) dejection
    (d) revelation

37. The earthquake was so strong it ___________ windows in hundreds of buildings.

    (a) splintered
    (b) crumbled
    (c) shattered
    (d) kindled

38. Suzie was so ___________ upon learning that she would not receive the scholarship that her friends could barely console her.

    (a) extolled
    (b) resilient
    (c) garnered
    (d) distraught

39. After waging war for decades, Napoleon was finally ___________ at the Battle of Waterloo, the defeat effectively ending his military career.

    (a) decomposed
    (b) unimpaired
    (c) vanquished
    (d) culminated

40. Unwary investors have been ___________ out of their savings by scam artists promoting dubious high-yield investments.

    (a) endeavored
    (b) redeemed
    (c) swindled
    (d) initiated

41. First published in 1711, the daily publication *The Spectator* had a modest ___________ of about 3,000 copies.

    (a) circulation
    (b) reciprocity
    (c) concurrence
    (d) replacement

42. Lisa threw a ball and watched her dog run to ___________ it so that she could throw it again.

    (a) clinch
    (b) probe
    (c) boost
    (d) fetch

43. Emperor Augustus ____________ the poet Ovid from Rome, forcing him to leave the city and live in Tomis.

(a) diverged
(b) banished
(c) bordered
(d) detached

44. With its emphasis on combining all aspects of learning, from physical to emotional to intellectual, Xavier School takes a ____________ approach to education.

(a) convalescent
(b) discursive
(c) syntactic
(d) holistic

45. Readers doubted the authenticity of Richard Wingman's autobiography, as it described many events that seemed highly ____________.

(a) presumptive
(b) implausible
(c) substantive
(d) infallible

46. Hegel's ambitions for himself were ____________, as he hoped he would be remembered as history's greatest philosopher.

(a) lofty
(b) aloof
(c) jovial
(d) cordial

47. In a show of ____________ with the hurricane's victims, citizens across the nation sent food aid and blankets to the devastated coastal area.

(a) torpor
(b) impetus
(c) temerity
(d) solidarity

48. The relationship between the houses of York and Lancaster was so ____________ that they fought a war that spanned decades.

(a) rancorous
(b) exuberant
(c) conducive
(d) imperious

49. Genetic evidence has been used to ____________ Darwin's theory of evolution, proving its veracity beyond a reasonable doubt.

(a) corroborate
(b) capitulate
(c) enunciate
(d) abrogate

50. Rather than planting crops every year, farmers leave their fields ____________ occasionally so that the soil can regain nutrients.

(a) surly
(b) fallow
(c) forlorn
(d) odious

This is the end of the Vocabulary section. Do **NOT** move on to the Reading Comprehension section until instructed to do so. You are **NOT** allowed to turn to any other section of the test.

READING COMPREHENSION

Part I Questions 1—16

Read the passage and choose the option that best completes the passage.

1. This weekend, residents of North Hills Apartment Complex are asked to
___________________________. With temperatures expected to exceed 40°C,
more people will be using air conditioners, and the government is worried about
meeting the demand for electricity. So select areas have been asked to lower their
energy consumption, and North Hills is included in this effort. If you must use your air
conditioner, please set it at no lower than 25°C.

(a) stay indoors to keep cool during the heat wave
(b) check that their air conditioners are working
(c) submit ideas for ways to conserve energy
(d) limit the use of air conditioners at home

2. The proprietor of Fantastis Circus, Guy Spight, has created a circus that
___________________________. Having spent years working as an organizer
at an animal rights advocacy organization, Spight knew about the abuse of animals in
entertainment venues, zoos and circuses particularly. So he went on to found a unique
human-only circus, where all the acts are performed by skilled acrobats, magicians, and
clowns. So far, the project has been successful, and it is even expanding with a second
touring troupe.

(a) embodies his values about the ethical treatment of animals
(b) takes great care to treat its animal performers humanely
(c) re-trains abused animals from zoos to perform in public
(d) has drawn criticism from opponents of animal cruelty

3. It is common for wine drinkers to open a bottle of wine to let it "breathe" before
drinking. However, it is important to remember that exposing wine to the air
___________________________. Exposure to oxygen can temper the tannins in the
wine and improve its character—but this is only true of younger wines. More aged and
fragile wines are a different story. The delicate aroma and flavor of a very old wine are
in danger of collapsing just hours, or even minutes, after being opened.

(a) amplifies muted tannins to improve the wine's taste
(b) has a different effect depending upon the wine's age
(c) can damage the character of even the youngest wines
(d) enhances the subtleties of an older wine's flavor profile

4. As a teacher, I've often witnessed parents praising their children, even though the children have done nothing especially remarkable. This kind of blanket positivity is thought to increase children's self-esteem, but I consider it frivolous. Instead of giving children empty praise for mediocre work or for being attractive, parents should compliment specific actions and actual achievements, such as successfully completing an important project. Praise is of course important for self-esteem, but ______________________.

(a) parents can be too stingy in offering it
(b) only when it is applied to innate talents
(c) it should focus on genuine accomplishments
(d) parents should avoid commending specific deeds

5. In 2011, residents in the Romanian city of Constanta learned that ______________________. After finding a flock of dead birds near the city, residents worried that an avian flu outbreak was brewing, and they quickly alerted authorities. Caution was warranted since a 2010 outbreak of avian flu in Romania led to a large poultry cull. However, a medical analysis by Constanta's veterinary authorities revealed that residents were safe; the birds had actually died of alcohol poisoning after eating fermented grape waste left over from wine-making.

(a) their quick action prevented a bird flu outbreak
(b) a 2010 strain of avian flu had spread to their area
(c) a suspected public health hazard was a false alarm
(d) grape waste can be used as a remedy for sick birds

6. At yesterday's city council meeting, Stanfield mayor Michael Goldsmith declared that he would not approve the budget for the coming year until the council ______________________. Goldsmith meticulously dissected individual lines of the budget to underscore his point, detailing numerous instances where imprecise estimates and definitions made it impossible to evaluate the budget's viability. Noting that the city was currently in surplus, he warned council members that poor accounting would create a deficit. Council members, who have unanimously supported the budget, have one month to address Goldsmith's concerns.

(a) agrees to resolve the deficit in the city's current budget
(b) clarifies sloppy explanations of certain items in the budget
(c) gives him a chance to publicly critique their budget proposal
(d) reaches a consensus among themselves over budgetary disputes

7. American entrepreneur George Eastman is known for
_________________________. He patented the first roll holder film in 1885
with William Walker, which allowed cameras to advance multiple exposures. Prior
to his invention, cameras were only capable of taking single shots and often required
technical knowledge and heavy equipment, which made them the exclusive domain of
professionals. In 1888, Eastman launched the first mass-produced Kodak camera, which
sold for $25. The simplicity of using this device sparked a photography craze.

(a) patenting the technology for stationary single-shot cameras
(b) creating easy-to-use film and cameras that popularized photography
(c) pioneering new ways to teach photography to amateur photographers
(d) developing specialized features on cameras for professional photographers

8.

Dear Professor Lemmon,

I have finished reviewing your proposed syllabus for next semester's survey
course in women's literature. Although I found your inclusion of certain
controversial modern works refreshing, I felt that too many of the readings were
contemporary texts. For a general survey course, the historical breadth of the
syllabus should be as comprehensive as possible. Before you submit the syllabus
to the department for formal approval, I suggest that you adjust it so that it

_________________________.

Sincerely,

Dr. Blake Stevens
Dean, English Department

(a) excludes texts which may be too controversial
(b) focuses more on contemporary women's issues
(c) includes a balance of classic and modern works
(d) gives less attention to outdated traditional texts

9. When astronomers first began observing planetary systems outside our solar system, gas giants were among the first planets they detected, so they believed that gas giants were the most common type of planet. However, these astronomers could only observe solar systems close to our own, where conditions seem to be particularly conducive to the formation of gas giants. Recently, the Kepler observatory, which is on a mission to search for Earth-like planets in more distant areas of the galaxy, has transmitted data showing that small, rocky planets are actually much more common. Thus, many astronomers now believe that gas giants _______________________________.

(a) are less prevalent than once estimated
(b) orbit stars that are smaller than expected
(c) exist in abundance in the galaxy's outskirts
(d) share many similarities with smaller planets

10. In most Slavic languages, the terms used to indicate foreigners and natives _______________________________. For instance, the name which Slavic peoples apply to themselves as a group—*Slovenin*—is believed to derive from "*slovo*," meaning "word," and describes Slavs as "people who can speak." Meanwhile, the term used to denote foreigners in most Slavic languages has the root "*nemec*," meaning "dumb, mute," suggesting that people from other geographic locations cannot speak. While crude by today's sensibilities, the terms probably reflect the lack of linguistic exchange between early Slavs and other ethnic groups.

(a) refer to whether a person knows a Slavic language or not
(b) derive from historical names for places in medieval Europe
(c) trace their roots back to labels given by non-Slavic outsiders
(d) reflect Slavic culture's traditional dedication to multilingualism

11. *A Sense of Aging* by George Arthur is a _______________________________. Readers follow Eugene, a man going through a midlife crisis. With few dreams left in life, he revisits his past only to find his memories and beliefs challenged. This is a tightly woven meditation on the intricate web of causes and effects that can dictate one's sense of self. As a short work involving big ideas, it is necessarily dense, with every word working to capacity. By the novella's end, you will feel as if you have read a modern classic.

(a) moving exploration of a young man's memory loss
(b) long-winded tale of a man with a troubled past
(c) rapturous meditation on the pursuit of dreams
(d) concise but complex narrative of middle age

12. Various species of eucalyptus trees grow in Australia, many of them in rain forests. The seeds of these trees have evolved a unique ability to withstand wildfires, and so the Australian government places eucalyptus in a conservation category separate from other rain forest trees. However, this has had unintended effects: while other rain forest tree species receive protection from over-harvesting, the eucalyptus, which is valuable to the timber industry, is not protected from logging. Thus, the eucalyptus tree's evolutionary advantages have actually _______________________________.

(a) played an unfavorable role in its conservation
(b) made it less valuable to industries that harvest it
(c) created a risk of logging for other rain forest trees
(d) harmed its ability to survive fires in the rain forest

13. The Sophists of ancient Greece were itinerant intellectuals who traveled and taught philosophy, often charging a hefty fee. They have a modern reputation for being deceptive rhetoricians, but it is possible that the portrayal of these Sophists as greedy, intellectually bankrupt instructors was biased. Most of the extant descriptions of their work are by contemporaries who strongly opposed the Sophists' techniques. Particularly, Socrates and Plato considered the Sophists' practice of charging money for education deplorable and thought their ideas were a kind of pseudo-philosophy. Thus, modern ideas about the Sophists may actually _______________________________.

(a) be based on gross misrepresentations of their work
(b) come from a description they applied to themselves
(c) stem from criticisms they made of their contemporaries
(d) have arisen from challenges to Plato's and Socrates's works

14. Research on capsaicin, the chemical that makes peppers hot, has taken a step toward proving _______________________________. The primary purpose of peppers—as with all fruits—is to disperse seeds. However, just as fruit attracts helpful organisms which spread the seeds, like birds, it also attracts harmful microbes that destroy seeds, like fungus. Studying wild pepper plants, a group of international researchers found that in areas with a high prevalence of fungus, peppers contained more capsaicin, a natural anti-fungal agent. These findings support the hypothesis that environmental factors trigger adaptive responses in the chemistry of fruits.

(a) why only some people find the spicy hot taste of peppers attractive
(b) that plants' adaptive responses have an influence on their environment
(c) that fruits' chemistry is influenced by the microbes in their environment
(d) how helpful and harmful organisms interact to affect the chemistry of fruit

15. All living languages are in flux. As speakers innovate new forms, both the vocabulary and syntax of living languages are continually altered. And though these changes are often so subtle that they are nearly imperceptible, they become apparent over long spans of time. _______________________________, when modern readers read Shakespeare, they can clearly see that English has undergone changes both in the words it uses and in its sentence structure.

(a) Even so
(b) Thereafter
(c) Meanwhile
(d) For instance

16. As I've gotten older, I've come to see my family's interest in music fade. When I was a child, everyone in my family could sing or play at least one instrument proficiently. Music was a pastime that we enjoyed together. _______________________________, these days my grandchildren are so distracted with readily available entertainment that they have little interest in learning instruments for more than a short time. They therefore never develop their musical skills enough to experience the thrill of playing together. I'm afraid they are missing out on a great experience.

(a) Hence
(b) Likewise
(c) By contrast
(d) Put another way

Part II   **Questions 17—37**

Read the passage, question, and options. Then, based on the given information, choose the option that best answers the question.

17.

Dear Ms. Huston,

Douglas McIntyre, who was previously employed at your firm, has applied for the position of head teller here at Global Savings & Trust and has identified you as a reference. It would be of tremendous assistance if you would verify your reference of him. If you wish to do so, please download and complete the attached reference questionnaire and send it back to us at your earliest convenience. Thank you.

Sincerely,

James O'Reilly

Q: What is the main purpose of the letter?
(a) To ask for an employment application
(b) To verify an applicant's current employment
(c) To obtain information about a vacant teller position·
(d) To request a reference from an applicant's former employer

18. Chaim Potok's *The Chosen* is unambiguously bound to Brooklyn's Jewish culture of the mid-twentieth century. Even so, it is eminently relatable. Main characters Reuven and Danny, though their experience is foreign to many readers, go through the same kind of emotional turmoil as readers might. Even Brooklyn, with its distinct culture, somehow manages to resemble a hometown anywhere. It is because *The Chosen* speaks to the greater human experience that it is able to be simultaneously universal and personal.

Q: What is the writer's main point about *The Chosen*?
(a) It shows Brooklyn as a multicultural society.
(b) It has characters that relate to each other well.
(c) It describes the immigrant experience convincingly.
(d) It appeals to a diverse audience despite its specificity.

19. Anything that diverts a driver's attention from the road can be risky because it can undermine driving ability. Among all distractions, drinking coffee is perhaps the most common—and the most dangerous. As a hot liquid, coffee presents a particularly distracting hazard if spilled. Recent laws have banned the use of handheld electronic devices while driving, and it seems that coffee, as a similarly dangerous distraction, should also be off-limits to drivers.

Q: What is the writer's main point?
(a) Coffee-related car accidents have recently increased.
(b) Handheld devices should not be used when driving.
(c) Bans for drinking coffee while driving should be instated.
(d) Drivers tend to underestimate the dangers of multitasking.

20. In workplaces, team members' new ideas are often criticized and dismissed because initial proposals are often not fully formed and usually have some problems. But carefully considering an idea's potential and trying to enhance its strengths is far more productive than finding fault with its weaknesses. Brainstorming and constructive criticism can eliminate weaknesses and transform a good idea into a great one. The best workplaces harness the power of new ideas and refine them until they are usable.

Q: What is the passage mainly about?
(a) How to know when to dismiss an idea for being too problematic
(b) The importance of challenging an idea to identify its weaknesses
(c) How focusing on positive over negative criticism can improve ideas
(d) Techniques for transforming negative relationships into positive ones

21. Graphic designer Alphonse Mucha was such an embodiment of the Art Nouveau movement that many referred to it as *le style Mucha*. However, Mucha himself did not associate with the movement. He believed that the name Art Nouveau—meaning "new art" in French—was absurd, since in his view art was eternal and could not be appropriately labeled "new." Nevertheless, the intricate lines and muted colors of Mucha's work are regarded as the epitome of Art Nouveau by art lovers today.

Q: What is the writer's main point about Alphonse Mucha?
(a) His art typified Art Nouveau though he rejected the label.
(b) His artwork contradicts the philosophy behind Art Nouveau.
(c) His artwork was renounced by Art Nouveau for its muted colors.
(d) His artistic style was affected by his disillusionment with Art Nouveau.

22. Edgemark Grocery has been reluctant to embrace digital media. However, the growth of online food retailing can be a boon for our company. By analyzing consumers' online purchase habits, we can tailor advertising to appeal to the individual and reach certain demographic groups more effectively. Moreover, purchase data can be used to help us manage our stock more efficiently. For the sake of our continued profitability, we must take advantage of the positive aspects of digital retailing.

Q: What is the main purpose of the passage?
(a) To detail how Edgemark can capitalize on digital media
(b) To state the positive aspects of advertising with Edgemark
(c) To express Edgemark's rationale for renouncing digitization
(d) To provide support for Edgemark's resistance to digital media

23. Do you love traveling to exotic locales and photographing them? If so, you could win a two-week all-expenses paid vacation for two at the world-renowned Peithos Resort in Cyprus. To participate in the contest, send your best travel photo to travelphoto@ medtravelmag.com by June 15. The winning entry will be featured in the August issue of *Mediterranean Travel* along with the editors' twenty other top picks. Limit one photograph per entrant. Multiple entries will be disqualified.

Q: Which of the following is correct about the contest according to the announcement?
(a) The prize is a two-week vacation for two people.
(b) Photos mailed before June 15 will not be eligible.
(c) The best entry will be printed in the June issue.
(d) Participants can send in more than one picture.

24. The modern practice of venture capitalism, where a company assesses business
proposals and funds the best ones, started with French academic Georges Doriot. Having
immigrated to the United States to complete his MBA at Harvard Business School,
Doriot later became a professor there. After serving in the US Army in World War II, he
returned to Harvard and founded the American Research and Development Corporation,
which accepted investments and backed promising business ventures. When his company
merged with a competitor in 1972, he had invested in over 150 companies.

Q: Which of the following is correct about Georges Doriot according to the passage?
(a) He emigrated from France after earning his MBA degree there.
(b) He immigrated to the US to accept a faculty position at Harvard.
(c) He developed contemporary venture capitalism while at Harvard.
(d) His company went bankrupt in 1972 because of intense competition.

25. One fun and easy way to make soap is the melt-and-pour method. This uses a material
called glycerin. Since caustic chemicals are needed to derive the otherwise harmless
glycerin, simply buy blocks of ready-made glycerin base. Once you have it, melt the
glycerin down. Fragrance and dye can be added to this base. Next, pour the soap into
the mold of your choice and wait until it hardens. Your new homemade soap will leave
traces of moisture-attracting glycerin on your skin and help keep it soft.

Q: Which of the following is correct according to the instructions?
(a) The melt-and-pour method uses a pre-made glycerin base.
(b) Ready-made glycerin soap base contains caustic chemicals.
(c) Fragrance and color are added before melting the glycerin.
(d) Glycerin-based soaps repel moisture from skin's surface.

26. Hurricanes in the Atlantic Ocean used to be named after saints or by their latitude-longitude positions. However, such identification methods were often confusing and subject to error. In 1953, the US National Hurricane Center began using a list of women's names, and in 1979, the list expanded to include men's names. Today, an international committee of the World Meteorological Organization is in charge of maintaining and updating the list, and there are six lists containing 21 names each, which are recycled. Names are sometimes retired if a hurricane causes severe damage: for instance, Irene was retired in 2011.

Q: Which of the following is correct according to the passage?
(a) Saints' names started to be given to hurricanes in 1953.
(b) Men's names were included in the first hurricane name list.
(c) There are a total of 21 names being reused to name hurricanes.
(d) The name Irene will never be used to name a future hurricane.

27. A favorite musician of Pope Julius III, Giovanni da Palestrina transformed the religious music of sixteenth-century Italy. His most famous compositions were masses. These masses, which were unaccompanied by instruments, explored the possibilities of the human voice as a heavenly instrument used to glorify God. Though these works were a cappella like earlier Gregorian chants, they differed from them. While chants consisted of a single melody, Palestrina's masses used a technique called polyphony, in which multiple melodies harmonize with each other. Palestrina's distinct contribution to religious music lasted well beyond the Renaissance.

Q: Which of the following is correct about Giovanni da Palestrina according to the passage?
(a) His vocal music was disdained by Pope Julius III.
(b) His masses were instrumental pieces without words.
(c) His music combined different vocal lines in harmony.
(d) His effect on music's style ended with the Renaissance.

28. In the 1960s, a tonsillectomy was one of the first options a doctor would consider for patients with recurrent throat infections, and thus the surgery was very common. Today, merely having a tendency towards infection is no longer considered a sufficient reason to perform a tonsillectomy. The medical profession now believes the procedure does not adequately prevent infections. However, doctors will still remove infected and swollen tonsils if an individual's breathing or ability to swallow is impaired.

Q: Which of the following is correct about tonsillectomies according to the passage?
(a) They were a rarely performed procedure in the 1960s.
(b) They were abandoned since they exacerbated throat infections.
(c) They are now believed to be the best way to prevent throat infections.
(d) They are still performed when breathing is hindered by enlarged tonsils.

29. Have the cold and snow got you down? You're in luck because Skyblue Airline is offering special winter vacation fares. You can fly to any of our domestic locations for the low cost of $89. You can even earn double BlueMile Rewards if you complete our online customer satisfaction survey. Regular baggage fees apply for all customers, and in-flight meal costs are not included. These fares are only valid through the end of the month, so act now!

Q: Which of the following is correct according to the advertisement?
(a) Domestic fares start at $89 and increase by distance.
(b) Filling out a survey confers extra BlueMile Rewards.
(c) In-flight meals are provided at no cost to customers.
(d) Discounted flights will be available after the month ends.

30. Joe Rosenthal's World War II photo of six soldiers, five US Marines and one Navy corpsman, hoisting a flag on Iwo Jima on February 23, 1945, instantly became iconic. But that was not the only flag-raising event of the day. Earlier in the day, a flag was raised atop the same mountain, and the event was photographed by Louis Lowery. However, Colonel Chandler Johnson deemed that flag too small and gave orders to raise a second, larger flag. Because both events were photographed, confusion ensued after the publication of Rosenthal's image.

Q: Which of the following is correct according to the passage?
(a) Rosenthal's photo depicts six US Marines raising a flag.
(b) The two flags were raised on different mountains on Iwo Jima.
(c) Lowery's photo was taken prior to Rosenthal's iconic photo.
(d) Colonel Johnson was unaware that a flag had already been hoisted.

31. The TotalMaxx is the lightest, most powerful vacuum on the market today, with two layers of dust filtration and a weight of just 4.5 kg! We're so sure that you'll love it that we'll give you a full 30 days from the time of delivery to test it. If you're not satisfied, send it back for a full refund, minus any shipping and handling charges. We'll even send you a complimentary iron with your trial, yours to keep even if you return the vacuum.

Q: Which of the following is correct according to the advertisement?
(a) The vacuum boasts the heaviest weight on the market today.
(b) The trial starts 30 days after initially ordering the vacuum.
(c) The shipping cost of the trial vacuum will not be refunded.
(d) The iron must be returned along with the trial vacuum.

32. With the exception of those born before January 1, 1957, all new Duade University students must provide proof of immunization for measles, rubella, and mumps. Religious exemption letters and vaccine contraindication statements written by a physician can be submitted in lieu of the Student Immunization Record form. Should an outbreak occur, however, students who have not been vaccinated will be asked to leave campus. First term students may register without immunization records, but those who do not comply with immunization requirements by the beginning of their second academic term will be blocked from registration.

Q: Which of the following is correct according to the passage?
(a) Students born before 1957 must provide proof of immunization.
(b) A physician's statement may be used as a substitute for the form.
(c) Vaccinated students must vacate campus in the event of an outbreak.
(d) Students must have proof of immunization to register for their first term.

33. The financial struggles of fast-food franchise Pizza Palace have led to the hiring of management guru Craig Murray. Murray, formerly of Burgermeister's, is known for innovative techniques to reduce employee turnover. Pizza Palace currently has a sky-high turnover rate, which Murray attributes to incompetent management, and the cost of training new employees has meant major profit losses for the franchise. Given Murray's previous successes, it is likely that the employee retention rate and the company's profits will soar again soon.

Q: What can be inferred about Craig Murray from the passage?
(a) He does not believe that employee satisfaction affects profits.
(b) He caused a decrease in employee turnover at his past jobs.
(c) He feels more money should be allotted to train new hires.
(d) He believes high employee turnover has positive effects.

34.

> Dear Laura,
>
> Thanks for inviting us to dinner last week. It was fun hearing about your vacation—so much so that Martin and I are eager to check out Tahiti as soon as the twins are old enough to travel. Also, it was great to see Jonathan while he was home from college. If he'd like to earn some extra money, we'd be happy to hire him to mow our lawn like last summer. Have him call us!
>
> All the best,
>
> Margaret

Q: What can be inferred from the letter?
(a) Martin and Margaret have been to Tahiti before.
(b) Margaret recommended that Laura go to Tahiti.
(c) Jonathan has no prior lawn cutting experience.
(d) Jonathan is older than Margaret's twins.

35. Mobsters and outlaws are often the heroes of films, but businesspeople seldom are. Instead, they are portrayed as manipulative and underhanded. Though many businesspeople are philanthropists who use their wealth to improve communities, this is hardly ever depicted in films. And films virtually never show how businesspeople conduct the workaday affairs that make our economy run. Filmmakers should give up the "greedy businessperson" stereotype—and should trade in the "heroic outlaw" one while they are at it.

Q: Which statement would the writer most likely agree with?
(a) Films have overplayed businesspeople's philanthropic acts.
(b) Movies cast an unreasonably negative light on businesspeople.
(c) Greed is unfairly portrayed as a characteristic of only mobsters.
(d) Filmmakers should focus more on criminal activity by businesspeople.

36. Much has been made of India's growing middle class, but it is only the wealthiest of the urban population who can claim a typical Western middle-class lifestyle. By and large, India's population is still rural and impoverished, and this poorer demographic is driving India's continued population growth. In fact, by 2030 India's population is projected to surpass that of China. The majority of this population will be concentrated in the poorest regions, where basic necessities are scarce.

Q: What can be inferred about India from the passage?
(a) Its middle class population is rapidly dwindling.
(b) Its birth rate is currently lower than that of China.
(c) Its wealth is slowly gravitating toward its rural areas.
(d) Its rural areas have higher birth rates than urban areas.

37. The philosophical discipline of bioethics is supposed to guide the moral direction of medical research. Its exponents used to function as expert gatekeepers, ensuring that advances in medical technology stayed on the path of humane decision making. However, modern bioethics has become entangled, most unfortunately, with politics, which has had a negative effect on bioethicists' governance. The field cannot properly function while politicians continue to not only question but also contradict and legislate against the judgments of bioethics experts.

Q: Which statement about bioethics would the writer most likely agree with?
(a) Politicians have little incentive to meddle with it.
(b) Bioethicists should be the sole arbiters of the field.
(c) It has little practical application in modern medicine.
(d) It has a negative effect on politicians' ability to legislate.

Part III **Questions 38 — 40**

Read the passage and identify the option that does NOT belong.

38. Perfectionism is not usually a problem unless that desire is combined with a tendency to put things off. (a) Perfectionists often suffer from procrastination, stemming from the fear that they cannot fulfill their own expectations. (b) Perfectionists may demand perfection from others, which can further hinder their ability to form relationships. (c) The problem is that by doing this, perfectionists are only able to temporarily delay shame and embarrassment. (d) Procrastination eventually backfires when they rush to complete tasks and end up completing them poorly.

39. As apex predators, sharks are erroneously viewed by humans as aquatic killing machines, devouring huge quantities of prey. (a) In actuality, because they are cold-blooded, sharks require relatively little food energy and eat far less than expected. (b) They eat only about 2% of their body weight daily, while dolphins eat up to four times as much. (c) Dolphins, of course, are warm-blooded, so extra food is needed to maintain their body temperature. (d) The probability of sharks attacking humans increases in areas where there are more people in the water.

40. For nearly two centuries, the Warsaw Confederation of 1573 ensured that Poland and Lithuania were the most religiously tolerant nations in Europe. (a) Prior to the signing of the confederation, religious freedom existed in the Polish-Lithuanian Commonwealth, but it was not officially recognized. (b) After the death of King Zygmunt II, nobles created the confederation because they feared this religious tolerance would be eliminated. (c) Because the king had no heir, Henry III of Valois was elected King of the Polish-Lithuanian Commonwealth. (d) The document guaranteed that the religiously diverse peoples of the region would continue to coexist peacefully.

This is the end of the Reading Comprehension section. Please remain seated until the proctor has instructed otherwise. You are NOT allowed to turn to any other section of the test.

서울대
최신기출

6

Listening Comprehension

Grammar

Vocabulary

Reading Comprehension

LISTENING
COMPREHENSION

Part I **Questions 1—15**

You will now hear fifteen individual spoken questions or statements, each followed by four spoken responses. Choose the most appropriate response for each item.

Part II **Questions 16—30**

You will now hear fifteen short conversation fragments, followed by four spoken responses. Choose the most appropriate response to complete each conversation.

Part III **Questions 31—45**

You will now hear fifteen complete conversations. For each conversation, you will be asked to answer a question. Each conversation and its corresponding question will be read twice. Then you will hear four options which will be read only once. Based on the given information, choose the option that best answers the question.

Part IV **Questions 46—60**

You will now hear fifteen short talks. After each talk, you will be asked to answer a question. Each talk and its corresponding question will be read twice. Then you will hear four options which will be read only once. Based on the given information, choose the option that best answers the question.

GRAMMAR

DIRECTIONS

This section tests your grammar skills. You will have 25 minutes to complete the 50 questions. Be sure to follow the directions given by the proctor.

Part I   Questions 1—20

Choose the option that best completes each gap.

1. A: Should we try fixing the printer?

B: No, neither of us __________ qualified to do that.

(a) is
(b) are
(c) was
(d) were

2. A: You have __________ handwriting I've ever seen.

B: Thanks. It's because my teachers stressed penmanship in school.

(a) lovely
(b) most lovely
(c) more lovely
(d) the loveliest

3. A: Will the drinks stay cold till lunchtime?

B: Yes. __________ in a cooler, they'll be fine for a couple of hours.

(a) Kept
(b) To keep
(c) Keeping
(d) Having kept

4. A: Why didn't you buy the shirt?

B: I __________, but my size wasn't in stock.

(a) wanted
(b) wanted to
(c) wanted it to
(d) wanted to do

5. A: I wonder what Terry's up to—she hasn't called me in a while.

B: I'll see if I can contact her, since I __________ from her in ages, either.

(a) won't hear
(b) didn't hear
(c) hadn't heard
(d) haven't heard

6. A: I'm worried about all my overdue parking tickets.

B: Well, it's not too late __________ them all off.

(a) pay
(b) paid
(c) to pay
(d) paying

7. A: How fast __________ at the time of the accident?

B: Not that fast. Around 30 kilometers per hour.

(a) had you driven
(b) are you driving
(c) have you driven
(d) were you driving

8. A: Let's go sailing today.

B: __________,

we should wait until tomorrow.

(a) What of the darkening with skies
(b) What with the skies darkening
(c) With skies what are darkening
(d) With what of darkening skies

9. A: Dave had better not come to work
       late again.
    B: I know. He's going to get himself
       ___________.

    (a) fire
    (b) fired
    (c) firing
    (d) to be fired

10. A: The bake sale is going great!
    B: Yeah, we're doing ___________
       better than any of us imagined.

    (a) so
    (b) far
    (c) very
    (d) such

11. A: Can you tell me the movie listings
       for this week?
    B: Yes, we ___________ *Snipes* and
       The Bank Job.

    (a) show
    (b) showed
    (c) have shown
    (d) are showing

12. A: Why did you come home so late?
    B: I lost track of time, ___________ in
       a laboratory experiment.

    (a) absorb
    (b) absorbed
    (c) absorbing
    (d) having absorbed

13. A: Is Sue going to stay with Joe?
    B: No. She still wants to break up with
       him ___________ I tried to talk her
       out of it.

    (a) even though
    (b) as long as
    (c) provided
    (d) unless

14. A: How long does it take to get to
       Boston from Philadelphia?
    B: That depends on ___________ of
       transportation you choose.

    (a) some mode
    (b) the mode
    (c) a mode
    (d) mode

15. A: Why did you take an aptitude test?
    B: I wanted to find out ___________
       for me.

    (a) a career what is suited
    (b) suited careers are what
    (c) a suitable career what is
    (d) what careers are suitable

16. A: Your puppy is really cute! Has she
       been housebroken?
    B: Not quite. I've been trying for
       weeks, but ___________.

    (a) she just seems impossible to train
    (b) I just seem impossible to train her
    (c) it just seems impossible her training
    (d) training her just seems to impossible

17. A: How did you find the hotel after getting lost in Rome?

    B: _____________ for hours, we finally stumbled upon it.

    (a) Wander
    (b) Wandered
    (c) Having wandered
    (d) To have wandered

18. A: I think it's time we moved.

    B: But I'm satisfied _____________ .

    (a) where do we live now
    (b) with now where do we live
    (c) with living where we do now
    (d) now living with where we do

19. A: Why are you revising your book?

    B: My editor had _____________ about the ending.

    (a) some reservations
    (b) the reservations
    (c) any reservation
    (d) the reservation

20. A: What do you think of the proposal to raise the minimum wage?

    B: It would be a blow _____________ companies that are already struggling to pay workers.

    (a) to
    (b) of
    (c) up
    (d) by

Part II **Questions 21–40**

Choose the option that best completes each gap.

---

21. _____________ young people these days aspire to be movie stars or famous pop singers.

    (a) Each
    (b) Many
    (c) Much
    (d) Every

22. Shannon _____________ as an engineer for more than five years before she realized she wanted to open her own business.

    (a) works
    (b) is working
    (c) has worked
    (d) had been working

23. Jason was not very hopeful when he asked his mother if he _____________ borrow her car, so he was elated when she consented.

    (a) will
    (b) shall
    (c) could
    (d) would

24. Researchers say that medical costs _____________ much lower if people did not smoke so much.

    (a) were
    (b) would be
    (c) will have been
    (d) would have been

25. The worker was caught __________ unemployment benefits unlawfully and was ordered to pay back $20,000.

(a) claim
(b) claimed
(c) to claim
(d) claiming

26. The resort __________ the couple chose to stay featured a private beach.

(a) that
(b) what
(c) which
(d) where

27. The legislative branch of government is called the Parliament in the UK __________ in the US it is known as the Congress.

(a) until
(b) since
(c) while
(d) wherever

28. Highland High School's basketball team won the state championship despite __________ for the competition.

(a) qualifying barely successful
(b) it barely succeeded to qualify
(c) it barely qualified successfully
(d) barely succeeding in qualifying

29. After the fire, the residents worked hard to rebuild the downtown area, much of which __________.

(a) is razed
(b) was razing
(c) had been razed
(d) had been razing

30. The city councilors __________ terms were ending soon were careful not to support any controversial policies.

(a) whose
(b) which
(c) when
(d) who

31. Many tourists fail to heed warnings about petty crime because they __________ and so do not fully appreciate the risks.

(a) are never victimizing
(b) have never victimized
(c) are never being victimizing
(d) have never been victimized

32. The actress offended animal lovers by carrying a small dog in her handbag __________ an accessory.

(a) if it were
(b) as it were
(c) as if it were
(d) it were as if

33. John's numerous career changes made for an unusual work history, __________ none of the standard résumé styles seemed appropriate.

(a) which
(b) whom
(c) for which
(d) for whom

34. __________ people what they hate most about politics, many would say corruption.

(a) You were to ask
(b) Were you to ask
(c) Were to ask you
(d) To ask you were

35. To achieve gender equality, it is essential that every woman ___________ the same opportunities as men.

(a) receive
(b) received
(c) will receive
(d) has received

36. The South American nation of Venezuela has ___________ of natural resources such as petroleum.

(a) abundance
(b) an abundance
(c) the abundance
(d) some abundance

37. The sudden dismissal of the company's three top executives last week ___________ precipitated by a series of abysmal earnings reports.

(a) was
(b) were
(c) is being
(d) are being

38. Bylaw enforcement officers have been instructed to crack down on those found ___________.

(a) of violation in parking rules of city
(b) violating of rules of city parking
(c) violating in parking rules of city
(d) in violation of city parking rules

39. The student's father requested a meeting with the school principal ___________ her earliest possible convenience.

(a) to
(b) at
(c) on
(d) for

40. Attempts ___________ a universal intelligence test that can be administered to humans, animals, and even artificial intelligence programs.

(a) devising are underway
(b) underway are devising
(c) are underway to devise
(d) to devise are underway

Part III   Questions 41—45

Read each sentence carefully and identify the option that contains a grammatical error.

41. (a) A: I haven't been able to concentrate on my work at all today.
(b) B: Why? Is the stress of the job making you lose focus?
(c) A: No, I keep getting calls asking me to buy random products.
(d) B: Oh, those calls can be really distracted, especially at work.

42. (a) A: Has Don introduced you to his new girlfriend yet? I heard she's from Japan.
(b) B: I met her last week. She's actually an American speaks Japanese like a native.
(c) A: Oh, do you know how she managed to become so proficient in the language?
(d) B: Yes, her mother is Japanese, so she learned the language while growing up.

43. (a) A: I can't believe how quickly four years of college have gone by!
(b) B: True! Who would've thought we graduated in a few weeks?
(c) A: Speaking of which, are you going to attend the graduation ceremony?
(d) B: Of course I am! My parents wouldn't have it any other way.

44. (a) A: My daughter told me that your son is tied with her for first place in their math class.
(b) B: Yes. Harry has been working exceptionally hard all semester to get to where he is now.
(c) A: Addie's desire to be number one among her classmates mean she's been studying harder than ever, as well.
(d) B: That's great! Let's hope their grades go up even more due to a little friendly competition.

45. (a) A: Excuse me, what's this 10% charge tacked on at the bottom of my bill?
(b) B: That's a standard service charge we add for parties of eight or more people.
(c) A: Oh, but I wasn't aware of that charge was automatically added, so I left a tip.
(d) B: I apologize for the confusion. I'll see to it that your service charge is refunded.

Part IV Questions 46—50

Read each sentence carefully and identify the option that contains a grammatical error.

46. (a) According to marriage counselors, nagging is among the top reasons why marriages dissolve. (b) In fact, experts say it is almost as toxic to relationships as adultery or financial woes. (c) It causes to argue couples rather than communicate about the root problems in their marriage. (d) For this reason, experts recommend establishing effective communication patterns early on.

47. (a) Scientists have discovered that plastic breaks down much more quickly in sea water than previous thought. (b) Despite a reputation for sticking around for centuries, plastic has been found to decompose in sea water in less than a year. (c) While this might seem like good news, the fact that plastic breaks down quickly is actually of concern to scientists. (d) The decomposition process releases harmful chemicals that can seriously damage the natural environment.

48. (a) Favoring the use of limbs on one side of the body is common among such animals as monkeys and birds. (b) Recent research has added walruses to the list, as they mainly rely on their right flipper to forage for food. (c) Researchers in Greenland found that walruses used their right flipper 90% of the time when unearthing clams. (d) The physiological reason behind this behavior is that the bones in their right flipper are longer than that in their left.

49. (a) Studies have found a positive correlation between the use of university support services and student success. (b) These services include everything from counseling students on academic problems to providing assistance with computer issues. (c) One problem is that male students much less likely to access support services than their female counterparts. (d) It has been suggested that this difference could be contributing to poor academic achievement among males.

50. (a) Although rarely mentioned as a weight-loss strategy, eating hot peppers can help people burn extra calories. (b) Research has shown that a chemical called capsaicin is responsible for the calorie burning power of hot peppers. (c) People given a compound related to capsaicin have also been shown to burn more calories than usual. (d) Still, scientists are quick to warn that consuming hot peppers would not be seen as a simple path to weight-loss.

This is the end of the Grammar section. Do NOT move on to the next section until instructed to do so. You are NOT allowed to turn to any other section of the test.

Vocabulary

Part I　Questions 1—25

Choose the option that best completes each gap.

1. A: Can I pay with my credit card?
B: Sorry, we only ___________ cash.

(a) perform
(b) occupy
(c) accept
(d) elect

2. A: Why is this road to the city closed?
B: There are fallen trees from the storm ___________ the way.

(a) checking
(b) blocking
(c) catching
(d) holding

3. A: Hello, could you put me through to Dr. Kane, please?
B: Sorry, he's on vacation now and can't be ___________.

(a) gained
(b) neared
(c) reached
(d) attached

4. A: Did you hear that a gas pipe downtown blew up last night?
B: Yes. Thankfully no one was hurt when it ___________.

(a) lightened
(b) exploded
(c) shocked
(d) abused

5. A: Can you send me a copy of the Henderson file?
B: Sure, I'll ___________ it to you as soon as I can.

(a) display
(b) expand
(c) forward
(d) approach

6. A: Did Stella smash up her car?
B: Yes, she made a total ___________ of it.

(a) bunch
(b) wreck
(c) batch
(d) load

7. A: Daniel was so ___________ of your project proposal.
B: I know. He found fault in every little thing.

(a) crisp
(b) daring
(c) critical
(d) reformed

8. A: How long will it be until the Internet is working again?
B: The technicians should ___________ service within an hour.

(a) relay
(b) recall
(c) relieve
(d) restore

9. A: Traveling can be a great learning
    experience, right?
    B: Yes, it certainly does ___________
    one's outlook.

    (a) spread
    (b) convey
    (c) broaden
    (d) regenerate

10. A: Have I missed Flight 107 to Dubai?
    B: Not yet, but you'll have to go to the
    gate ___________ to make it.

    (a) rashly
    (b) swiftly
    (c) concisely
    (d) thoroughly

11. A: Is Tom a close friend of yours?
    B: No, he's more of an ___________ .

    (a) evidence
    (b) utterance
    (c) observance
    (d) acquaintance

12. A: Did Jim say he wants to move offices?
    B: Not outright, but he strongly
    ___________ it.

    (a) implied
    (b) conformed
    (c) symbolized
    (d) hypothesized

13. A: Your company is really turning
    things around this year!
    B: Yes, our stock price has ___________
    by 20% from last year's low.

    (a) derived
    (b) attained
    (c) compiled
    (d) rebounded

14. A: Why did Vincent quit eating red
    meat?
    B: His doctor said it was ___________
    to his health.

    (a) conspicuous
    (b) detrimental
    (c) susceptible
    (d) exorbitant

15. A: I didn't like that new movie. I don't
    understand what the hype's all
    about.
    B: Oh, really? It was highly
    ___________ by movie reviewers.
    They loved it.

    (a) acclaimed
    (b) fabricated
    (c) instigated
    (d) procured

16. A: I hate flying economy class. There's
    never enough leg room.
    B: Try business class. It's less
    ___________ .

    (a) scarce
    (b) durable
    (c) cramped
    (d) insulated

17. A: I wish the presenter would speak
    more loudly.
    B: I know. I can't ___________ a word
    he's saying.

    (a) take after
    (b) make out
    (c) dwell on
    (d) put off

18. A: I haven't had any energy lately.

B: I'm also feeling so ___________ that I don't want to do any work.

(a) retired
(b) sluggish
(c) adamant
(d) divergent

19. A: How will you pay your bills if you quit your job?

B: I have some money saved to ___________ in case of an emergency.

(a) tell me off
(b) buy me out
(c) tide me over
(d) stand me up

20. A: Fairfield's CEO was accused of ___________ millions of dollars!

B: Yes, I heard he siphoned funds into an offshore account.

(a) riveting
(b) curtailing
(c) embezzling
(d) reprimanding

21. A: I told Joyce the driver's test is easy, so she shouldn't worry.

B: That's good. I'm sure it helped ___________ her fears.

(a) allay
(b) malign
(c) exculpate
(d) dissemble

22. A: Did you hear Mark's angry speech at the meeting?

B: Yes, I thought his ___________ would never end.

(a) tirade
(b) refuge
(c) fissure
(d) deluge

23. A: Heather loves to give people advice.

B: I know, but I wish she didn't ___________ so freely.

(a) lop it off
(b) take it up
(c) dish it out
(d) count it in

24. A: Be careful, or your boat will float away!

B: No, it won't. It's ___________ to the dock with a rope.

(a) baffled
(b) tethered
(c) consigned
(d) infatuated

25. A: Another report on the city's budgetary problems came out.

B: Yes, the city is certainly ___________ by financial problems.

(a) salvaged
(b) ensconced
(c) beleaguered
(d) incarcerated

Part II   **Questions 26—50**

Choose the option that best completes each gap.

26. Stanley Brewer's art had a great ______________ on later painters, setting the style that was popular for many years.

(a) shift
(b) extent
(c) herald
(d) impact

27. This year's Oktoberfest celebration is expected to ______________ millions of visitors to Munich, Germany.

(a) draw
(b) devote
(c) submit
(d) produce

28. During severe winters, some animals go so long without finding food that they die of ______________.

(a) prominence
(b) starvation
(c) expiration
(d) obedience

29. Those not given a spot at Everton Academy this year may reapply next year, by which time ______________ may be possible.

(a) succession
(b) enrollment
(c) concurrence
(d) reconciliation

30. As part of their lease, ______________ must pay for any damage they do to their apartment while living there.

(a) shelters
(b) patrons
(c) tenants
(d) rentals

31. In a successful ______________ on a counterfeiting operation, police confiscated thousands of dollars in fake $100 bills.

(a) raid
(b) descent
(c) enterprise
(d) recollection

32. Objects that are too small to be seen with the naked eye can be made visible if ______________ with a microscope.

(a) inflated
(b) disposed
(c) extended
(d) magnified

33. The global tiger population is thought to be around 3,200, but an actual census has not been done, so this is just a(n) ______________.

(a) allegory
(b) premise
(c) deletion
(d) estimate

34. The protesters, determined to see the dictator removed from power, staged a demonstration to have him ___________.

(a) instated
(b) amended
(c) undertaken
(d) overthrown

35. The hinge on the old chest was stuck, so Lyle had to ___________ it open with a crowbar.

(a) pry
(b) halt
(c) evoke
(d) dodge

36. Teachers should strive to ___________ student engagement in the classroom, since active participation improves learning outcomes.

(a) foster
(b) ordain
(c) portray
(d) relegate

37. The pace of the action film built up gradually until it ___________ in a thrilling finale.

(a) exasperated
(b) encroached
(c) culminated
(d) harangued

38. The theater apologizes for postponing the start of the show, which will now ___________ at 8 o'clock and end at 10 o'clock.

(a) dispense
(b) originate
(c) commence
(d) encapsulate

39. The Dalai Lama is ___________ by followers of Tibetan Buddhism, who regard him as their spiritual leader.

(a) recapitulated
(b) personified
(c) epitomized
(d) venerated

40. Far from asking superficial questions, the psychologist ___________ deeply into the reason behind his patient's depression.

(a) probed
(b) faltered
(c) deviated
(d) skimmed

41. The story of the protagonist's birth, which was mysterious at the outset, gradually ___________ throughout the course of the novel.

(a) elongated
(b) detached
(c) unfolded
(d) reprised

42. As team leader, Linda ___________ full responsibility for the team not meeting its deadline, sparing her subordinates blame.

(a) prefaced
(b) assumed
(c) allocated
(d) prioritized

43. Medieval knights swore their ___________ to a lord in order to confirm their loyalty.

(a) allegiance
(b) constraint
(c) admonition
(d) compulsion

44. In response to concerns over its
aging _____________ of airplanes,
Blue Airways just purchased ten new
jetliners.

(a) sect
(b) fleet
(c) scale
(d) forte

45. Reports of excess amounts of pesticide
on some of its vegetables _____________
the otherwise sterling reputation of the
produce company.

(a) tarnished
(b) rendered
(c) berated
(d) grazed

46. The remote tribe was notoriously
_____________ to outsiders, attacking
anyone who was not a member of their
group.

(a) prudent
(b) grievous
(c) repentant
(d) antagonistic

47. The scientists disagreed about the
storm's _____________, some arguing
that it would veer west and others that it
was headed north.

(a) embankment
(b) vanguard
(c) trajectory
(d) locution

48. Although the company had many
small debts, when added together, the
_____________ amount was beyond its
means to repay.

(a) aggregate
(b) syndicated
(c) acquiescent
(d) collaborative

49. The boundary between the two
properties was clearly _____________ by
a fence separating them.

(a) extirpated
(b) perforated
(c) demarcated
(d) underpinned

50. Following the massive hurricane,
the prime minister _____________ the
international community to provide
humanitarian assistance.

(a) saluted
(b) revered
(c) beseeched
(d) elucidated

This is the end of the Vocabulary section. Do NOT move on to the Reading
Comprehension section until instructed to do so. You are NOT allowed to turn
to any other section of the test.

READING COMPREHENSION

○ 정답 P 339

Part I Questions 1—16

Read the passage and choose the option that best completes the passage.

1. Starting October 20, Savannah Adventures is closing temporarily as the zoo undergoes construction to _______________________________. The individual enclosures currently housing most of our animals will be replaced by carefully concealed fences around the park's edges. Those visiting after the reopening will not feel like they are in a zoo, but instead like they have stepped out into the wilds of Africa. Future visits will be by guided tour only, using custom off-road vehicles to give visitors animal encounters just like those on actual African safaris.

   (a) make the safari experience more affordable
   (b) separate the animals into individual enclosures
   (c) allow visitors to bring their vehicles into the park
   (d) give customers a more authentic safari experience

2.

Dear Leonard,

I'm writing to _______________________________. I started feeling really sick Saturday evening and couldn't bring myself to leave the house. I didn't call because I figured you were busy with guests, and didn't want to disturb your birthday celebrations! Andrea told me it was fun, so I'm sad to have missed it. Anyhow, I'll make it up to you by buying you dinner—just name the day.

Take care,

Lisa

   (a) say I'm sorry I couldn't make it to your birthday party
   (b) apologize for forgetting your birthday last Saturday
   (c) find out how Andrea's birthday party went
   (d) invite you out for dinner on my birthday

3. With its tropical climate, pristine blue waters, and white-sand beaches, the Caribbean is one of the world's busiest tourist destinations. But you can still have a peaceful vacation in the Caribbean by choosing one of its lesser known islands like Dominica, Grenada, or Bonaire. Visitors will experience pure bliss as these islands boast secluded beaches and water-front bungalows without the tourist bustle. So book your trip to one of these destinations today and ____________________________________.

(a) learn why they are now the busiest in the Caribbean
(b) see what the Caribbean offers besides just the beaches
(c) find out why they are a better option than the Caribbean
(d) enjoy a tranquil Caribbean vacation away from the crowds

4. The fisheries of Galton Bay are in serious decline, and quick legislative action is needed to correct the situation. Over the past two decades, the catch allowance for commercial fishing boats has remained constant. However, the number of such ships that have received permits to ply the bay's waters has swelled. This has placed mounting pressure on fish stocks, which are currently at precarious levels. It is time to ease the strain on the bay's fisheries by reversing this damaging trend of ____________________________________.

(a) raising the catch allowance for individual fishing boats
(b) allowing fishing boats to harvest unlimited numbers of fish
(c) concentrating fishing rights in the hands of fewer companies
(d) granting fishing permits to ever more commercial fishing vessels

5. The seventeenth-century English poet John Milton contended that ____________________________________. After being deserted by his wife, Milton published a series of pamphlets on the legal conditions for divorce at the time, in which he claimed there was no need to prove that a spouse was at fault to obtain a divorce. Citing Scripture for support, he defended the right to terminate a marriage if a couple found each other's company unbearable. This shocked conservatives, who unleashed a storm of protest against Milton and tried to have his pamphlets banned.

(a) divorce laws had made it too easy for spouses to separate
(b) incompatibility alone is a legitimate reason to end a marriage
(c) divorces should be banned since Scripture strictly forbids them
(d) married couples should resolve their differences rather than separate

6. A recent study looked at the effect of ocean acidification on the ability of marine organisms to build and maintain their shells. The study found that ocean acidification, caused by rising levels of carbon dioxide in the atmosphere, dissolved the shells of clams, oysters, and some sea snail species. Yet the effect was reversed for other species, such as lobsters, crabs, and prawns, which were able to build thicker shells in acidic water conditions. These findings show that shell-building sea creatures ____________________________.

(a) exhibit changing patterns of migration due to more acidic oceans
(b) are declining as a result of the rise in the acidification of sea water
(c) respond differently to ocean acidification depending on the species
(d) have evolved into forms not requiring shells because of acidic oceans

7. The Northern Miners' Union has gone on strike to ____________________________. This comes after a strike last spring, during which miners in the south refused to work until they received a promise of improved salaries and retirement benefits. The current strike in the north, however, follows a series of deadly accidents which gave rise to the perception that the company has failed to invest in minimizing dangers to workers. The union claims its members have no alternative but to walk off the job until the company commits to the investments necessary to rectify the situation.

(a) secure government sponsorship of unions
(b) petition for safer working conditions for miners
(c) demand wage increases on par with southern miners
(d) protest inadequate medical coverage for union members

8. Valerie Lee's *Wyoming Dreams* depicts a world in which people's visions of the future are never realized. Her characters cultivate romance only to be torn apart by random accidents. They have to give up scholarships they worked their whole lives to earn when their parents are stricken by mysterious illnesses. This is a world where fate is cruel — where free will bows under inexorable powers beyond one's control. In essence, the book tells of characters who ____________________________.

(a) pursue dreams that are ever thwarted by chance misfortunes
(b) take control of their destinies to avoid being ruled by fate
(c) learn that persistence ultimately pays off with fulfillment
(d) compromise their moral integrity to achieve success

9. In Finland, urban planners examine parks and other public spaces following a snowfall in order to ___________________________. The freshly fallen snow obscures constructed pathways, so people choose their own ways to navigate the area. The footprints they leave in the snow yield valuable information about the most natural paths for visitors. These so-called desire lines are then used by planners to make actual footpaths that are as efficient and user-friendly as possible.

(a) discover routes for trails that pedestrians find natural
(b) gauge which paths are most hazardous in snowy weather
(c) clear user-friendly paths so that visitors can use them safely
(d) find inspiration for ideas about how to beautify public spaces

10. Geologists studying the Hawaiian Islands have recently found that ___________________________. In trying to predict the islands' future, the scientists observed erosion patterns, with a keen interest in how water circulation strips the islands of minerals. They discovered that more minerals are removed from the island by water circulating beneath its mountains than by water running over its surface. This internal loss of materials will be the main cause of the mountains' disintegration over millions of years.

(a) water currents around the island are eroding its coastlines
(b) the island's mountains are slowly being eroded from within
(c) the island's water supply is being contaminated by minerals
(d) soil erosion from mountains' surfaces is flattening the islands

11. The fungus species *Cordyceps unilateralis* has developed a surprising method of spreading through the jungle. The fungus's spores enter the bodies of a specific ant species and slowly consume the ants' soft tissues. This process changes the ants' behavior—forcing them to climb a plant and clamp onto it before being killed by the fungus. This aids the fungus: when it finishes growing inside the ant, it sprouts from its host and releases its spores, and because the spores fall from a height, they are spread over a wider area. Essentially, the fungus modifies its host's behavior in a way that ___________________________.

(a) provokes violent conflicts between individual ants
(b) contributes to the propagation of its own species
(c) helps its host populate wider areas of the jungle
(d) protects its host against infection from spores

12. Researchers interested in the relationship between intelligence and learning tracked 3,500 German students from fifth to tenth grade. Surprisingly, they found that while a high IQ is a predictor of initial math skills, it does not necessarily foretell long-term development of math ability. The students with higher IQs got better math scores at the beginning of the study, but the students who took an interest in math and put in more effort made the most gains. Ultimately, the findings show that success for young math students ______________________.

(a) is based on commitment to the subject more than aptitude
(b) proceeds from strict supervision of school work by parents
(c) depends on possessing higher than average intellectual ability
(d) is uninfluenced by intellectual ability in early stages of learning

13. The German philosopher Arthur Schopenhauer argued that the contemplation of art allowed people to ______________________. According to Schopenhauer, people are driven by a powerful sense of desire that causes them almost endless suffering. He argued that one of the only times this desire ceased was when the mind was engrossed in artistic representations of the world. When the mind is focused on artworks, people enter a state where their desire is suspended, and they enjoy a respite from suffering through their dispassionate aesthetic contemplation.

(a) effectively grasp the consequences of prolonged suffering
(b) become conscious of the pervasive suffering around them
(c) learn to desire things that genuinely satisfy their passions
(d) temporarily escape from the pain that accompanies desire

14. In mid-nineteenth-century America, an education in the classics involved reading ancient literary works that were provocative by the conservative moral standards of the time. Such works were regarded as essential to give young men a solid grounding in the humanities, but they were denied to many young female readers because women were viewed as too easily corrupted by the depictions of lust and seduction in them. In effect, the widespread belief that women should uphold their supposed moral purity resulted in their ______________________.

(a) being depicted in ancient literature as impervious to seduction
(b) receiving support to study harmless subjects such as literature
(c) being deprived of a portion of the curriculum afforded to men
(d) obtaining more encouragement than men to study the classics

15. In today's popular culture, the ancient Japanese mercenaries known as ninjas are typically presented as dressed all in black and carrying large swords. This is not a historically accurate portrait of the ninjas. While they truly were stealthy warriors tasked with spying on enemies, the ninjas would not have dressed all in black very often. ________________________________, they were more likely to dress as ordinary people, such as merchants or peasants, in order to blend in with their surroundings.

(a) Otherwise
(b) Granted
(c) Namely
(d) Indeed

16. For many years, the government was the only major player in the space industry because only it had the financial and technological muscle to launch space missions. After years of research into low-cost propulsion methods, Buckley Industries is now offering a private-sector alternative, delivering heavy payloads, such as commercial satellites, into space for lower fees. ________________________________, companies no longer have to rely on the government rockets to launch their products into orbit.

(a) Particularly
(b) Consequently
(c) That being said
(d) As an illustration

Part II Questions 17–37

Read the passage, question, and options. Then, based on the given information, choose the option that best answers the question.

17. The East Coast Circus is coming to our town of Centerville for one week on their yearly whirlwind tour, so don't miss it! Come enjoy next Monday's opening show or any other performance held every evening throughout the week. As a special performance, on Saturday the circus will perform alongside musicians from Centerville High's Brass Band! Every night will bring something wonderful and different!

Q: What is mainly being advertised?
(a) A one-time performance of Centerville's circus
(b) Upcoming performances of a local brass band
(c) A touring circus's visit to a local town
(d) Audition dates for a traveling circus

18. Increasingly, companies are using online videos to attract attention to their products and services. For example, videos that teach viewers specific skills can promote a company's products indirectly yet effectively. Testimonials from satisfied customers can convince skeptics to use a company's services. Another category, often overlooked, is the employee profile video, which serves to establish an emotional bond between a company and its target customers.

Q: What is the main topic of the passage?
(a) The pros and cons of posting videos for promotional purposes
(b) How various types of videos are used to gain customer interest
(c) The kinds of videos consumers most often seek out on the Internet
(d) How video viewers are increasingly forced to view advertisements

19. In recent years, the issue of climate change has contributed to increased demand for energy-efficient homes. Instead of moving into new "green" or "eco" buildings, many homeowners are retrofitting their existing properties with solar energy panels, cavity wall insulation, and even wind turbines in a quest to achieve energy sustainability. Many people feel that this is sensible, given not only the world's environmental problems but also the likelihood that gas heating will become prohibitively expensive.

Q: What is the main topic of the passage?
(a) How homes are being modified to be more environmentally friendly
(b) Why building methods need to change to help fight climate change
(c) How new sources for home heating are better for the environment
(d) Why people are buying new homes with energy-efficient features

20. Of all the train rides I've taken, the Trans-Siberian Railway tops my list. It is one of the longest train journeys in the world, so it affords travelers the opportunity to cover a huge amount of terrain. Along the way, there are stops at places of stunning natural beauty, such as Lake Baikal. Plus, the length of the journey itself allows travelers to really get to know fellow explorers. This is one journey not to be missed!

Q: What is the passage mainly about?
(a) The changing landscape visible along the Trans-Siberian Railway
(b) What travelers should take onboard the Trans-Siberian Railway
(c) What makes the Trans-Siberian Railway appealing for travelers
(d) The different Trans-Siberian Railway routes travelers can take

21. Have you been hurt in a work-related accident only to find your company unwilling to compensate you for your pain? Buford Law can help! Our long track record of clients who have been awarded damages in excess of their demands speaks for itself. Regardless of the size of the company where you work, if you feel you have a legitimate claim to compensation in response to an accident, contact Buford Law.

Q: What is mainly being advertised about the law firm?
(a) It defends companies against workplace accident lawsuits.
(b) It helps employers establish effective workplace safety guidelines.
(c) It specializes in advising people about obtaining accident insurance.
(d) It helps injured workers reach a financial settlement with employers.

22. The concept of the cyborg—a fusion of man and machine—has been around in science fiction literature for a while. But do cyborgs already exist? Millions of people are equipped with hearing aids, pacemakers, and prosthetic limbs, many of which incorporate digital electronics. These people are not fundamentally unlike cyborgs in that their bodies have been fitted with synthetic components for the purpose of enhancing their natural capacities.

Q: What is the writer's main point?
(a) Cyborg technology promises to eliminate widespread disabilities.
(b) Science fiction literature shows how cyborgs are being developed.
(c) People long to enhance their natural abilities with cyborg technology.
(d) Common devices make many people today no different from cyborgs.

23. Sacagawea, a native Shoshone-language speaker, was a guide who accompanied the Lewis and Clark Expedition between 1804 and 1806 from present-day North Dakota to the Pacific coast and back. Sacagawea's most important contribution was when the party entered the Rocky Mountains and met Shoshone warriors. Serving as an interpreter, Sacagawea discovered the tribe was led by her older brother, Cameahwait. Though she could have remained with her people, she helped the explorers secure horses and guides and accompanied them for the rest of the journey.

Q: Which of the following is correct about Sacagawea according to the passage?
(a) She acquired the Shoshone language during the expedition.
(b) She did not return to North Dakota after the expedition.
(c) She translated exchanges between the Shoshone and explorers.
(d) She abandoned the explorers to reunite with her tribe.

24. BerryBrite Laundry Services has opened a new route servicing Paloma University's freshman dormitory! Just write your name and room number on any old laundry bag, and leave it in the designated bin in the dormitory's main lobby before 2 p.m. each Saturday. BerryBrite vans will swing by at that time to pick up the laundry, and all clothes will be washed, dried, folded, and returned at the same time the following day! Call 771-641-8365 for more information.

Q: Which of the following is correct according to the advertisement?
(a) Clothes need not be placed in BerryBrite laundry bags.
(b) Bags should be left in the dormitory's laundry room.
(c) BerryBrite pick-up is not available on weekends.
(d) Clothes are picked up and returned on the same day.

25. During the last ten years of his life, painter Vincent van Gogh received most of his support, financial and emotional, from his younger brother Theo. Though Theo had no formal art training, he found employment as an art dealer and promoted Vincent's paintings. Theo sent Vincent money for living expenses, paid for Vincent's brief residency with painter Paul Gauguin, and even allowed Vincent to live with him, his wife, and his daughter in their Paris apartment. Theo was only able to sell one of Vincent's paintings before Vincent's early death at age 37.

Q: Which of the following is correct according to the passage?
(a) Vincent's elder brother Theo provided most of his support.
(b) Theo became an art dealer after receiving formal training in art.
(c) Vincent's stay with Paul Gauguin was funded by Theo.
(d) Theo's wife resided elsewhere when Vincent lived with him in Paris.

26. Carlson's Auto Zone is having an unbeatable sale this week only! Take 30% off select seat covers, floor mats, and other accessories! Purchase four tires, and we'll throw in a flat tire repair kit, a $29 value, at no extra charge. Also, for the month of December, bring in this ad and receive $20 off any single item costing $100 or more. Please note that coupons cannot be used in conjunction with any other sales or promotions.

Q: Which of the following is correct about Carlson's Auto Zone according to the advertisement?
(a) Its accessories have all been marked down by 30%.
(b) It sells repair kits for $29 with the purchase of four tires.
(c) It is offering 20% off all sales that add up to more than $100.
(d) Its coupons are valid for regular-priced items only.

27. In 1919 Franz Boas, a renowned American anthropologist, alleged that four unnamed colleagues had abused their professional positions to conduct espionage during World War I. Ten days later, the American Anthropological Association voted to censure Boas, and three out of the four accused, whose names came to light decades later, supported the vote. The fourth did not, however. Later he personally wrote Boas a letter explaining that his espionage, of which he remained proud, had been entirely out of patriotism.

Q: Which of the following is correct according to the passage?
(a) Boas initially named those accused of World War I espionage.
(b) The accused colleagues unanimously voted to censure Boas.
(c) The identities of three of the four accused remain unknown.
(d) One of the accused justified his espionage as a patriotic duty.

28. The 2010 US Census shows that America's ethnic and racial makeup is changing. Compared to 2000, the percentage of the population identified as white shrank, from 75.1% to 72.4%. Every other ethnic category increased, except for Native Americans, which remained unchanged at 0.9%. The biggest growth came from the Hispanic population, which grew from 12.5% in 2000 to 16.3% of the population ten years later. Those identified as belonging to two or more racial categories also climbed to 2.9% in 2010 from 2.4% ten years earlier.

Q: Which of the following is correct according to the passage?
(a) The white population made up 75.1% of the US population in 2000.
(b) Every minority group in the US increased between 2000 and 2010.
(c) The Native American population rose by 0.9% between 2000 and 2010.
(d) The 2010 census did not allow for multiple racial group identifications.

29. My job involves recruiting and screening new employees for my company. Over the past few years, I've turned to social networking websites for help. I don't have time to check every applicant's online profile, but I do search for those who are shortlisted. This has never caused me to reject an applicant, but it has revealed attractive personal qualities that were not obvious from their applications. Unfortunately, this has become harder lately, as people seem to be using privacy filters and removing old posts and photos.

Q: Which of the following is correct about the writer according to the passage?
(a) She uses online profiles to screen each application she receives.
(b) She has discarded applications because of people's online profiles.
(c) She has found positive points about shortlisted candidates online.
(d) She has noticed people showing less concern for privacy lately.

30. Exponents of the theory of punctuated equilibrium contend that evolution is not simply a gradual accumulation of minor genetic changes, as the original theory of evolution had proposed. They argue that sudden environmental changes also initiate relatively short bursts of rapid evolutionary growth, with long periods of stasis, or genetic stability, in between. Their view is not theoretically at odds with the original conception of evolution; the two processes, they note, are actually complementary.

Q: Which of the following is correct about punctuated equilibrium theory according to the passage?
(a) It predates the view that genetic changes accumulate gradually.
(b) It claims that evolution occurs in quick bursts of genetic change.
(c) It states that abrupt environmental changes deter evolutionary growth.
(d) It is mutually incompatible with the original theory of evolution.

31. The massive tsunami that devastated many parts of Asia in 2004 was the result of a huge undersea earthquake. The quake was centered off the west coast of the Indonesian island of Sumatra in the Indian Ocean. It caused a crack on the seafloor stretching 1,000 kilometers and sent waves rolling across the sea at the speed of a jet. The waves first hit Indonesia, then Thailand, India, and Sri Lanka, and later the Maldives. In all, 11 countries were struck by waves that reached 15 meters high and traveled 5,000 kilometers from the quake.

Q: Which of the following is correct about the 2004 tsunami according to the passage?
(a) It was triggered by an earthquake off the east coast of Sumatra.
(b) It resulted in a rupture on the seafloor 5,000 kilometers long.
(c) It made landfall in Thailand before crashing into the Maldives.
(d) It caused waves that were a maximum of 11 meters tall.

32. Formed by the combination of two amateur groups, the Hillsburg Shakespeare Troupe is getting rave reviews for recent performances. Though they formed less than a year ago, they have already joined Hillsburg's League of Resident Theaters, becoming its most junior member in November of last year. Since its inception, the troupe has aimed at having several works—those by Shakespeare and others—ready at the same time, thus being capable of "audience choice" performances, in which audiences select by popular vote the work to be performed on a given evening.

Q: Which of the following is correct about the Hillsburg Shakespeare Troupe according to the article?
(a) It was created when two amateur groups combined two years ago.
(b) It is the oldest group in Hillsburg's League of Resident Theaters.
(c) Its objective is to have multiple works prepared simultaneously.
(d) Its repertoire consists exclusively of the works of Shakespeare.

33.

Dear Mr. and Mrs. Larson,

I'm writing about your daughter Marcy. While she is a very capable student, her homework grade is unnecessarily low in comparison with her other scores. This is because her assignments, while often exemplary, are turned in very inconsistently. It would be helpful if you made sure she stayed on task at home. Please contact me if you would like ideas other parents have found helpful over the years.

Sincerely,

Gillian Webster

Q: What can be inferred from the letter?
(a) Marcy achieves satisfactory scores on work done in class.
(b) Marcy's assignments have all been poor in quality.
(c) Gillian Webster assigns homework inconsistently.
(d) Gillian Webster has recently become a teacher.

34. After sailing around the globe seven times, 77-year-old Minoru Saito was in search of a new challenge. So he decided to attempt the journey from west to east. When he finally completed this trip, after long delays in various ports for repairs, he had set three new world records. He became the oldest person to sail the globe alone, the first person to do so eight times, and the oldest to do so in an eastward direction.

Q: What can be inferred about Minoru Saito from the passage?
(a) He brought a crew aboard his ship for his latest journey.
(b) His latest trip was his first one in an eastward direction.
(c) His latest journey took less time than his previous ones.
(d) He completed his journey without damage to his ship.

35. A new production of Tchaikovsky's celebrated ballet *The Nutcracker* opened at the Dunville Cultural Center last night. The ballet is a holiday tradition for many families, delighting audiences with its light mixture of magic and sentimentality. Yet its story goes back to the German author E.T.A. Hoffmann, whose telling has a more menacing tone. It is to this source that the Center looked for inspiration, depicting its villainous mice as red-fanged beasts. This version is not one for a family outing at Christmas, but it will be welcomed by mature audiences tired of having seen it done the same way for decades.

Q: Which statement about the new production of *The Nutcracker* would the writer most likely agree with?
(a) It has distorted the intention of the story's original creator.
(b) It is too dark to be appropriate for children's entertainment.
(c) It will appeal to viewers who prefer to watch sentimental performances.
(d) It will be less satisfying than a repeat viewing of the traditional production.

36. The Kingdom of Genevia relies heavily on expatriate workers, yet it has a huge untapped domestic labor force—women. The traditional roles of Genevian women, wife and mother, have limited their participation in the workforce, and currently less than 15% of them have jobs. Yet they are making gains. They have literacy rates comparable to those of men and attend university in higher numbers than men. Encouraging these women to find employment would be a boon to the country. With the right opportunities, they would be able to fill many of the skilled jobs that currently go to outsiders.

Q: Which statement about Genevian women would the writer most likely agree with?
(a) Their role in society is increasingly that of wife and mother.
(b) They are unemployed because expatriates will not hire them.
(c) Their opportunities to attend school lag behind those of men.
(d) They have the potential to fill positions occupied by expatriates.

37.

To the Editor:

When I renewed my driver's license yesterday, I noticed I was deprived of a convenient way to remain a potential organ donor. The option is now missing from the renewal. Instead, I have to apply to the government for a special card. This more complicated system will deter people from becoming donors. Just one donor can potentially save ten lives, so becoming one shouldn't be a hassle. Already thousands of people die a year waiting for organ transplants. This doesn't have to be the case. Consider Spain, where everyone is classified as a donor unless they say otherwise. Now that is common sense.

Dr. Ralph Marvin

Q: Which statement would the writer most likely agree with?
(a) Citizens have a duty to report their organ donor status to the government.
(b) Special cards are an irksome but necessary means of identifying donors.
(c) Organ donation status should be separated from driver license renewal.
(d) Spain's policies on organ donation should stand as the exemplar.

Part III   **Questions 38—40**

Read the passage and identify the option that does NOT belong.

38. Panic attacks, or involuntary rushes of intense fear, have many possible causes. (a) In some cases, genetic predisposition seems to be to blame, as the disorder runs in families. (b) Stress from life events such as romantic troubles or personal loss can also trigger attacks. (c) Other times, an attack can be brought on simply by encountering a situation that causes fear. (d) Attempting to bring back a measured pattern of breathing is a good way of ending an attack.

39. In medieval Europe, consumption of beer and wine was important for maintaining one's health. (a) They were safe to drink because their production process killed harmful bacteria that often lingered in unboiled drinking water. (b) Beer and wine also provided certain nutrients that were difficult to obtain elsewhere. (c) Wine was generally more expensive than beer on account of its relative scarcity and greater prestige. (d) Moreover, these drinks were rich in calories and so provided ample energy, particularly in winter months.

40. Tattooing of the arms and lips was a deeply symbolic practice for Japan's indigenous Ainu people. (a) According to Ainu lore, the sister of the creator god brought tattooing to earth, so tattoos connect people to the divine. (b) This led the Ainu to believe tattoos had magical properties such as the power to repel evil spirits and protect women from disease. (c) The tattoos got their characteristic bluish hue from the soot of birch bark, which was rubbed into cuts made by a razor. (d) They were also central to the Ainu people's concept of female beauty and signified a woman's readiness for marriage.

This is the end of the Reading Comprehension section. Please remain seated until the proctor has instructed otherwise. You are NOT allowed to turn to any other section of the test.

Listening Comprehension Scripts

Listening Comprehension Scripts

1

M　Want to go to the gym?

W　_______________________

(a) Try exercising it.
(b) It's at the gym.
(c) Thanks, but not today.
(d) No, I'll keep it.

2

W　I heard you had a bike accident.

M　_______________________

(a) Yes, but it wasn't serious.
(b) No, it was my bike.
(c) Be more careful.
(d) I hope not.

3

M　How was last night's concert?

W　_______________________

(a) Great! I wouldn't miss it.
(b) Oh, you'd have loved it.
(c) I'm glad you did.
(d) You're tough to please.

4

W　Let's paint the house soon. It's badly needed.

M　_______________________

(a) Too bad it's being painted.
(b) Nah, it can wait awhile.
(c) Yeah, I think it's too soon.
(d) Your brush needs more paint.

5

M　Is your shirt inside out? I see the seams.

W　_______________________

(a) I'll iron it for you.
(b) It's the right size.
(c) Actually, they're supposed to show.
(d) It's too hot to wear outside.

6

W　Pam looks so much like her mother!

M　_______________________

(a) No, she couldn't find her.
(b) Yes, there's a strong resemblance there.
(c) Not unless they look alike.
(d) How nice of them.

7

M　I ordered a vegetarian meal for this flight, but this has meat.

W　_______________________

(a) Do that when booking your ticket.
(b) My apologies. I'll fix that immediately.
(c) We'll be serving meals soon.
(d) Sorry, no nonvegetarian meals are left.

8

W　Do you mind if I put ketchup on our fries?

M　_______________________

(a) You're right, the ketchup tastes weird.
(b) Not at all. Put some ketchup on them instead.
(c) Go ahead. I love the stuff.
(d) I wish we'd ordered the fries.

9

M　Hello. Is this the right number for James Munroe?

W　_______________________

(a) I lost his number.
(b) It is, but he's not in right now.
(c) I'll try calling back.
(d) He gave me the message.

10

W Isn't this toy supposed to come with batteries?

M ___________________________

(a) No. They were included when I purchased it.
(b) Yeah, choose any toy you like.
(c) No, that's why I bought some separately.
(d) Replacing the batteries should fix it.

11

M You must hate the company's new ban on cell phones.

W ___________________________

(a) Believe it or not, I'm all for it.
(b) Sorry, I don't make the rules.
(c) Plus, hearing other people's calls is distracting.
(d) Yeah, it's a big relief.

12

W What a shame your holiday got canceled last-minute.

M ___________________________

(a) Mine might get canceled, too.
(b) For all that, the trip had few complications.
(c) I know, I was really looking forward to it.
(d) Hardly. No one could do it but me.

13

M The school is finally updating its curriculum. It's about time!

W ___________________________

(a) I agree, a change is long overdue.
(b) You're right, there isn't time.
(c) At least the curriculum hasn't changed.
(d) The students studied hard for it, too.

14

W Would you say downtown Hong Kong is pedestrian-friendly?

M ___________________________

(a) You can make it by then.
(b) Very. It's easy to get around on foot.
(c) Take your time. There's no hurry.
(d) Of course, but you'd better walk.

15

M How reliable are these online travel booking sites?

W ___________________________

(a) As far as I know, it's an online agency.
(b) I see the issue—you forgot to book it.
(c) I've never had any problems with them.
(d) That's how you know they're legitimate.

16

M Should I bring anything to the party?
W Maybe a dessert.
M How about cupcakes?
W ___________________________

(a) That would be fantastic!
(b) Wow, they were delicious.
(c) They're not ready.
(d) That's why I made them.

17

W I'm sorry you didn't get into Briar University.
M It's OK. I was accepted at a few other places.
W Have you made a choice?
M ___________________________

(a) I've decided on Briar.
(b) I will, if I'm accepted.
(c) I'm still considering my options.
(d) That's after I apply.

18

M Do you know a good web designer?
W Yes, but she's usually busy.
M My project isn't big. Would she have time for it?
W ___________________________

(a) In fact, that's her web design.
(b) I'll ask her if she's available.
(c) Sorry, I can't do that project.
(d) Not if it's that big.

19

W   I didn't expect to see you here on campus.

M   I'm actually here for a job interview.

W   For the vacancy in the history department?

M   _______________________________

(a) No, for a position in the administration office.

(b) Well, you should consider it.

(c) Yeah, I'm looking for a replacement.

(d) Don't worry. You'll do fine.

20

M   Are you ready for today's Spanish test?

W   Didn't you hear? Class is canceled.

M   Oh? Where'd you hear that?

W   _______________________________

(a) The teacher emailed everyone this morning.

(b) It's being announced after the test.

(c) I forgot to call and check.

(d) Something must've come up.

21

W   How was your business trip?

M   Great, Hawaii was amazing.

W   You must've done a lot of sightseeing.

M   _______________________________

(a) At least it wasn't a business trip.

(b) I did, between meetings.

(c) Someday, if I ever visit Hawaii.

(d) No, actually, a friend recommended it.

22

M   How's the project with Alvin coming?

W   He's not contributing enough.

M   Why don't you confront him?

W   _______________________________

(a) That's not what he told me.

(b) I'm afraid of how he'll react.

(c) If it helps, put in more effort.

(d) What a nice contribution.

23

W   Thanks for house-sitting during my vacation.

M   Don't mention it.

W   I'll buy you lunch sometime as a thank-you.

M   _______________________________

(a) I appreciate the advice.

(b) No need. My vacation got canceled.

(c) Thanks, but I've already eaten.

(d) Really. That's unnecessary.

24

M   Have you seen Philip's laptop?

W   No. Didn't he take it to school?

M   He called and asked me to email him a file
    from it.

W   _______________________________

(a) Then it must be somewhere around here.

(b) Search his laptop for it.

(c) He'll send the file if he said so.

(d) That's why I'm sure he won't mind.

25

W   Excuse me. Isn't Kelman's Deli near here?

M   Kelman's is on Third Avenue—this is Third
    Street.

W   There's a Third Avenue and a Third Street?

M   _______________________________

(a) Yes, and Third Avenue is three blocks away.

(b) No, Kelman's moved to Third Street.

(c) Actually, it's a three-way intersection.

(d) Right, you should try Third Street.

26

M   Do we need to hold a staff meeting today?

W   Yes, but the work schedule seems pretty
    tight.

M   Should I move some things around to make
    time for the meeting?

W   _______________________________

(a) Attendance wasn't bad, if I recall correctly.

(b) If it's not too much trouble, yes.

(c) I'll let you know after the meeting.

(d) That's not in the meeting agenda.

27

W Whose song is this?

M It's by my friend's band. This is their demo tape.

W Wow! Have they recorded anything else?

M _______________________________

(a) Nope, never heard of them.
(b) Tons. I'll get you some to listen to.
(c) Yeah, so long as they play live.
(d) All the original members are there.

28

M Has your family adjusted to life in Beijing?

W We're still struggling. Everything's so hectic.

M You're not too fond of living in the city, then?

W _______________________________

(a) At first, but now we've adjusted.
(b) No, we prefer a slower pace.
(c) Maybe, but I wouldn't know.
(d) Yes, although only when we visit.

29

W You make public speaking look easy.

M Thanks, but I put a lot of effort into making it look effortless.

W I wish I had such ease in front of people.

M _______________________________

(a) As I said, it takes a lot of work.
(b) I wish I did, too, but I could never do it.
(c) Maybe you can give me some tips.
(d) In fact, the presentation is postponed.

30

M What would you say constitutes a good life?

W You have to decide that for yourself. Everyone has to.

M How do I know what's right for me?

W _______________________________

(a) I suppose that's the difference between right and wrong.
(b) It takes some serious reflection.
(c) Overall, it's good that you did.
(d) That's because I do what's expected of me.

31

M Any plans for tomorrow night?

W No. Got any ideas?

M How about seeing a basketball game?

W That could be fun.

M I have two tickets from my friend.

W Great, it's a date!

Q What is the conversation mainly about?

(a) Playing basketball with friends
(b) Going to a basketball game
(c) Where to buy basketball tickets
(d) Finding the basketball arena

32

M Lena, about that book you lent me.

W Did you like it?

M It's great, but I accidentally spilled coffee on it.

W Oh, no. Well, it was old anyway...

M But I feel terrible—I've ordered another copy to replace it.

W That wasn't necessary, but thanks.

Q What is the man mainly doing in the conversation?

(a) Explaining why he is replacing the woman's book
(b) Apologizing for losing the woman's book
(c) Offering to exchange books with the woman
(d) Complaining about his book being damaged

33

W Can you help me distribute posters for our charity drive?

M Happy to. Where?

W All over town. I'll do the campus.

M Then I'll go downtown. What about shopping areas?

W If you take the City Square, I'll do Northtown Mall.

M Sure, that should cover the whole city.

Q What are the man and woman mainly doing in the conversation?

(a) Considering locations to hold their charity event
(b) Dividing the task of putting up posters
(c) Choosing the best poster to advertise their event
(d) Discussing whether they should distribute posters together or separately

34

W Where are our seats? Check the tickets.

M Uh oh. Looks like we're in 231 and 222.

W Those aren't next to each other.

M I must've made a mistake when reserving them.

W So we have to sit apart?

M I guess so. I'm sorry.

Q What are the man and woman mainly doing in the conversation?

(a) Deciding where to sit

(b) Reserving concert tickets online

(c) Trying to change their seats

(d) Discovering their seats are not together

35

W That movie was just one chase scene after another.

M Oh, come on! They added drama to the story.

W What story? It didn't have a plot.

M What do you expect from an action flick?

W Some semblance of a storyline, at least.

M Wow, even the critics weren't as harsh as you!

Q What is the woman mainly doing in the conversation?

(a) Correcting the man's misunderstanding of a movie's plot

(b) Defending why she dislikes action films

(c) Pointing out how a movie's plot was weak

(d) Asserting that action movies are too violent

36

M Why are you so opposed to our office being renovated?

W Because the proposed layout isn't practical.

M Everyone else loves it, though.

W The floor plan just doesn't make sense.

M You really think so?

W I do. The renovation shouldn't go ahead as planned.

Q What is the woman mainly doing in the conversation?

(a) Choosing which office layout will work best

(b) Pointing out flaws in the office's current layout

(c) Expressing her skepticism about a proposed renovation

(d) Refusing to halt a planned renovation to the office

37

W What do you think about the proposal to pump oil to refineries on the west coast?

M Well, the pipeline's ecological impact needs to be assessed first.

W Exactly, and by impartial scientists, not a group of insiders.

M They would also need contingency plans.

W Like specific spill scenarios?

M Right. All that should be considered before proceeding any further.

Q What are the man and woman mainly discussing?

(a) The measures needed to ensure the safety of a proposed oil pipeline.

(b) The negative impact an oil spill is having on the environment.

(c) Their opposition to an environmentally hazardous pipeline.

(d) Their dissatisfaction with the assessment of a pipeline.

38

M   I'm going to visit my sister in Texas.

W   Really? I heard that area's having bad rainstorms.

M   Oh, I didn't know.

W   Are you flying there?

M   Driving. But the trip's not until next week.

W   Oh, then maybe it'll be fine. The storms should end by then.

Q   Which is correct about the man according to the conversation?

(a) He is leaving Texas to see his sister.

(b) He was not aware of the rainstorms.

(c) He will fly to Texas.

(d) He is leaving for his trip tomorrow.

39

M   I heard your brother got a job with Digimax software!

W   Yeah, and right out of college! He starts next week.

M   I hear Digimax is the best tech employer out there.

W   They offer much better perks than my company!

M   Well, it must be nice to have a relative in the same industry.

W   Yes, I'm looking forward to that.

Q   Which is correct about the woman according to the conversation?

(a) Her brother is a recent college graduate.

(b) Her brother has already begun working at Digimax.

(c) Her employer offers better benefits than Digimax.

(d) She no longer works in the tech industry.

40

M   I just filed my tax papers with the American government.

W   But you work here, in Singapore. Why do you have to pay US taxes?

M   I don't pay anything. I just have to send in paperwork.

W   You do pay income taxes in Singapore, right?

M   Yes, I do.

W   At least you don't have to pay in both countries!

Q   Which is correct about the man according to the conversation?

(a) He opted out of filing his taxes to the US this year.

(b) He does not pay taxes to the US.

(c) He lives and works in the US.

(d) He does not pay income taxes in Singapore.

41

W   Thank you for calling Seaside Resort. How can I help you?

M   I'd like to cancel my reservation. It's under Brian Smith.

W   OK, I've got the reservation right here. But there'll be a small cancellation fee.

M   And how much is that?

W   Ten percent, since you're giving us less than two weeks notice.

M   OK. That was part of the agreement.

Q   Which is correct according to the conversation?

(a) The resort does not have a record of the reservation.

(b) The man must pay a small charge for cancelling his reservation.

(c) The reservation is more than two weeks away.

(d) The man does not agree to pay the cancellation fee.

42

M   Do you know of any available part-time jobs?

W   Why? Did you quit your full-time one?

M   No, but with my wife not working I need extra income.

W   Doesn't your contract forbid you from working elsewhere?

M   It does, but I'm hoping my boss will give me permission.

W   I'll keep an eye out for opportunities for you.

Q   Which is correct about the man according to the conversation?

(a) He resigned from his full-time position.

(b) He hopes to supplement his income with part-time work.

(c) His contract permits him to work for other employers.

(d) His boss has granted him permission to work a second job.

43

W   Jack just asked me to lend him another $500.

M   Did he pay you back from the last time?

W   Eventually, but I had to nag him.

M   Didn't you set up a repayment schedule beforehand?

W   No, but this time, I definitely will.

M   Yeah, make the conditions clearer this time.

Q   What can be inferred about the woman from the conversation?

(a) She has borrowed money from Jack in the past.

(b) She was surprised how quickly Jack paid back his loan.

(c) She lacks the financial stability to lend money to Jack.

(d) She plans to grant Jack's request for a loan.

44

M   Excuse me, do you sell camera film?

W   Yes. What kind do you need?

M   Oh, I didn't know there were different kinds. I wanted some as a gift for a friend.

W   Well, do you know what kind of camera your friend has?

M   Not sure—my friend is a professional photographer, though.

W   Sorry. Without the specific film or camera type, I can't really help.

Q   What can be inferred about the man from the conversation?

(a) He prefers using film over digital cameras.

(b) His friend did not ask him to buy camera film.

(c) He used to work as a professional photographer.

(d) His friend is less knowledgeable about cameras than he is.

45

W   Have you picked a topic for the English final paper?

M   Not yet. The topics from the professor's handout don't appeal to me.

W   Well, why don't you create your own topic?

M   Maybe I will. Have you picked a topic?

W   Yes, I'm writing about female characters in Shakespeare.

M   Oh, I love Shakespeare. I did my last essay on him.

Q   What can be inferred from the conversation?

(a) The man has not seen the handout with the topic list.

(b) Students need not select a topic from the handout.

(c) All essay topics must be on Shakespeare.

(d) The man is retaking the course.

46

Professional athletes are turning to a procedure called "whole body cryotherapy" in the hopes of reducing muscle inflammation after working out. But does this process, which has athletes stand inside a chamber cooled to -110 degrees Celsius, actually work? Apparently so. Research has shown that athletes who used cryotherapy had fewer indicators of inflammation than those who didn't. This is good news for athletes who want to recover faster and train harder.

Q   What is the speaker's main point about whole body cryotherapy?
(a) It is still in the testing phases.
(b) It cannot treat serious injuries.
(c) It should be administered with care.
(d) It reduces muscle inflammation effectively.

47

As employees, you know our company is experiencing severe budget problems. So we're taking steps to reduce expenses in an attempt to avoid layoffs. First, to minimize paper waste, workers are encouraged to use the double-sided printer feature. Also, to save energy, lights will work on motion sensors. Finally, computing staff will be adjusting the power settings on all computers. Thanks for your cooperation.

Q   What is the main purpose of the talk?
(a) To inform workers of layoffs
(b) To give an update about office renovations
(c) To announce cost-saving measures
(d) To describe recent budget cuts

48

For most of the 1960s and '70s, Atlantic cod were devastatingly overfished in Canadian waters. To restore the cod population, the Canadian government banned commercial fishing in its waters in 1993, but this action was very slow to produce results. In fact, the cod population was showing little promise of recovery until 2011. It was then that reports showed that the marine environment was starting to stabilize enough to allow the fish to make steady gains.

Q   What is the speaker's main point?
(a) Reversing the effects of overfishing took a long time.
(b) Environmental changes have caused Canada's cod population to migrate.
(c) An explosion in Canada's cod population endangered other fish species.
(d) Cod populations would have eventually stabilized on their own.

49

Hospitals are typically noisy and busy around the clock. However, this type of hectic environment is detrimental to patients' recovery because it inhibits their sleep, and things need to change. Overhead announcements and alarms need to be designed to be quieter. Also, staff should never wake a patient to administer medication that isn't urgent. Minimizing both noise and interruptions will allow hospitals to better serve patients and speed their recovery.

Q   What is the talk mainly about?
(a) What hospitals should do to improve patients' sleep
(b) How hospitals are endeavoring to help patients sleep better
(c) Why sleep is essential to recovery from illness
(d) How to tailor treatments to each patient's needs

50

The District of Columbia prison announced its intention to transition completely from in-person visits to video visitation sessions, claiming that such a move saves money and enhances security. But this totally disregards human beings' essential need for tangible, meaningful interaction with loved ones. The effects of such measures on inmates' psyches would be devastating. Seeing loved ones in person is an invaluable experience, one that should be available to inmates.

Q   What is the speaker's main point?

(a) Prisoners should not be deprived of crucial human contact.

(b) Inmate visits require video monitoring for security purposes.

(c) Family visits are a privilege inmates need to earn.

(d) Jails need more rehabilitation programs for prisoners.

51

The construction and operation of the US transcontinental railroad was a great boon not only for the nation but also for businessmen. Railroad owners, who had previously been wealthy merchants, became staggeringly rich by taking advantage of government loans doled out to build the rail lines. Without government oversight of these businesses, inflated prices and transportation monopolies were rampant, and railroad owners and operators were transformed into moguls with free reign over the flow of goods and products throughout the land.

Q   What is the speaker's main point about the US transcontinental railroad?

(a) It was crucial for the economic expansion of the country.

(b) It afforded businessmen a chance to amass fortunes.

(c) Its construction was impossible without governmental financing.

(d) Its economic effects spanned several financial markets.

52

A recent study on deaf subjects confirmed the remarkable plasticity of the brain. In the study, researchers took neurological scans of deaf subjects while presenting them with tactile and visual stimuli. Researchers found that the region of the brain used by the non-deaf to process sound was activated during these trials. That is, the sound-processing portion of the brain was not shut off in deaf people—it was actively used in processing other stimuli. This surprising finding shows that the brain is not as limited in its design as previously thought.

Q   What is the main point of the talk?

(a) Science can manipulate the visual portions of the brain to process sound.

(b) Different brain areas are responsible for different sensory tasks.

(c) The sound-processing area of the brain deteriorates upon the loss of hearing.

(d) Auditory areas of the brain can be reassigned to process other stimuli.

53

Third Hand, an on-campus store for previously owned goods, is pleased to announce its grand opening next week. We are still accepting donations of gently-used clothes, office supplies, and books to be resold in our store. All proceeds go toward store operations and funding future initiatives. Although we do not accept donations brought to the store on a daily basis, we will hold drop-off events each month during which one of our volunteer staff members will inspect the condition of the items and decide whether or not to accept them.

Q   Which is correct about Third Hand according to the announcement?

(a) It has been open for business for one week.

(b) All of its profits go to paying its employees.

(c) It welcomes everyday in-store donations.

(d) Items that do not pass the inspection will be turned away.

54

Thank you all for coming to our annual shareholders' meeting. You should've already received an information packet by mail, but if you haven't or didn't bring yours, please see Stacy Kimble in the lobby for an extra copy. In just a few minutes, CEO Martin Garland will brief you on the company's performance last year. He will also answer any questions you might have regarding last year's earnings. We'll start at nine, as scheduled, so you still have a few minutes to grab some coffee in the lobby.

Q Which is correct according to the announcement?
(a) Information packets were distributed before the meeting.
(b) All questions will be answered by Stacy Kimble.
(c) Martin Garland's talk will focus on the projected budget.
(d) The meeting's scheduled start has been pushed back.

55

Surprisingly, there are a disproportionately larger number of cases of autoimmune disease in industrialized nations compared with developing ones. This phenomenon has been attributed to advanced sanitization practices in the developed world, which limit exposure to parasites. It has been recognized that exposure to parasites alleviates the symptoms of certain autoimmune diseases. And so a modern therapy for autoimmune diseases, while seemingly backward, has met with success: deliberately infesting patients with certain parasite larvae.

Q Which is correct about autoimmune disease according to the talk?
(a) More cases are reported in developing nations than in developed.
(b) It has been shown to increase with exposure to parasites.
(c) Advanced sterilization reduces its prevalence in societies.
(d) Application of parasites has been shown to mitigate its effects.

56

The nuclear power plant in Bentonport is known to routinely give off steam, so residents were not particularly alarmed last week when the plant emitted white plumes. When local police and emergency vehicles sped through the city's streets and sealed the plant's gates, however, panic started to spread. After 25 years of leak-free operation, the plant had sprung a leak for the first time and was spouting radioactive steam. Fortunately, plant operators were quick to respond, and had the leak sealed within half an hour.

Q Which is correct according to the report?
(a) Steam emissions were unprecedented at the power plant.
(b) The white fumes immediately put residents on alert.
(c) The plant had no prior incidents of radiation leakage.
(d) It took hours to seal the radioactive breach.

57

In the United States, a census is mandated once per decade and determines the makeup of the House of Representatives. The census was initiated in 1790, but the results of this census were questionable. For one thing, it only named heads of households. Also, at the time, slaves were supposed to be counted as 3/5 of a person, yet it is unclear whether this rule was strictly adhered to. Approximately four million people were recorded, but today historians consider the population to have been undercounted.

Q Which is correct about the United States census according to the talk?
(a) The government requires it to be held once a year.
(b) It originally named all males of a household.
(c) Its earliest version did not assign equal value to everyone.
(d) Historians deem the 1790 census to be an accurate record.

58

Not all of your old, non-functioning electronics belong in the trash. Come to the Get Your Fix clinic, where our certified technicians will teach you how to disassemble, reassemble, and, if it comes to it, reuse parts in your electronics items. If your belongings are beyond repair, we'll even take them off your hands for free, saving you the cost and hassle of taking them to a recycling center yourself. We offer the know-how, workspace, and tools, so all you need to bring are your broken electronics and the desire to try and fix them yourself.

Q   What can be inferred about the Get Your Fix clinic from the advertisement?
(a) It does not accept items that are several years old.
(b) It has an in-home repair service for electronics.
(c) It has an on-site electronics recycling center.
(d) It does not guarantee all goods will be fixed.

59

According to a recent study, the growing demand for organic foods has been accompanied by a misconception that could harm people's health. That is, many people are choosing organic foods not because they want foods uncontaminated with pesticides but because they assume organic foods contain fewer calories than non-organic alternatives. The study showed that such people are liable to gain weight, as they adjust their diet to reflect their beliefs about the low caloric content of organic foods.

Q   What can be inferred from the talk?
(a) Organic foods contain fewer calories than non-organic foods.
(b) False impressions about organic foods have caused overeating.
(c) Non-organic foods have been shown to contain fewer vitamins.
(d) The misconception about organic foods was caused by inaccurate labeling.

60

As you know, Mark Twain's classic *The Adventures of Huckleberry Finn* has been released in a newly sanitized version, in which racial slurs have been replaced with milder alternatives. The revised version is nothing but a patronizing attempt to water down history, and it distorts the context of the novel. The fact that the language used in Twain's novel reflected the actual language commonly used in nineteenth-century America seems lost on advocates of the revised edition, who are clearly more concerned with self-righteous political correctness than with maintaining historical accuracy.

Q   Which statement would the speaker most likely agree with?
(a) Mark Twain's use of language was patronizing.
(b) The text's language should not have been altered.
(c) Political correctness is more important than literary merit.
(d) Schools libraries should replace Twain's original with the newly revised version.

Listening Comprehension Scripts

1

W   Welcome back! How was your vacation?

M   ______________________________

(a) Next Saturday at the latest.
(b) By plane, actually.
(c) It was fantastic.
(d) I'd love to.

2

M   Hello. I'm calling to speak to David.

W   ______________________________

(a) I'd rather ask David.
(b) Sorry, I misdialed.
(c) He's unavailable at the moment.
(d) Yes, I've talked to him, too.

3

W   Want me to close the window?

M   ______________________________

(a) No, I opened it for the breeze.
(b) Oh, let me open it for you.
(c) I wasn't the one who closed it.
(d) No, I was just about to open it.

4

M   Great job organizing this fundraiser!

W   ______________________________

(a) I don't think I will.
(b) I couldn't have done it without you.
(c) You'd better organize it, then.
(d) Of course you're invited.

5

W   Where can I get a cheap computer?

M   ______________________________

(a) Try selling it on the Internet.
(b) I bet you're regretting that decision.
(c) Shopping online is your best bet.
(d) It's probably worth more than that.

6

M   I've been calling you all day.

W   ______________________________

(a) Take a message for me.
(b) I was too busy to answer.
(c) But we haven't talked since then.
(d) I'll give you my number.

7

W   How should we announce the schedule
      change to the staff?

M   ______________________________

(a) Let's send out a group email.
(b) I appreciate the announcement.
(c) The news came suddenly.
(d) Check the schedule changes.

8

M   How did you pay your tuition this semester?

W   ______________________________

(a) Just under $5,000.
(b) I got a scholarship.
(c) With a full course load.
(d) Since my parents can't afford it.

9

W   You can't enter this club wearing sandals.

M   ______________________________

(a) I didn't know about the dress code.
(b) Then I'll put my sandals on inside.
(c) Good thing I wore sandals today.
(d) You can always change later.

10

M   Why are you rushing to finish your
      homework?

W   ______________________________

(a) I handed it in on the due date.
(b) So I'll be free to go out later.
(c) I just like taking my time on it.
(d) Because I got it done earlier.

11

W   Movies today aren't what they used to be.

M   _________________________

(a) I'll wait for the movie.
(b) Agreed—so few are worth seeing.
(c) You can bet it will.
(d) Some are more recent than that.

12

M   That tennis player showed poor sportsmanship.

W   _________________________

(a) True. He didn't take losing very well.
(b) I could use that kind of exercise.
(c) Right. He was a model of courtesy.
(d) That would improve my game.

13

W   Excuse me. Can I go ahead of you in line?

M   _________________________

(a) Thanks for letting me cut in.
(b) Not at all. I'll be right ahead of you.
(c) Sorry, I'm in a hurry myself.
(d) Oh, I hadn't noticed you did.

14

M   What possessed you to dig up these old family photos?

W   _________________________

(a) I can take more of them, if you'd prefer.
(b) Exactly where I'd left them last time.
(c) I wanted to make them into a slideshow.
(d) From an old album my mother made.

15

W   Oh, no! This chair's assembly instructions are only in Chinese!

M   _________________________

(a) No wonder we put it together.
(b) It's a good thing they're not in Chinese.
(c) Let's try to make do without them.
(d) They all got together by themselves.

16

W   Any plans for Thanksgiving?

M   None so far.

W   You're welcome to come to my place.

M   _________________________

(a) I appreciate the offer.
(b) Really, it was my pleasure.
(c) Sure, I'd be glad to host you.
(d) Thanks. I enjoyed it.

17

M   How's your recovery after surgery?

W   Good. My leg should be better soon.

M   You must be eager to leave the wheelchair behind.

W   _________________________

(a) Yes, I'm glad I finally got rid of it.
(b) No, that's for the doctor.
(c) Yeah, I can't wait to walk again.
(d) Well, not before the surgery.

18

W   Would you like some cake?

M   No, thanks, I'd better not.

W   Oh, are you avoiding sweets?

M   _________________________

(a) No, I just prefer cake.
(b) It must be delicious then.
(c) No, it's the sweets I'm avoiding.
(d) It's just that I'm full.

19

M   Drew's school called. He cut class today.

W   Really? Has that happened before?

M   Never. I don't know how to handle it.

W   _________________________

(a) Have a serious chat with him.
(b) That's what I would do in your place.
(c) At least he's not skipping classes.
(d) I know you had your reasons.

20

W   Why don't you change your own motor oil?

M   I prefer getting a mechanic to do it.

W   But you could save money doing it yourself.

M   __________________________

(a) You can pick it up later.

(b) Once the oil's been changed.

(c) I wouldn't know where to start.

(d) True, but I don't want to rely on mechanics.

21

M   Is there an Italian restaurant nearby?

W   There's one a few blocks over.

M   Do you remember which street?

W   __________________________

(a) It always gets a five-star rating.

(b) They don't take reservations.

(c) I can look it up for you.

(d) Just give me some directions.

22

W   Hello, Dr. Lipman's office.

M   Can I reschedule my appointment?

W   OK, when was your original appointment?

M   __________________________

(a) I'm not available today.

(b) It was supposed to be on Friday at 10:30.

(c) It was rescheduled as soon as possible.

(d) Until 4 pm is best for me.

23

M   How's your volleyball team doing?

W   Terrible. Our team captain is out with an injury.

M   Can't someone fill in for her?

W   __________________________

(a) She has leadership potential.

(b) No one who can play like her.

(c) That's why she's irreplaceable.

(d) Sure, she can take your place.

24

W   No one will try the new diner with me.

M   Why not go on your own?

W   Wouldn't eating alone be awkward?

M   __________________________

(a) Anytime the diner is open.

(b) There's no need to share yours.

(c) If so, try going alone this time.

(d) You don't need company to enjoy yourself.

25

M   How's your new neighborhood?

W   Great. I just wish I knew more people there.

M   You haven't met your neighbors?

W   __________________________

(a) Not until they know each other, I guess.

(b) Only one, and it was very brief.

(c) No, they don't live in town anymore.

(d) It's OK, they're from the neighborhood.

26

W   My room doesn't have a balcony, but I requested one when I reserved it.

M   Hmmm...I'm sorry. There's no record of your request.

W   Well, is it possible to get one anyway?

M   __________________________

(a) As I've been saying, the record is right here.

(b) I'm afraid yours is the only room with a balcony.

(c) Yes, it's outside on the balcony.

(d) Let me see what I can do.

27

M   Pardon me. This is my table.

W   Oh! But...no one was here when I arrived.

M   I stepped away to greet a friend, but I left my coat on the chair, right here.

W   __________________________

(a) Oops, I hadn't noticed—my apologies.

(b) That's exactly where I left it.

(c) I see your friend's saving the table.

(d) I appreciate you taking care of this.

28

W That deli on the corner is always packed.

M Trust me, though, the food is terrible.

W How do you explain its popularity then?

M ______________________________

(a) The price is the reason it's so unpopular.

(b) It was too full for me to get a seat anywhere.

(c) Lack of choice. There're no other restaurants for blocks.

(d) Customer service. That's what needs improvement.

29

M Personal email is blocked on our work computers now.

W I guess emails were affecting productivity.

M Were they really that distracting?

W ______________________________

(a) Enough to warrant this measure, apparently.

(b) That's why I don't email confidential documents.

(c) Too little time was being spent on them, I guess.

(d) They needed to be for people to work properly.

30

W What's with this hand-drip coffee craze?

M Its flavor is better than regular coffee.

W The difference can't be that noticeable.

M ______________________________

(a) True. They taste nothing like each other.

(b) To serious coffee lovers, it certainly is.

(c) If that's what you prefer, it's yours.

(d) Actually, everyone's noticed the craze.

31

W Let's get the big box of detergent.

M No, that won't save us any money.

W But buying in bulk is cheaper.

M Not in this case. The small packages cost less by weight.

W Wow. I just assumed bigger packages would be the better deal.

M See, you should always check.

Q What is the man mainly doing in the conversation?

(a) Comparing different brands of detergent

(b) Determining how much a box of detergent costs

(c) Showing that the small box of detergent costs less

(d) Claiming that buying detergent in bulk is cheaper

32

W We need to talk about Veronica. She's called in sick.

M Oh, no. Again?

W Yes. It's the fourth time this month.

M She's going through a tough time now.

W Even so, she can't keep missing work like this.

M I'll have a word with her about it.

Q What is the main topic of the conversation?

(a) Veronica's frequent use of sick days

(b) Why Veronica habitually leaves work early

(c) Veronica's insistence on working despite being sick

(d) How Veronica intends to make up lost work time

33

M Do you think I could earn much by selling this clock?

W Not really. It looks pretty common.

M It's old, though. It was my grandmother's.

W That doesn't automatically make it valuable.

M Well, some people pay a premium for antiques.

W Still, don't get your hopes up.

Q What is the woman mainly doing in the conversation?

(a) Expressing doubt about the value of a clock

(b) Cautioning the man about fake antiques

(c) Convincing the man to sell a clock

(d) Insisting the man get an antique appraised

34

W My luggage hasn't come down the carousel.

M Sorry, ma'am, but it should arrive shortly.

W But I've been waiting 20 minutes.

M Bags are still being unloaded.

W Are you sure it hasn't been misplaced?

M It's unlikely. Please wait a few more minutes.

Q What is the man mainly doing in the conversation?

(a) Explaining where the woman can find her luggage

(b) Reassuring the woman that her luggage is on its way

(c) Advising the woman to collect her luggage quickly

(d) Suggesting that the woman's luggage might have been misplaced

35

M The advanced text editing software I bought is fantastic.

W Well, the basic version is free. How is this one better?

M It makes it much easier to manipulate source code.

W Does that help you produce any better work?

M No, but it does save me plenty of time.

W Well, that is one thing that could justify the price.

Q What are the man and woman mainly doing in the conversation?

(a) Questioning the capabilities of free text editing software

(b) Praising work the man has done with advanced software

(c) Discussing how the advanced text editing software is beneficial

(d) Deliberating about upgrading to a better type of software

36

W Did you get the insurance money for your lost parcel?

M No. They're not paying because the courier claims they delivered it.

W But it never arrived!

M Well, I opted not to pay extra for delivery confirmation.

W So now it's your word against theirs?

M That's what it seems. This is so frustrating.

Q What is the man mainly doing in the conversation?

(a) Soliciting advice on how to file an insurance claim

(b) Explaining why his insurance claim has been rejected

(c) Complaining about the cost of having insured a delivery

(d) Describing a courier's efforts to recover his parcel

37

M Have you heard about colleges teaming up to offer free online courses?

W Yeah, but it seems pointless if they won't even carry credit.

M Still, it will help provide quality education on a mass scale.

W Provided that students have Internet access.

M Well, more people will be able to take college courses.

W We'll see. Earlier efforts proved financially unsustainable.

Q What is the woman mainly doing in the conversation?

(a) Attributing a program's failure to the limitations of online learning

(b) Touting the benefits of collaboration on online learning ventures

(c) Expressing skepticism about an attempt to offer free courses online

(d) Pointing out the drawbacks of low enrollment in online courses

38

M Is this your first visit to Seoul?

W Yes! It's my first time in Asia, actually.

M Great! So where are you staying?

W At the Han Hotel downtown.

M And for how long?

W One week in Seoul, but I'll be in Korea for a month.

Q Which is correct about the woman according to the conversation?

(a) She is a frequent visitor to Seoul.

(b) She has been to other Asian cities.

(c) She is staying downtown while in Seoul.

(d) She has just one week in Korea.

39

W It's strange Dave hasn't shown up for the concert.

M Yes, especially since he convinced me to buy these tickets.

W I tried calling him. No answer.

M Weird. He's usually punctual.

W I know. Should we keep waiting for him?

M You go in. I'll stay here until he arrives.

Q Which is correct according to the conversation?

(a) Dave persuaded the man to buy concert tickets.

(b) Dave answered the woman's phone call.

(c) The man knows that Dave is usually late.

(d) The man resolves not to wait longer for Dave.

40

M Are you still living in the campus dormitory?

W Yes, but I'd like to live off campus.

M Why don't you get an apartment then?

W I'd have to find a roommate first.

M Jane is looking to move out of her homestay.

W Really? I'll see if she's interested in renting with me.

Q Which is correct about the woman according to the conversation?

(a) She wants to remain on campus.

(b) She needs to find a roommate before getting an apartment.

(c) She would like to find a homestay with Jane.

(d) She and Jane have already agreed to become roommates.

41

W Are you offering any calligraphy courses this term?

M Yes, one. Are you new to calligraphy?

W I took a lesson once, but I'm still a novice.

M That's fine. Most of our students are.

W Really? So the class is for beginners?

M It's for everyone, from beginner to advanced.

Q Which is correct according to the conversation?

(a) Several calligraphy classes are being offered this term.

(b) The woman has never taken a calligraphy lesson.

(c) The majority of the calligraphy students are advanced.

(d) The calligraphy class admits students of all levels.

42

W There's a film festival coming up consisting entirely of Ken Wong's films.

M I've heard of him. He's an actor, right?

W Nope. He's directed many well known martial arts flicks.

M Ah yes. Didn't he do one called Fire and Fists?

W Actually, it's called Fury and Fire. It's being screened at the festival.

M Let's go, then! That's the only film of his I know, and I'd love to see more.

Q Which is correct according to the conversation?

(a) The festival includes films by multiple directors.

(b) Ken Wong is better known for acting than directing.

(c) The man was mistaken about the title of a Ken Wong film.

(d) The man has seen several films by Ken Wong.

43

W Three months of lessons, and my Korean is still terrible.

M I've seen you improve so much since you started.

W I wish I could hold a conversation like you.

M At least you're getting by with Korean waiters and taxi drivers now.

W But they usually have a hard time understanding me.

M Find a Korean friend. That's what helped me the most.

Q What can be inferred from the conversation?

(a) The woman speaks Korean better than the man does.

(b) The man has known the woman for less than three months.

(c) The woman has not tried using Korean outside of class.

(d) The man's first language is not Korean.

44

M I heard you're moving. Is it a furnished place?

W No. I hired movers to take my stuff there next week.

M Are you taking everything to the new place?

W I can't. There isn't room for everything.

M Really? I could use some extra furniture in my house.

W Come over tonight, and I'll show you what I'm giving away.

Q What can be inferred from the conversation?

(a) The man has no space for more furniture at home.

(b) The woman is moving into a smaller place.

(c) The woman is planning to replace all of her furniture.

(d) The man needs to pay for the woman's old furniture.

45

W With all this overtime, I feel like I'm living at the office this month!

M Why don't you bring some work home with you?

W I would if I could, but the files I work on contain sensitive information.

M Oh, so you never take them outside?

W No, it's company policy to keep them on the office intranet system.

M Well, at least your paycheck this month will be higher.

Q What can be inferred about the woman from the conversation?

(a) Her company encourages employees to work from home.

(b) She does not receive compensation for her overtime work.

(c) She is prohibited from copying her files to her personal laptop.

(d) She prefers working from her office to working from elsewhere.

46

For decades, archaeologists have posited that the "first Americans" came to populate the Americas by crossing the Bering Land Bridge, a strip of land that connected Asia and North America during the Ice Age. Other archaeologists, however, link the first Americans to the Solutrean culture of ancient Europe, implying early sea travel across the Atlantic. Yet another suggestion points to linguistic and cultural similarities between Australia, Asia, and South America, arguing that the first settlers crossed the Pacific.

Q What is the main topic of the talk?
(a) How the first Americans survived during the Ice Age
(b) Competing theories about how the Americas were first populated
(c) Evidence disproving that there was migration over the Bering Land Bridge
(d) The development of sea travel by the early Americans

47

Before an important exam, make sure to gather everything you need, including writing instruments and a watch. Don't rely on cell phones to tell the time, as they are not usually permitted in exam rooms. Also, dress in layers so that you can remove clothing in response to the room's temperature, if you need to. Finally, arrive at the test center early so you can settle your mind before the exam commences.

Q What is the main purpose of the talk?
(a) To direct students to seek help before tests
(b) To suggest ways of getting ready for an exam
(c) To describe actions prohibited during tests
(d) To give advice on how to study for an exam

48

Ancient Chinese medicine is giving new hope to people with Parkinson's disease. Studies show the ancient herbal remedy gou teng is effective at reducing the disease's symptoms, including tremors and difficulty moving. The herb is thought to work by removing a certain protein from people's bodies. This protein is responsible for destroying the brain cells that produce dopamine. A shortage of this chemical is believed to be a major cause of Parkinson's disease.

Q What is the lecture mainly about?
(a) What happens when Parkinson's sufferers stop taking gou teng
(b) Concerns about the side-effects of a popular Chinese remedy
(c) The discovery of dopamine in an ancient Chinese medicine
(d) How gou teng alleviates the symptoms of Parkinson's disease

49

Nowadays, more people are working on a freelance basis. For these people, it's important to find ways of dealing with a fluctuating income. The most important step is to realize that they won't have a steady source of income and plan their spending accordingly. When work is abundant, it's tempting to spend freely on luxuries. But there's no guarantee the good times will last. So freelancers need to live on less than they earn so they can set some aside for less successful periods.

Q What is the speaker's main point about freelancers?
(a) They need to negotiate to secure higher incomes.
(b) Their spending too often exceeds their current salary.
(c) They need to plan to manage their inconsistent incomes.
(d) Their income is too small to provide them with luxuries.

50

While grading papers, I'm often appalled by students' inability to compose grammatically correct sentences. But they're not entirely to blame. Their deficiency is largely due to introductory college English courses that include scant training in the mechanics of writing. Instead of teaching the rules of language, these courses often focus on discussions about novels, movies, and current issues. Composition courses should return to the basics—grammar, organization, and rhetoric—and cut out all the distractions.

Q   What is the speaker's main point about college composition courses?
(a) They fail to prepare students to produce good writing.
(b) The writing topics they use fail to appeal to students.
(c) They provide insufficient time for student discussions.
(d) The assignments they use stress grammar too much.

51

Despite knowing the health risks of tanning, many people continue to enjoy the activity. Why? A new study points to people's neurological response to ultraviolet light. Experiments show that tanning elevates activity levels in regions of the brain associated with cravings. After prolonged exposure to sunlight, people naturally yearn for repeated exposures. So beyond the desire to look good, there is a biological reason people keep tanning.

Q   What is the speaker's main point?
(a) Tanning leads to increased cravings for ultraviolet light.
(b) The risks of tanning are offset by positive effects on the brain.
(c) Lack of exposure to sunlight decreases neurological functioning.
(d) People remain unaware of the health risks of tanning.

52

Agricultural products from the US became available to Cubans in 2000, when the US lifted its forty-year export ban on sales of food to Cuba. However, Cuba continued to avoid purchasing crops from the US for political reasons. This changed in 2001 when a hurricane devastated Cuba's farmland. It was then that Cuba began purchasing large quantities of food from the US. By 2002, the US had become the source of more than a quarter of the food imported by Cuba.

Q   What is the main topic of the talk?
(a) How Cuba's farmers sought to rebuild following a hurricane
(b) Why the US decided to lift its restrictions on trade with Cuba
(c) How the US helped Cuba restore its farmland after a hurricane
(d) Why exports of US agricultural products to Cuba have increased

53

The Congolese Cultural Society is pleased to announce the start of traditional Congolese dance classes. Semesters begin in March and September and last from 12 to 13 weeks. Classes are free for Congolese Cultural Society members. Non-members pay family or individual rates. Those under age 14 must register with and be accompanied by an adult for all classes. Hope to see you there!

Q   Which is correct about the dance class according to the announcement?
(a) There are two semesters per year.
(b) Semesters run for 12 to 14 weeks.
(c) Classes are free for all participants.
(d) Children are not allowed to enroll.

54

Pacific Fireworks would like to apologize for the incident at the Fourth of July fireworks show in Sparrow Bay. A virus within our computer system caused the fireworks on three barges to discharge prematurely. Fortunately, the safety precautions instituted to protect both the public and our employees were effective. As a result, the incident resulted in zero injuries. After hundreds of shows, and ten years doing the Sparrow Bay show, this is the first such mishap in company history. We are committed to ensuring it is also the last.

Q   Which is correct according to the announcement?

(a) A computer error postponed the launch of the fireworks.

(b) The fireworks were all launched from a single barge.

(c) The company's employees were unharmed in the incident.

(d) It was the firm's first time doing the Sparrow Bay show.

55

In a 1997 case, the Supreme Court unanimously struck down the anti-indecency provisions of the Communications Decency Act. These provisions had been the first to restrict the distribution of online materials deemed harmful to minors. In ruling against the provisions, the Supreme Court argued that they infringed on adults' constitutional right to free speech. Two of the judges, while agreeing to strike down the ruling, published a separate opinion encouraging Internet companies to establish online zones accessible only to adults.

Q   Which is correct about the anti-indecency provisions of the Communications Decency Act according to the talk?

(a) The judges were divided over whether to strike them down.

(b) They were the first to shield minors from harmful online material.

(c) They were not ruled to unlawfully hinder freedom of speech.

(d) The judges unanimously rejected exclusive online zones for adults.

56

Over the last twenty years, London-based artist Banksy has gained an international reputation for his graffiti artwork. Yet, his practice of stenciling politically subversive images on the sides of public buildings without authorization has proved highly controversial. While some of his works have been preserved with plexiglass covers and sold for six-figure sums, others have been destroyed by public officials who regard them as simple vandalism. His depiction of two gangsters clutching bananas, for example, was painted over by London's transit officials despite public support for preserving the work.

Q   Which is correct about Banksy according to the talk?

(a) His work remains unknown outside England.

(b) He created his works without official permission.

(c) None of his graffiti art has been sold.

(d) A public outcry saved his depiction of gangsters.

57

The removal of the Costa Concordia shipwreck off the Tuscan coast promises to be one of the most challenging in history. Financed by the ship's insurers and managed by two construction companies, the operation is expected to take up to a year and cost more than half the ship's value. Removing sections of the ship separately would have been easier and less costly, but this plan was abandoned when it was found it would cause excess debris. The current plan is to raise the partially submerged vessel in one gigantic piece and drag it away.

Q   Which is correct about the Costa Concordia according to the report?

(a) Its removal is being funded by two construction companies.

(b) The salvaging operation will cost double the ship's value.

(c) A proposal to divide the ship into sections was rejected.

(d) The wreckage currently lies completely under the ocean.

58

Sick of endless searching for parking downtown and paying exorbitant prices at parking garages? Then Parking Match is for you. Our online service enables drivers to reserve parking spots from private owners. Those with spots to rent post a picture and address on the site, and customers make bookings with their license plate number. The times and prices are there for easy comparison, and advance payment is made through our secure online booking service. Try it next time you're in the city!

Q   What can be inferred about Parking Match from the advertisement?

(a) It lists the location of all parking garages downtown.

(b) It charges a fixed rate for all its parking spot rentals.

(c) It offers an inexpensive alternative to parking garages.

(d) It owns all the spaces that are advertised on its website.

59

The Brownstone School Board recently adopted a plan to cut class sizes for elementary schools by hiring dozens of new teachers. This was a move in the right direction, but now the board is scrambling for ways to pay for the additional teachers. Board members are already eyeing the easy targets, including school budgets for arts, sports, and field trips. But these cuts would directly impact the children. Meanwhile, the board refuses to even consider reducing its administrative workforce. It's time to prioritize the cuts with the least impact on our children!

Q   Which statement would the speaker most likely agree with?

(a) The school board has placed too much value on arts and sports.

(b) Arts and sports programs should not be sacrificed to pay for the new teachers.

(c) Reducing class sizes is not going to improve elementary education.

(d) Government funding should be sought to hire more administrators.

60

A new production of Janet Horton's classic comedy What the Traveler Said debuted at the Grace Theater last night. It was a clear departure from the subtlety of earlier performances. Trying every cheap trick to get a laugh, the company's seasoned actors shouted their lines and grossly overacted their parts. It all fell flat. The only laughter heard last night was the awkward tittering that greets an embarrassing spectacle.

Q   What can be inferred about the new production of What the Traveler Said from the review?

(a) Its subtle humor is lost on contemporary audiences.

(b) The intensity of the performance captivated onlookers.

(c) The actors embraced an exaggerated performance style.

(d) More experienced actors are needed for the production.

Listening Comprehension Scripts

1

M   Hello, could I book dinner for two tonight?
W   _______________

(a) Sorry. We don't accept reservations.
(b) Sure, I'd love to join.
(c) Dinner was excellent, thanks.
(d) I'd like to sit by a window.

2

W   When are you leaving for Houston?
M   _______________

(a) I haven't gone lately.
(b) I'll be back in a week.
(c) My family lived there for a year.
(d) My flight's tomorrow evening.

3

M   You're early to the office this morning!
W   _______________

(a) That's fine. I'm almost there.
(b) No, I'm at the office.
(c) My commute was unusually fast.
(d) Let's just meet here, then.

4

W   I'd like to check in to the suite I reserved.
M   _______________

(a) I just need your name, please.
(b) Great. I'm glad you've enjoyed your stay.
(c) No need. Just leave the key in the room.
(d) You'd better reserve it soon, then.

5

M   Does John really practice tennis every day?
W   _______________

(a) That's right. He gave up.
(b) Yeah, he's trying to improve.
(c) Sure, but not on a daily basis.
(d) Only when he's not busy practicing tennis.

6

W   I heard Suzie isn't teaching this semester.
M   _______________

(a) That's just a rumor—I'm still here.
(b) Right. She'll be too busy teaching.
(c) That's a lot of students for her.
(d) Yes. She's on leave.

7

M   I'm looking to buy some extension cords. Do you sell them?
W   _______________

(a) I'll take two if they're in stock.
(b) They can't be extended any more.
(c) They're in the electronics section.
(d) Try selling them at the hardware store.

8

W   Wasn't that last question on the test tough?
M   _______________

(a) No, it wasn't on the test.
(b) It sure was tricky.
(c) It wasn't that hard to find.
(d) Yeah, I didn't find it challenging, either.

9

M   Your presentation seemed rushed.
W   _______________

(a) OK. I'll try to speed things along.
(b) Sorry, I won't go so slowly next time.
(c) Yeah. I couldn't even attend!
(d) I know. I was pressed for time.

10

W   Professor, could we meet this Thursday?
M   _______________

(a) Unfortunately, the department was closed all day.
(b) Sure, come during my office hours.
(c) Let's make it Thursday instead.
(d) Definitely. I'll tell the professor.

11

M Sorry for losing my temper earlier. I was stressed.

W _______________________

(a) Thanks for staying patient.
(b) Don't be offended. It's normal.
(c) I operate better under pressure, too.
(d) I understand. I've felt that way, myself.

12

W Do you want to use my discount card to buy your movie tickets?

M _______________________

(a) OK, I'll take you up on that.
(b) I can't offer a big discount.
(c) Yeah, the card was free with the tickets.
(d) Sorry I forgot to buy them.

13

M Did you ask Annie before borrowing her laptop?

W _______________________

(a) No, but she'd offer if she had one.
(b) Sorry. I thought we were done with it.
(c) She won't mind. She said I can use it.
(d) Don't worry. I gave mine away.

14

W It's hot in here. Is the air conditioner on?

M _______________________

(a) Oops. I forgot to turn it off.
(b) Yeah, but it's not really working.
(c) Be patient. You'll feel warmer soon.
(d) I guess so. Just wear a sweater.

15

M We should expand our internship program.

W _______________________

(a) No, it's already too small.
(b) I don't think we have the capacity to.
(c) But I thought you advocated internships.
(d) I agree. It should be curtailed.

16

W I'm unhappy with this haircut.

M Why? It's nice.

W Isn't it too short, though?

M _______________________

(a) Yeah, you should make it shorter.
(b) No, the length is fine.
(c) I'll take whatever you don't want.
(d) Not really. It took a while.

17

M Have you seen the movie Untold Story?

W Yes, it's one of my favorite British films.

M It wasn't made in the US?

W _______________________

(a) No, it's already out in theatres.
(b) It's actually from England.
(c) I thought it was a commercial film.
(d) Then it must have been filmed in Britain.

18

W Let's go to a sauna today.

M No, I'd rather do something outdoors.

W Like hiking?

M _______________________

(a) I was thinking of a bike ride.
(b) I can't. I'm going to the sauna.
(c) No. I'd prefer to stay inside today.
(d) Fine. Let's just keep hiking then.

19

M They've started road work on route 75.

W Thankfully, it won't inconvenience me much.

M Don't you usually drive that way to work?

W _______________________

(a) I guess I could start going that way.
(b) Yes, but I can take an alternate route.
(c) That's why it won't affect my commute.
(d) Sometimes, when it's under construction.

20

W   Is someone at the door?

M   I don't think so. Why?

W   I could swear I heard a knock.

M   ___________________________

(a) I'll go check just to be sure.

(b) Still, I don't think anyone's home.

(c) No, I made sure the door was closed.

(d) Try a little louder, then.

21

M   Are you renewing your apartment lease?

W   I haven't decided. It expires in a month.

M   Doesn't the landlord require a month's
    notice?

W   ___________________________

(a) He's making an exception for me.

(b) Only if I've already signed a lease.

(c) Yeah, he made me renew early.

(d) I guess I can wait a month.

22

W   How is your steak?

M   It's a little overcooked.

W   Complain to the waiter, then.

M   ___________________________

(a) No, I won't let that one pass.

(b) I don't want to make a fuss.

(c) OK, I'll compliment the chef.

(d) Cooking it a little more will solve the problem.

23

M   Hello, I'm Mark, the new reporter.

W   I'm Vanessa. I'll be coordinating your training.

M   Are you the staff supervisor here?

W   ___________________________

(a) I look forward to meeting him.

(b) Yes, I'm head of this department.

(c) I'll find out for you.

(d) No, you'll have to ask the supervisor.

24

W   You're dressed up today. What's the
    occasion?

M   Nothing special.

W   But you rarely wear a suit.

M   ___________________________

(a) I should've worn one today.

(b) That's OK. I'm more about comfort.

(c) Thanks, I appreciate the offer.

(d) I just felt like looking nice today.

25

M   I had a hard time with that article for our
    sociology class.

W   I really liked it.

M   You didn't find it confusing?

W   ___________________________

(a) It seemed clearer than the article.

(b) It was complex, but interesting.

(c) I'll tell you once I've read it.

(d) I'm not ready to submit it yet.

26

W   Do you see any parking spaces?

M   No, try heading toward the back of the lot.

W   Will there be spaces there?

M   ___________________________

(a) Sure, all of them have been taken.

(b) We won't be staying long enough.

(c) No. There's still plenty of room.

(d) Maybe. It's often empty back there.

27

M   Are you organizing the office party?

W   Yes, why?

M   Do you need volunteers?

W   ___________________________

(a) Yes. Just tell me what to do.

(b) Sure, we could use help cleaning up
    afterwards.

(c) No, but I'm happy to help.

(d) Maybe. Check with whoever's organizing the
    party.

28

W   Hello, Deerpath Middle School.

M   Hi, this is Steven Jones. My daughter Stacey will be absent today.

W   I see. And what's her homeroom?

M   ________________________

(a) She'll be in around 9:30.

(b) She's just feeling a bit sick.

(c) She's in Mrs. Spiegel's class.

(d) She caught the cold there, I think.

29

M   I wish work started an hour earlier.

W   Why don't you suggest it?

M   Wouldn't our colleagues balk at the idea?

W   ________________________

(a) You never know what they might say.

(b) So that's why you're constantly late.

(c) Try getting more sleep.

(d) They've asked for the time off.

30

W   Are you entering the creative writing contest?

M   Do they accept non-fiction submissions?

W   No, just fiction and poetry.

M   ________________________

(a) Then my work won't qualify.

(b) Whichever category I chose to submit my work in.

(c) Oh. Too bad fiction is all I write.

(d) Either that, or I'll submit some non-fiction.

31

M   Why don't you come work for my company?

W   I'm happy where I am right now.

M   We could offer you a higher salary.

W   It's not about money. I like my employers.

M   Loyalty's admirable, but don't be afraid to make a change.

W   I'll give it some thought.

Q   What is the man mainly trying to do?

(a) Get the woman's help in finding a position

(b) Convince the woman to be loyal to her company

(c) Suggest that the woman ask for a raise

(d) Lure the woman away from her current position

32

M   Do you know Tim Davis?

W   Yeah, he works at our university. You know him?

M   We've been friends for years.

W   Do you know his wife, Theresa?

M   Yes, we've met.

W   We were best friends in college.

M   What a small world!

Q   What are the man and woman mainly discussing?

(a) The universities where they work

(b) Their shared experiences at a university

(c) Their impressions of their colleagues

(d) Acquaintances they have in common

33

W   Were you invited to Alicia's wedding?

M   Yeah, but I don't think I can go.

W   You have to! You've been friends for years.

M   Well, it's going to be expensive to fly to Cancun.

W   Come on. Destination weddings are fun.

M   I'll think about it.

Q   What is the woman mainly trying to do?

(a) Convince the man to take her to Cancun

(b) Entice the man to visit her in Cancun

(c) Persuade the man to attend a friend's wedding

(d) Encourage the man to have a destination wedding

34

W Have we received all the design bids for the City Hall renovation project?

M Yes. We'll start reviewing them today.

W I'm guessing cost will be the deciding factor.

M Not necessarily. The mayor said he's concerned with style.

W So we can select something really innovative?

M As long as it's functional, since that's a big concern, too.

Q What are the man and woman mainly discussing in the conversation?
(a) Their proposal for redesigning City Hall
(b) The merits of various design submissions
(c) Criteria for evaluating design project bids
(d) Why City Hall needs to be renovated

35

M The price of Bellview's real estate has surged.

W Really? We should've bought property there.

M Yeah, what an opportunity that was!

W We had the money, and the time was right.

M I can't believe we didn't take the plunge!

W Well, it's too late now.

Q What are the man and woman mainly doing in the conversation?
(a) Discussing the prospect of purchasing property
(b) Lamenting a missed opportunity to buy property
(c) Complaining about Bellview's exorbitant property prices
(d) Expressing regret about investing in property in Bellview

36

W Hi, I have a question about my bank account balance.

M Certainly. What's your account number?

W It's 858-931. I think I'm missing a deposit.

M The last record of a deposit was two days ago.

W But I should've received another one yesterday.

M Processing takes up to 24 hours, so check again tomorrow.

Q What is the woman mainly doing in the conversation?
(a) Requesting that a payment from her account be cancelled
(b) Inquiring about a recent deposit into her account
(c) Setting up a transfer between her accounts
(d) Explaining why her account balance is low

37

M They're going to dredge the lake of pollutants.

W Finally! It's been seriously contaminated for years.

M They should just leave it alone.

W And forget about all the dangerous toxins?

M Dredging could stir up the pollution and make the lake even worse!

W Well, it's not going away by itself. Something has to be done.

Q What are the man and woman mainly discussing?
(a) Whether dredging is the best response to the lake's pollution
(b) Whether the lake's pollution has become more serious
(c) How dredging limits the spread of toxins in the lake
(d) A less dangerous alternative to dredging the lake

38

W   What's your airline's free baggage allowance?

M   Is this for an international flight?

W   Yes, from Seoul to Vancouver.

M   For international flights, we allow two bags.

W   And the maximum weight is 32 kilograms per bag, right?

M   For first class. But you're in economy, so the limit's 23 kilograms.

Q   Which is correct according to the conversation?

(a) International passengers are allowed only one bag.

(b) The woman's trip originates in Vancouver.

(c) The baggage allowance for economy class is 32 kilograms.

(d) The woman does not have a first class ticket.

39

M   Can I borrow your lawnmower?

W   Didn't you buy one last week?

M   I did, but it broke down this morning.

W   Oh no! Can you exchange it for a new one?

M   No, but it's still under warranty, so I took it to get it repaired.

W   Well, use mine whenever you need it.

Q   Which is correct about the man according to the conversation?

(a) The lawnmower he bought broke down last week.

(b) He exchanged his lawnmower for a new one.

(c) The warranty for his lawnmower has expired.

(d) He has taken his lawnmower out to be repaired.

40

W   Honey, I can't believe how high last month's gas bill came out!

M   It was January. Heating is expensive in winter.

W   Well, the bill shows a comparison with last January, and we're paying more now.

M   That's because gas prices have risen.

W   True, but we've also consumed more.

M   Really? Then we should turn the thermostat down.

Q   Which is correct according to the conversation?

(a) The woman is surprised by the gas bill's low cost.

(b) The couple's gas bill was higher last January than now.

(c) Gas prices went up while the couple's gas consumption went down.

(d) The man suggests lowering the thermostat.

41

W   Let's all go to Viva for Danielle's twentieth birthday.

M   No way. Their food is good, but their service is horrible!

W   The service was fine when I ate there last week.

M   But it was awful when I went on opening night last month.

W   Have you been back? They've obviously sorted their problems out.

M   No, but I still wouldn't trust them with a large party.

Q   Which is correct according to the conversation?

(a) The man was dissatisfied with Viva's food.

(b) The woman found no problems with Viva's service.

(c) The woman went to Viva before the man.

(d) The man has dined at Viva multiple times.

42

M Hi, this sweater is too small. Can I exchange it for a large?

W Sorry, that style is out of stock.

M Can I get a cash refund, then?

W Do you have the receipt?

M No, it was a gift from my sister.

W Oh, then we can only offer you store credit.

Q Which is correct about the man according to the conversation?

(a) The sweater he wants to exchange is too large.

(b) The store ran out of the sweater he wants.

(c) He got the sweater as a gift for his sister.

(d) He cannot get store credit without a receipt.

43

W Is that painting a Matisse? It must have cost a fortune!

M It's been in my family for years, but actually, I found out it's a fake.

W Wow, it looks so real!

M I know. Even my appraiser was taken in for a bit.

W Why do you keep it, if it's not worth anything?

M I just like how it looks.

Q What can be inferred about the man from the conversation?

(a) He had the painting evaluated by an expert.

(b) He keeps the painting for its high monetary value.

(c) He wants his painting to be known as a genuine Matisse.

(d) He purchased the painting knowing it was not genuine.

44

M Honey, what was City Auto's estimate to repair your car?

W They quoted $100.

M That's suspiciously low. Did they inspect it carefully?

W I don't know. Should we wait and take it to our regular mechanic?

M Yeah, I want his opinion.

W OK. But you'll need to drive me to work until he's available.

Q What can be inferred from the conversation?

(a) The woman obtained an estimate from their regular mechanic.

(b) The couple's regular mechanic works at City Auto.

(c) The man suspects City Auto will not provide quality repairs.

(d) The woman will continue to drive her car without getting it repaired.

45

M How's the grant application? Was everything I wrote OK?

W Yes! I'll finish my revisions with time to spare.

M Can I take another look at the budget section?

W I haven't changed anything, but go right ahead.

M I think I forgot to account for equipment maintenance.

W We shouldn't forget that!

Q What can be inferred from the conversation?

(a) The man created the draft of the grant proposal.

(b) The woman is late finalizing the grant application.

(c) The man and woman are applying for different grants.

(d) The woman already added maintenance costs to the budget.

46

Attention, everyone! As you know, the bus trip to the beach is next weekend. Last time we all went there, a few people weren't at the departure spot on time, and we ended up having to wait for half an hour. So next weekend, we're going to adhere to our program strictly. The bus leaves for the beach at seven o'clock, so please come on time.

Q   What is the main purpose of the announcement?
(a) To invite people to a trip to the beach
(b) To warn people that the beach trip could start late
(c) To remind people of what time the beach trip will finish
(d) To advise people to be punctual for the bus to the beach

47

Jobs in the meatpacking industry have long been among the most hazardous in the world. During the twentieth century, various countries implemented labor reforms that reduced the number of worker injuries in meatpacking plants, but such jobs are still dangerous by nature. Since it involves fast, repetitive work with sharp tools and wet surfaces, workers today often suffer repetitive-motion disorders, cuts, and falls.

Q   What is the main topic of the talk?
(a) The history of labor disputes involving meatpacking workers
(b) The persistent dangers of working in the meatpacking industry
(c) Reasons why more stringent food-safety regulations are needed
(d) Ways to prevent injuries in meat-processing plants

48

Good effort in the last volleyball match, team! As you know, next up is the championship, so we need to be at the top of our game. Where we fell short last time was our defensive coverage. Fortunately, our opponent's offense was weak, so we got away with it. But in the tournament's final match, we'll be facing our toughest opponent yet, so we have to stay on our toes. We have the discipline and focus to win, so let's do it!

Q   What is the main purpose of the talk?
(a) To motivate the team to perform well in their next match
(b) To explain changes in the team's offensive strategy
(c) To congratulate the team on a recent victory
(d) To announce the team's next volleyball tournament

49

US military forces have been stationed in Japan for over sixty years. Following World War II, the two nations signed treaties specifying the presence of US troops in Japan. This was both a safeguard against a resurgence of Japan's imperialistic sentiments, and a strategic alliance during the Cold War. But both of these concerns are history, and there is no reason for US forces to remain. Japan now has the resources to provide its own security, and the American military is needed elsewhere in the world.

Q   What is the speaker's main point?
(a) Japan's military is incapable of self-defense.
(b) Japan should not receive US monetary aid.
(c) The US is obligated by treaty to defend Japan.
(d) The US forces' presence in Japan is no longer justified.

50

For years, Cambodia's coastal city of Sihanoukville languished in the bottom tier of Southeast Asia's beach destinations. But now, new domestic flights from more popular destinations in Cambodia have kick-started the city's tourism industry. Entrepreneurs once frustrated by the lack of air connections to Sihanoukville have spotted a new opportunity there, and they are investing in prime beach-side land to build luxury hotels and restaurants.

Q   What is the main topic of the talk?
(a) The positive impact of air travel on Sihanoukville's tourism sector
(b) New investment opportunities in Cambodia's air travel industry
(c) The growth in demand for beach-side property in Southeast Asia
(d) Construction of a new airport near Sihanoukville

51

Every year, our company provides numerous professional development training opportunities, yet few people register for them. Many staff members are simply unaware of these offerings, so we're going to start circulating a monthly listing of training events. Additionally, we're asking department managers to remind staff that our policy is — and has always been — to offer paid time off for training. With these steps, we hope that more people will engage in professional development.

Q   What is the main purpose of the announcement?
(a) To circulate an update on policy changes for time off during training
(b) To give details about what training opportunities are available
(c) To request that managers start conducting more staff training
(d) To explain measures to increase participation in training opportunities

52

With the recovery of gray wolf populations in the US, the federal government has removed it from the endangered species list and ceded responsibility for its conservation to individual states. In Wyoming, this has resulted in a dispute between state officials on how best to manage the iconic predator. State officials recently lifted a decades-long hunting ban, since the wolf threatens the state's livestock. But a few officials assert that the wolf is an important state symbol in Wyoming and its protection from hunting should be reinstated.

Q   What is mainly being stated about the gray wolf?
(a) Wyoming residents cannot decide who has responsibility for protecting it.
(b) State and federal officials cannot agree on how to manage it.
(c) Removal of federal protection has caused a controversy over hunting it.
(d) Officials in Wyoming have successfully defended it from hunting.

53

Taking a group tour? Destinations Plus can help! Design your own custom itinerary with the support of our knowledgeable agents. Or save yourself the hassle of planning and join one of our preplanned tours, which are guaranteed to depart no matter what — even including protection from cancellation due to under-booking. No matter how many people you have in your group, we have a trip for you — and for groups over twenty, the group leader always travels absolutely free!

Q   Which is correct according to the advertisement?
(a) Destinations Plus offers preplanned tour packages only.
(b) Destinations Plus caters to any size of group wanting to travel.
(c) Preplanned tours will be cancelled if they are underbooked.
(d) The leader travels free in groups with fewer than twenty people.

54

Russia is planning to become the main transportation corridor for trade between Europe and Asia. One component of this plan is upgrading the Trans-Siberian Railway, a single-rail line already operating at full capacity. Billions of dollars of investment are needed for logistics facilities along the route. The plan's other component is doubling the cargo that passes through Russia's ports by the end of the decade. Shipments currently face long delays clearing customs, taking nearly two weeks compared to just a single day in Singapore.

Q   Which is correct according to the talk?

(a) The Trans-Siberian Railway cannot currently accommodate any more traffic.

(b) Russia is preparing to scale back logistics facilities on the Trans-Siberian Railway.

(c) Russia is planning to increase shipments in its ports by half this decade.

(d) Shipments to Russian ports clear customs faster than in Singapore.

55

Doctors fear that the drug Adderall is being prescribed too freely. Though the drug was developed to treat clinical attention deficit disorder, a small but growing minority of Adderall prescriptions are being used to reduce inattentiveness in normal children who are struggling at school. As government insurance covers prescription costs for low-income families, the drug is often the most affordable and quickest way to improve struggling children's academic performance. However, Adderall comes with serious side-effects, including stunted growth, hypertension, and very rarely, psychotic episodes.

Q   Which is correct about Adderall according to the talk?

(a) It was developed to augment attention in ordinary people.

(b) The majority of its prescriptions are now for normal children.

(c) Low-income families bear the full cost of prescriptions for it.

(d) Psychotic episodes are among its most uncommon side effects.

56

Colic, a condition characterized by extended, inconsolable crying in healthy infants, affects about 25% of babies. No one knows exactly what causes colic, and various explanations have been proposed. The most popular theory is that colic results from digestive distress; however, 90% of colicky babies have no observable gastrointestinal abnormalities. The condition typically peaks around six weeks of age, then gradually improves and tapers off by the time a baby is four months old.

Q   Which of the following is correct about colic according to the talk?

(a) It occurs because babies are unhealthy for other reasons.

(b) About 90% of babies develop it during early infancy.

(c) It has not been clearly linked to gastrointestinal problems.

(d) It continues to worsen until the baby is four months old.

57

Ukraine has rich, fertile soil that produces abundant harvests. However, the nation has no official market for agricultural property, since the sale of farmland was prohibited to both domestic and foreign buyers in 1992. This has led to the development of a black market trade—not in farmland itself, but in soil. With the tacit backing of local and regional officials, traders steal dirt from farms and sell it for prices that fluctuate with the seasons.

Q   Which is correct according to the talk?

(a) Ukraine prohibited the sale of agricultural land until 1992.

(b) The sale of Ukrainian farmland is permitted to residents but not foreigners.

(c) Black-market soil traders operate with the unofficial support of government officials.

(d) The price of black-market soil remains constant throughout the year.

58

Millston School is launching a new electronic nametag system to track students. As you know, student attendance affects the amount of funding. In the past, students who arrived late were often counted as absent because teachers failed to update their presence, and this needlessly lowered our funding. But now, using scanners throughout the school, we can ensure that everyone who comes to school is counted. Additionally, as seen in other districts, the system increases safety by allowing us to locate students quickly in an emergency.

Q   What can be inferred from the announcement?
(a) The school prioritizes students' privacy over their security.
(b) Other schools have already implemented the nametag system.
(c) Being late and absent are counted as the same for funding purposes.
(d) The cost of implementing the nametag system exceeds the school's funding.

59

For years, engineers have been trying to harness the power of ocean waves to generate clean electricity. Unfortunately, for every new device that has been conceived, ecological concerns have arisen. For instance, certain designs utilize hydraulic fluid, which could leak and pollute the water. Others involve electromagnetic forces that could disrupt animals' navigational abilities. However, one thing is clear: nothing could damage ocean ecosystems more than the continued use of fossil fuels and the resulting ocean acidification. For everyone's sake, it's time to choose the lesser of two evils.

Q   What would the speaker most likely agree with?
(a) There have been too many different designs for wave-energy capture devices.
(b) Devices that capture ocean energy are more harmful than fossil fuels.
(c) The engineering obstacles to capturing wave energy are insurmountable.
(d) Wave-energy capture devices should be implemented despite their downsides.

60

Welcome to Biology 101. Please note that this course offers a general overview; biology majors should take Biology 103 instead. Final grades will be based entirely on four quizzes and a final exam. Attendance does not count towards your grade, as monitoring absences of more than 200 students would be infeasible. The class is currently full and closed to registration, but for final-year students who still need to fulfill their Natural Science requirement, I can arrange for an override.

Q   What can be inferred about Biology 101 from the talk?
(a) It is more advanced than Biology 103.
(b) It places a strong emphasis on class participation.
(c) It satisfies a requirement necessary for graduation.
(d) It is open strictly to non-science majors.

1

W　Excuse me, is the subway nearby?

M　______________________

(a) I'll be right behind you.
(b) No, it runs all night.
(c) I'm already there.
(d) It's just ahead.

2

M　Wow, our hotel room has a spectacular view!

W　______________________

(a) OK, I'll ask for one.
(b) Yes, it's perfect for watching sunsets.
(c) Wait until I reserve it.
(d) Then let's ask to change.

3

W　Thanks for sending me these lovely flowers!

M　______________________

(a) They'll be delivered tomorrow.
(b) Sure, I welcome any suggestions.
(c) I'm glad you're enjoying them.
(d) No, I kept them in water.

4

M　Where can I exchange my foreign currency?

W　______________________

(a) There's a lot of money in it.
(b) That's what they said at the bank.
(c) There's a bank kiosk down the hall.
(d) The exchange rate is rising.

5

W　Hi, please transfer me to Brian Jones. This is his wife.

M　______________________

(a) I'll put you right through.
(b) I'll tell her Brian called.
(c) No, I'm afraid I can't hold.
(d) Sorry, they're both unavailable.

6

M　I need your help solving this math problem.

W　______________________

(a) Sure, as soon as you solve it.
(b) I'm no better at math than you are.
(c) I knew you'd get it right.
(d) Let's do math problems instead.

7

W　Do you always stretch before exercising?

M　______________________

(a) Really? I'd love to.
(b) Only before stretching.
(c) Yes, it's a must.
(d) I'll decide later.

8

M　Why did you miss school yesterday?

W　______________________

(a) Unfortunately, I wasn't feeling well.
(b) The school must've missed it.
(c) No, I decided to stay home.
(d) I took it when I was in school.

9

W　Your car's engine is making a rattling noise.

M　______________________

(a) It's a good thing I got rid of it.
(b) I've been meaning to get that checked.
(c) I'm surprised you can't hear it.
(d) No, it's coming from the engine.

10

M　When will I need another exam for my broken foot?

W　______________________

(a) Until it starts to heal.
(b) Not for another six weeks.
(c) When you break your foot.
(d) The first time you broke it.

11

W   Could you drop this package off at the post office?

M   ____________________

(a) Sorry, I've got too much to do.
(b) Thanks for going all the way.
(c) Don't mention it. It was easy.
(d) That's OK. I can't go anyway.

12

M   How'd you get so good at running meetings?

W   ____________________

(a) One more isn't necessary.
(b) I learned from the best.
(c) I'm sorry for being late.
(d) Please be sure to attend.

13

W   Why is Randy so fed up at his job?

M   ____________________

(a) He didn't complain until after he left.
(b) That's why he's looking for another one.
(c) He feels overworked and underpaid.
(d) I thought you were satisfied with your job.

14

M   Where'd you get the inspiration for your latest painting?

W   ____________________

(a) It won't take long to get it done.
(b) I'm not a painter by trade.
(c) It would make a good painting.
(d) I can't attribute it to a single source.

15

W   The critics hated James Lane's new book. Have you read it?

M   ____________________

(a) Not yet, but I will, no matter what the reviews say.
(b) Yes, but I want to finish his new book first.
(c) Not until I'm done reading his new one.
(d) I'd rather read books by James Lane.

16

M   Finally! A parking spot.

W   I don't think we can park there.

M   Why not? It's an empty space.

W   ____________________

(a) Let's wait until it's vacant, then.
(b) The sign above it says it's reserved.
(c) It's bigger than our car.
(d) We should take the car, instead.

17

W   Are you sure you're cooking those noodles right?

M   Yup. I've made spaghetti lots of times.

W   But you need to stir them more.

M   ____________________

(a) No, I don't think I'm stirring them too much.
(b) There's enough in the spaghetti already.
(c) Don't worry — I know what I'm doing.
(d) Good idea. Let's have spaghetti.

18

M   Let's join a dance class together.

W   I'm no good at that sort of thing.

M   Come on. It's not really that hard.

W   ____________________

(a) The class surprised me, too.
(b) Well, I guess I could give it a try.
(c) I went after I took the class.
(d) Actually, I'd rather try dancing.

19

W   Want to join me for dinner tonight?

M   Sure. Where should we go?

W   I'm still debating between a couple of places.

M   ____________________

(a) See you there, then.
(b) Let me know when you decide.
(c) Then be sure to eat first.
(d) In that case, let's eat together.

20

M   Your golf game's much better today.
W   Thanks, I've been practicing.
M   What do you say to playing again next Saturday?
W   ___________________________

(a) Sure, but let's try a new course next time.
(b) Of course, don't mention it.
(c) Sorry, I'm not sure where the game is.
(d) Thanks, but only if I learn how to golf.

21

W   Did you live in Japan long?
M   No, just six months.
W   Did you have any trouble adjusting?
M   ___________________________

(a) That's because I liked it there.
(b) The food took some getting used to.
(c) Probably not until after I leave.
(d) I'll let you know when I get there.

22

M   I need to pack for my camping trip.
W   Don't forget some warm clothes.
M   Isn't it supposed to be warm out?
W   ___________________________

(a) See, I said those clothes were too hot.
(b) But the temperature might drop at night.
(c) No, the weather's been getting warmer.
(d) In that case, you should go camping.

23

W   I want to write my term paper on Macbeth.
M   There are two suggested topics on that play.
W   Yes, but I don't like either of them.
M   ___________________________

(a) Then just propose a topic of your own.
(b) Yes, that's the only real viable topic.
(c) I agree. The suggested topics are better.
(d) Try writing about Macbeth instead.

24

W   I need a personal reference for a job application.
M   Would you like to use my name?
W   If you wouldn't mind, yes.
M   ___________________________

(a) Yes, I received your references.
(b) It would be no trouble at all.
(c) No, they're still hiring for the job.
(d) I've already applied for it, though.

25

M   I've been thinking about taking up yoga.
W   You can join the yoga studio I go to.
M   Are there beginners' classes?
W   ___________________________

(a) They cater to all ability levels.
(b) By then, you'd be pretty good.
(c) Even if I'm just warming up.
(d) I wish you'd try it, as well.

26

M   The speed limits should be lowered on highways.
W   The problem's not that they're too high—they're just not observed.
M   So how can authorities make highways safer?
W   ___________________________

(a) No wonder the number of accidents has declined.
(b) They didn't suffer any serious injuries.
(c) They should find ways to enforce existing limits.
(d) That would just make people's journeys longer.

27

M Is Scott usually able to work on a tight schedule?

W Why? Do you need him for an urgent assignment?

M Yes, I need him to write the sales report.

W ___________________________

(a) Then tell Scott to stop working in such a rush.

(b) Maybe that's why Scott's taken so long on it.

(c) Well, he's never let me down in a pressing situation.

(d) It's a relief he could finish it on time.

28

W Was the feedback on your philosophy essay helpful?

M I'd hoped for more comments on the content.

W Didn't the feedback address your arguments?

M ___________________________

(a) No, I've run out of comments already.

(b) It focused more on my writing style.

(c) Because I didn't want to argue about it.

(d) Not even my philosophy essay was helpful.

29

W The museum is packed today!

M Yes, we're lucky to have gotten tickets.

W Is it normally this crowded?

M ___________________________

(a) I suppose, but only when it's crowded.

(b) No, only when there's a big exhibit.

(c) There are even more at the museum.

(d) That must be why it's so busy.

30

M I wish I hadn't turned down my last job offer.

W The position was all wrong for you.

M But what if nothing better comes along?

W ___________________________

(a) Don't lower your standards out of fear.

(b) No, it's time you started looking for a job.

(c) That's the type of offer you should take.

(d) Then you will regret taking the job.

31

W Grandville Apartments Management Office.

M Hi, I live in 3A. My sink is clogged.

W OK, I'll have it fixed tomorrow morning.

M Could you send someone tonight?

W Let me make some calls and see.

M Thanks, I appreciate it.

Q What is the man mainly trying to do?

(a) Explain that a repairperson is late

(b) Request that someone come fix his sink

(c) Find out how his sink got clogged

(d) Borrow some tools to fix his sink

32

M I heard you're taking summer classes.

W Yeah, I want to get ahead for next year.

M Don't you want a vacation?

W I'd rather get my required courses out of the way.

M I couldn't imagine studying year-round.

W I want to graduate as soon as possible.

Q What are the man and woman mainly discussing?

(a) The woman's reasons for taking summer classes

(b) The classes they are taking this summer

(c) The man's upcoming summer vacation plans

(d) The difficulties of studying during the summer

33

W You're Timothy West, right? The designer?

M Yes. It's not often I'm spotted in a crowd.

W I was at your fashion show in New York.

M Oh, did we meet there?

W No, I just saw you take a bow at the end.

M Well, I hope you enjoyed the collection.

Q What is the woman mainly doing in the conversation?

(a) Explaining how she recognizes the man

(b) Reminding the man where they were introduced

(c) Complimenting the man's design collection

(d) Expressing her interest in men's fashion

34

M Hello, I'm calling about your subscription to Great Cooks magazine.

W Oh, it expired some time ago.

M Would you consider signing up again?

W Actually, I have no time to read it.

M I can offer you the first three months for free.

W It wouldn't make any difference—my mind is made up.

Q What is the woman mainly doing in the conversation?

(a) Declining to restart her subscription to a magazine

(b) Asking to cancel her magazine subscription

(c) Rejecting the offer to subscribe to a new magazine

(d) Denying she allowed her subscription to expire

35

W Greg told me that Denise split up with him.

M Yes, and he's been taking it pretty hard.

W I can imagine. They were together for so long.

M Right. He's trying not to think about it too much.

W I'll try not to ask him too many questions then.

M That would probably help him get over it.

Q What are the man and woman mainly discussing?

(a) How Greg has been coping with a recent breakup

(b) How Greg regrets deciding to split up with Denise

(c) What Greg has been telling people about Denise

(d) Why Greg decided to split up with his girlfriend

36

M Professor Harrison? I'm wondering about my history assignment.

W What's the issue exactly?

M I was hoping you could take a look at an early draft.

W Well, I can't read the whole thing.

M Would you have time to review an outline and the conclusions?

W Yes, feel free to bring it during office hours.

Q What is the man mainly trying to do?

(a) Request that the professor grade his paper ahead of schedule

(b) Seek feedback on an initial version of his assignment

(c) Ask the professor to reconsider the grade given to a paper

(d) Obtain permission to write an assignment on a specific topic

37

W Mr. Walsh, I apologize for the Clarkson contract.

M You were supposed to review all the figures before it was sent.

W I know, and I'm sorry I missed the mistake.

M That one slip-up could've cost us a lot of money.

W I know, and I accept full responsibility.

M The client was obliging this time, but this can't happen again.

Q Why is the woman mainly apologizing?

(a) She lost the company a client by sending the wrong contract.

(b) Her review of a contract overlooked a significant error.

(c) She has refused to take the blame for a mistake in a contract.

(d) Her mistake in a contract cost the company a lot of money.

38

M How do you like living with your roommates?

W To be honest, I don't really like sharing.

M So you're looking for a new place?

W Yes, somewhere closer to my job.

M Isn't that a more expensive neighborhood?

W Yes, but my recent raise can cover the difference.

Q Which is correct about the woman according to the conversation?

(a) She is currently living by herself.

(b) She would prefer to have roommates.

(c) She wants to find a place closer to work.

(d) She is looking at places in a less expensive area.

39

W Your garden looks even better than last year!

M Thanks. We hired a landscaper this time.

W Did you replace the gazebo?

M No. We just painted it.

W I love it. I wish I had the space for a gazebo.

M You do—a smaller one would look great.

Q Which is correct according to the conversation?

(a) The woman prefers the man's garden from last year.

(b) The man personally landscaped his garden.

(c) The man replaced his gazebo this year.

(d) The woman wants to add a gazebo to her garden.

40

W Have you finally booked your honeymoon to Mexico?

M Actually, my fiancée decided on Brazil instead.

W Oh, I was in Brazil last year. It was fantastic.

M It'll be the first time for both of us. Did you enjoy the beaches?

W Yes, I've been to Mexico, too, but I like Brazil's beaches better.

M Great. I'm really looking forward to going.

Q Which is correct according to the conversation?

(a) The man will go to Mexico for his honeymoon.

(b) The woman has been to Mexico but not Brazil.

(c) The man and his fiancée have never visited Brazil.

(d) The woman feels the best beaches are in Mexico.

41

M I'm sorry, Ms. Hendricks, but I have to resign.

W Oh, really? But you've never mentioned having problems here.

M I know. It's just that I've been offered a job overseas.

W You know you're up for a promotion here next year.

M I do, but this is an opportunity that I just can't pass up.

W Well, we'll be sorry to see you go.

Q Why is the man resigning from his job?

(a) His complaints about his current job have been ignored.

(b) His request for an overseas transfer was turned down.

(c) He wants to take the chance to work for a firm abroad.

(d) He lacks opportunities for promotion at his current job.

42

M Have you decided who you're voting for in this election?

W I'm voting for the Liberal Party again.

M Me, too. Did you vote for them in the last election?

W Yes. I've been a lifelong supporter of the party.

M I've gone with the Conservative Party on occasion.

W Well, some people do switch sides based on the issues.

Q Which is correct according to the conversation?

(a) The woman is undecided how to vote in this election.

(b) The man is supporting the Conservatives this time.

(c) The woman has always voted for the Liberals.

(d) The man is a consistent supporter of the same party.

43

W Where did you go for lunch today?

M Dianne wanted to go to the buffet again.

W Nice! The food there is great.

M It is. The problem is—I don't know when to stop.

W It's not like you have a weight problem.

M I know. I just hate feeling bloated all afternoon.

Q What can be inferred about the man from the conversation?

(a) He was dining at the buffet for the first time.

(b) He is concerned about putting on weight.

(c) He regrets having eaten too much at lunch.

(d) He did not find the food at the buffet tasty.

44

W Do you still have an electric drill?

M Dave asked for it when he was renovating his garage.

W Oh, do you think he still needs it?

M No, that was more than six months ago.

W I could really use it. I'm fixing up my kitchen.

M OK. Let me have a word about it with Dave.

Q What can be inferred from the conversation?

(a) Dave is continuing renovations on his garage.

(b) The woman already asked Dave to borrow the man's drill.

(c) Dave has not returned the drill he had borrowed.

(d) The man bought a new drill after giving his to Dave.

45

M Remember Freddy Gleeson from high school?

W Sure, he was always playing guitar with his friends.

M That's him. I read he was appointed CEO of FutureCorp.

W That's a surprise! I never really saw him as ambitious.

M He was always focused on making it big in the music world.

W Well, at least he made it big as a businessman.

Q What can be inferred from the conversation?

(a) The woman saw Freddy's promise in high school.

(b) Freddy failed to achieve fame as a musician.

(c) The man used to practice the guitar with Freddy.

(d) Freddy's interest in business was evident in high school.

46

Welcome to our hiking excursion! Before we set out, I'd like to stress the importance of sticking together in the wilderness. Our trail today is crisscrossed with other trails, and most of them see very few hikers and have virtually no signs. Unless you want to end up wandering around on your own—and let me assure you that you don't—I strongly suggest you keep the group in your sight at all times.

Q   What is the main purpose of the announcement?
(a) To advise hikers to begin their trip on time
(b) To warn hikers not to get separated from the group
(c) To encourage hikers to stick to well-marked trails
(d) To urge hikers to follow signs on the trails

47

As we at Bulldog Insurance continue to grow, we've identified a need for greater supervision of the administrative staff and closer coordination of company-wide projects. To this end, I am pleased to announce that Martin Buckley has been promoted to the newly created role of chief supervisor. Martin will oversee the administration and work alongside senior managers to coordinate related projects. Let's give a big welcome to Martin!

Q   What is mainly being announced?
(a) The start of a project to integrate different departments
(b) An employee's decision to step down from management
(c) The promotion of a staff member to a new leadership role
(d) A plan to recruit more workers for company projects

48

Dozens of sugary snack foods use cartoon characters and toy giveaways to market their products directly to children. The problem is that by targeting children, who can't make informed nutritional decisions, these companies undermine parents' efforts to feed their children a healthy diet. Instead of blaming parents for feeding their kids sugary foods, we should enforce measures to curb food companies' advertisements that try to manipulate children.

Q   What is the main purpose of the talk?
(a) To advocate restrictions on food advertising to children
(b) To identify snack foods containing excessive levels of sugar
(c) To promote restrictions on the amount of sugar in snack foods
(d) To describe the adverse effects of a poor diet on children

49

Teachers, it has come to my attention that most of the student assignments are individual projects. Such reliance on independent work does not reflect the educational goals here at Ridgeville High School, where we strive to develop students' capacity for teamwork. We ask that teachers assign more group projects, as they foster the skills of negotiation and collaboration that help students grow both academically and socially.

Q   What is the speaker mainly doing in the talk?
(a) Persuading teachers to give students more individual attention
(b) Justifying the amount of homework assigned at the school
(c) Urging that teachers assign more collaborative schoolwork
(d) Explaining the policy for grading group projects

50

Most medications that combat chronic sleeplessness have long been known to be addictive. For decades, drug companies have tried to create new insomnia medications that do not foster dependence, but subsequent testing has shown that these pills also hooked patients who took them for extended time periods. Now some scientists claim that it will never be safe to take prescription sleeping pills and that ultimately they do more harm than good.

Q   What is mainly being reported about prescription sleeping pills?
(a) They remain popular despite recently being proven addictive.
(b) Attempts to overcome their addictiveness have been unsuccessful.
(c) They aggravate the symptoms of sleeping disorders.
(d) Testing has shown they are only effective for short periods of time.

51

To start our sales meeting, let's talk about upselling, which refers to encouraging upgrades or recommending additional items to complement customer purchases. I know some customers grumble about us being too aggressive, but the fact is—upselling works. When our sales team does upselling, we see consistently higher profits—meaning that even though customers feel we're being pushy, they often see that our suggestions suit their needs.

Q   What is the speaker's main point about upselling?
(a) It requires sales staff who know how to use products.
(b) It results in increased profits despite it annoying customers.
(c) It is less effective when sales staff are seen as pushy.
(d) It causes customers to avoid shops with aggressive staff.

52

The highly anticipated rematch between boxers Bobby Smith and Nick Johansson took place at the Golden Bay Arena on Saturday. Defending his title as the reigning middleweight champion for the third time, Smith entered the fight as the clear favorite to win, despite having lost to Johansson in their first encounter three years earlier. The champion did not disappoint his supporters, delivering a commanding performance in which he took each of the first six rounds on points before winning with a knockout in the seventh round.

Q   What is the main topic of the report?
(a) How Johansson failed to earn a coveted rematch with Smith.
(b) How Smith successfully retained his boxing title in a rematch.
(c) How Smith won his middleweight boxing title from Johansson.
(d) How Johansson defied expectations that he would lose to Smith.

53

This weekend the Milton Public Library is hosting its second annual book sale. Doors open Saturday and Sunday at 9:30 a.m. and close at 5:00 p.m. The best books tend to go quickly, but if you're searching for real bargains, stop by on Sunday afternoon, as we'll be slashing prices at 2:30 p.m. Entry is free, and all proceeds will go to support our community outreach programs. Complimentary coffee will be available. See you this weekend!

Q   Which is correct according to the announcement?
(a) The sale is the first of its kind for Milton Public Library.
(b) The book sale is scheduled for one day.
(c) The prices for books will be lowered on Sunday afternoon.
(d) The library is offering coffee for a small fee.

54

The jumping spider has exceptional eyesight compared with other spider species, probably because it hunts its prey rather than capturing it in webs. Its visual system consists of four pairs of eyes, each thought to serve separate functions. Their principal eyes, the pair located in the center of their heads, detect fine detail and ultraviolet light. Those on either side of the principal eyes, called the anterior lateral eyes, are used to detect motion. What the remaining two pairs of eyes do is still unknown.

Q   Which is correct about jumping spiders according to the news report?
(a) They capture their prey mainly using their webs.
(b) Their visual system is based on four eyes in total.
(c) They use their principal eyes to sense ultraviolet light.
(d) Their anterior lateral eyes mainly detect fine detail.

55

The White Terror was a two-year period of political upheaval that gripped Hungary after World War I. The intent of its leadership, headed by former Hungarian navy commander Miklós Horthy, was to purge the country of communist sympathizers. Taking advantage of the ouster of the country's communist leadership by Romanian forces, Horthy gathered a military force known as the White Guard and seized power. Then he embarked on a campaign of revenge against communist sympathizers to frighten the population into loyalty.

Q   Which is correct according to the lecture?
(a) The White Terror preceded the outbreak of the First World War.
(b) Miklós Horthy sought to reinstate the leaders ousted by Romania.
(c) Hungary's communist government was overthrown by Miklós Horthy.
(d) Communists were the target of the White Guard's campaign of terror.

56

Newcomb's Speed Reading Guide is guaranteed to make you a faster reader! In just one week, you'll see its full potential—the ability to read three times as fast as before. And that's not all! You'll also remember more than ever before—twice as much, in fact! This system works for readers of any age, from young children to senior citizens. If you're not completely happy with the product, return it within a month for a full refund, minus shipping and handling costs.

Q   Which of the following is correct about the guide according to the advertisement?
(a) It takes about a month to produce results.
(b) It doubles the information people can remember.
(c) It is intended to be used by adults only.
(d) It can be returned for a refund including shipping.

57

The end of the American Civil War marked a turning point in the United States' development from an agricultural to an industrial society. The trend toward greater industrialization, which had begun before the war, progressed rapidly with the end of hostilities. The country's expansion was aided by its wealth of natural resources as well as the completion of a national railroad four years after the war. These factors contributed to increasing America's economic output tenfold in the half century following the war's end.

Q   Which is correct according to the lecture?
(a) The United States became an agricultural society after the Civil War.
(b) The Civil War was preceded by a trend toward greater industrialization.
(c) The national railroad was completed four years before the Civil War.
(d) The Civil War led to half a century of declining economic output.

58

The Hawthorne Studies were originally conceived to determine the effect of lighting conditions on factory workers. However, the project became famous for something else the researchers discovered. The initial results suggested that manipulating lighting increased worker productivity, but it soon became evident that the workers were actually responding to the presence of the researchers. In other words, workers were motivated simply by interest being shown in their work.

Q   What can be inferred about the Hawthorne Studies from the talk?

(a) They produced unexpected findings related to workplace motivation.

(b) They demonstrated that motivation has no impact on productivity.

(c) They were hampered by the resistance of workers to the researchers.

(d) They had the unintended effect of reducing workplace productivity.

59

Today, I want to look at the rise to prominence of amateur theater critics in the age of online blogging. Theater bloggers are on the increase, while professional critics are in decline. Some observers see the trend as bringing an influx of new talent, but I see it as a harbinger of less precise reporting—a drowning out of the authoritative voice of the professional. Theatrical reviews now reflect the confusion of undiscerning amateurs who cannot articulate their standards effectively.

Q   Which statement would the speaker most likely agree with?

(a) Bloggers generally outdo professional critics in terms of accuracy.

(b) Modern theatrical productions have lowered their standards.

(c) Experts are needed for accurate evaluation of theatrical productions.

(d) Professional theater critics are unnecessary in modern times.

60

Rodney Elliot's new TV series, Probable Cause, debuted last night on LBS. Set in a downtown police department, the show has all the ingredients for thought-provoking social commentary. Unlike Elliot's critically acclaimed previous work, however, the new series avoids serious engagement with pressing issues such as poverty and crime. Instead, Elliot relies on fast-paced dialogue crammed with five-syllable words to give his show the veneer of intellectual complexity. Whoever found his previous hit shows genuinely stimulating is bound to find Probable Cause disappointing.

Q   Which statement would the speaker most likely agree with?

(a) The dialogue of Probable Cause is uncommonly subtle and witty.

(b) Probable Cause is more superficial than thought-provoking.

(c) Probable Cause's first episode set a high standard for later ones.

(d) The acclaim for Rodney Elliot's previous work was unwarranted.

Listening Comprehension Scripts

1

W   Would you watch the baby while I run an errand?

M   _______________________

(a) Sure, take your time.
(b) Sorry, she was just here.
(c) I appreciate the offer.
(d) No problem, I'll be quick.

2

M   Hi, it's Jack calling. Can I talk to Alice?

W   _______________________

(a) Jack just stepped out.
(b) I think you should call her.
(c) I'll go get her for you.
(d) She gave me your number.

3

W   Was that the actress from Destiny who just passed us?

M   _______________________

(a) Could be. I heard she lives nearby.
(b) It never came through our city.
(c) Yeah, it's too bad she just passed away.
(d) No, I didn't catch the show.

4

M   When are you going to finish that book you're writing?

W   _______________________

(a) Whenever you finish it.
(b) It hasn't even been released yet.
(c) I should be done in about a month.
(d) I saw it at the store but didn't buy it.

5

W   Have you mailed Frank's package for him yet?

M   _______________________

(a) Yes, whenever he gives it to me.
(b) No, he's asked me to mail it instead.
(c) I sent it by courier an hour ago.
(d) I ordered it to my address.

6

M   Tanya? What brings you to Miami?

W   _______________________

(a) You should visit Miami, too!
(b) It's too bad I missed you.
(c) I only brought two suitcases.
(d) I just arrived on business.

7

W   Want to ride bikes with Josh and me?

M   _______________________

(a) OK, as long as bikes aren't involved.
(b) Sorry, I was too busy to join you.
(c) Yeah, I wish Josh could've come.
(d) Sure, I could use the exercise.

8

M   That girl looks familiar. What's her name?

W   _______________________

(a) She was in our grade, but I don't recall.
(b) I used to be called Lizzy.
(c) I doubt she'll remember.
(d) Now that I hear it, the name rings a bell.

9

W   Why were you late to the office meeting?

M   _______________________

(a) I just lost track of time.
(b) Because it ran over.
(c) Actually, I was supposed to attend.
(d) That's OK. You don't need to apologize.

10

M Did you buy us tickets to another romantic comedy?

W ________________________

(a) Well, only if you'd canceled.
(b) Sorry, I didn't know you wanted to see it.
(c) No, it's a funny love story.
(d) I didn't. This one's a social drama.

11

W Sorry I couldn't come to the beach with you yesterday.

M ________________________

(a) Thanks for waiting until I got there.
(b) No problem. We can meet up another time.
(c) It's OK, it'll be too hot, anyway.
(d) It was great to see you there.

12

M Isn't Greg too young to be the new head coach?

W ________________________

(a) No, he's not overqualified.
(b) That's because he waited until he was older.
(c) Perhaps when the players promote him.
(d) We'll see how he does with his first game.

13

W How did you learn to speak fluent Russian?

M ________________________

(a) I picked it up while living there.
(b) As soon as I start taking classes.
(c) I don't think I have time to learn it.
(d) Just enough to get by while on vacation.

14

M Should I toss these leftovers?

W ________________________

(a) No, I'm not hungry yet.
(b) Just wrap them up for later.
(c) I'm sure there'll be enough.
(d) Only if you plan to eat them.

15

W Thanks for dropping by. It's been great catching up.

M ________________________

(a) The weekend would be better.
(b) Sure! We'll catch up by then.
(c) I think that'd be for the best.
(d) Let's not leave it so long next time.

16

W Any plans for break?
M I'm just going home to see my parents.
W The entire week?
M ________________________

(a) I suppose you can ask them.
(b) No, only half the time.
(c) Yes, they're visiting for the entire week.
(d) The next day, actually.

17

M Do you turn your heating off during the day?
W No, it gets too cold if I do.
M Isn't keeping it on expensive, though?
W ________________________

(a) A bit, but comfort's my first priority.
(b) It's better than sweating all day.
(c) Yes, but you should conserve energy.
(d) No, a heater needs to be installed.

18

W I'm grateful you helped me move.
M It was no trouble.
W Can I take you out to dinner sometime as a thank-you?
M ________________________

(a) I'll never turn down a free meal!
(b) But dinner cost more than the furniture!
(c) I thought you cooked it yourself.
(d) Call me anytime you want my cooking.

19

M   Will you be free on Halloween?

W   There is one party I might go to.

M   Well, I'm going to be throwing one, too.

W   ___________________________

(a) Too bad your party got canceled.
(b) I'll send you an invitation once I decide.
(c) Good thing it's before Halloween.
(d) All right, then I'll be there for sure.

20

W   All ready for your trip?

M   No, I still need to pack.

W   Make sure you don't forget your passport.

M   ___________________________

(a) Oh, thanks for reminding me.
(b) I'll just fill in the paperwork.
(c) There's a separate line for foreigners.
(d) That's OK. Take mine instead.

21

M   I'm hungry. Are we almost at the diner?

W   The flyer says to make a right at Westview.

M   OK. Which side of the street is it on?

W   ___________________________

(a) Just across the street from the diner.
(b) That I don't know. It doesn't say.
(c) It's probably on the main street.
(d) I'm sure you made the right choice.

22

W   Pacific Airlines, how can I help you?

M   Hi, I just joined your frequent traveler club, and I have some questions.

W   Sure, do you have your membership card handy?

M   ___________________________

(a) No, but fortunately I do have my card.
(b) I'll send my membership application first.
(c) Yes, just let me know where I can find it.
(d) Hold on, I'll pull it from my wallet.

23

M   I can't believe how humid this summer is.

W   You should've been here last summer. It was much worse.

M   Really? Worse than this?

W   ___________________________

(a) It was more tolerable.
(b) Right, it wasn't as humid.
(c) Not sure. I just moved here myself.
(d) This year's nothing in comparison.

24

W   Why'd the city reschedule the Easter marathon?

M   It conflicted with the holiday parade route downtown.

W   Can't the marathon just be rerouted?

M   ___________________________

(a) Apparently it'd inconvenience a lot of businesses.
(b) Yes, the parade has been moved downtown.
(c) That's exactly what the parade is for.
(d) Not unless the parade runs its course.

25

M   Let's join the mountain temple group tour on Friday.

W   I called yesterday, but the tour's booked up.

M   Then how about we go on our own?

W   ___________________________

(a) OK, as long as you don't mind groups.
(b) Sure. That way everything will be guided.
(c) That might be better, since we'd have more flexibility.
(d) Only if the group tour is included.

26

W My car battery's dead. I must've left my headlights on.

M Oh, no! Do you have jumper cables?

W No. Can I borrow yours?

M _______________________

(a) I can just borrow them from you.

(b) At least your headlights weren't on.

(c) Thanks. I appreciate your advice.

(d) Let me check if I have them.

27

M What's wrong? You seem down.

W I messed up on my midterm.

M Ouch. How much does it count for?

W _______________________

(a) I'm not counting on my course grades.

(b) It's worth a quarter of the course.

(c) The final will be even harder.

(d) I'll just cram for the test.

28

W Victor ignored me at his party.

M Maybe he was too preoccupied with his other guests.

W To even acknowledge me?

M _______________________

(a) Yeah, that was nice of him.

(b) We've already been introduced.

(c) That he has no excuse for.

(d) But I'm not going to the party.

29

M Let's stop getting our milk delivered.

W Isn't it convenient, though?

M But it sometimes spoils because we forget to bring it inside.

W _______________________

(a) OK. Let's just cancel it, then.

(b) Tell the delivery guy to leave it.

(c) Just put it outside when you get home.

(d) Right, delivery is more convenient.

30

W I heard your assistant is quitting.

M Yeah. It caught me completely off guard.

W Really? Weren't there any signs?

M _______________________

(a) That's why I can't work for her anymore.

(b) She never gave the slightest hint.

(c) I haven't told her about it yet.

(d) That's how I knew well in advance.

31

W What's the most exotic thing you'd ever eat?

M I'd try anything at least once.

W Even snails? Or chicken feet?

M Sure! I've had those before.

W Wow. You're more adventurous about food than I am.

M I guess I just like trying new things.

Q What is the main topic of the conversation?

(a) The man's willingness to try exotic food

(b) Which exotic foods the man enjoyed the most

(c) The best way to enjoy exotic foods

(d) Why the woman refuses to eat exotic food

32

M Are you all moved into your new place?

W Not quite. I'm still waiting for my refrigerator to arrive.

M I thought you were getting it yesterday.

W I was supposed to, but they keep giving me excuses.

M So, when are they coming?

W Not sure. I have to call them again.

Q What is mainly being discussed in the conversation?

(a) A delay in the delivery of an appliance

(b) The woman's opinion of a delivery service

(c) Measures being taken to retrieve a lost item

(d) The woman's troubles with a faulty refrigerator

33

M I want to travel abroad but I'm on a budget. Any suggestions?

W What about a place where you have family or friends?

M I have friends in Istanbul.

W Could you stay with them? It'd save on hotel costs.

M Probably. Have you been there?

W Sure. There are so many sights to see.

Q What is the man mainly doing in the conversation?

(a) Debating whether to move to Istanbul

(b) Getting advice on where to take a vacation

(c) Asking about accommodations in Istanbul

(d) Determining his budget for an overseas trip

34

W Do your wrists still hurt from typing?

M Yeah, that's why I'm using this wrist-rest for my keyboard.

W Have you tried strengthening exercises?

M Yep, and I've been sleeping with braces on.

W Have you noticed any improvement?

M A little, but I'm still taking a pain reliever.

Q What is the main topic of the conversation?

(a) Problems the man is having with his computer

(b) Measures the man is taking to remedy his wrist pain

(c) How the man's wrist-rest aggravated his pain

(d) How the man improved his typing skills

35

W Excuse me, where's Gate 59?

M That's in the south terminal.

W This isn't the south terminal?

M No, you'll need to take a shuttle to get there.

W But they didn't mention a shuttle when I checked in for my flight.

M Well, it's not far. Just follow the red signs.

Q What is the man mainly doing in the conversation?

(a) Determining the woman's current location

(b) Trying to find his flight's gate

(c) Assisting a confused traveler

(d) Checking the woman in for her flight

36

M Let's put the new table over by the TV.

W But it would block the screen.

M Well, I thought you wanted to throw that TV out eventually.

W Still, no need to block it now. How about by the fireplace?

M Won't that look cluttered?

W No, it'll be cozy.

Q What is the conversation mainly about?

(a) Removing a table that is underutilized

(b) Deciding how to position a table

(c) Putting the TV in a more convenient space

(d) Decorating a remodeled apartment

37

W Remember that watch you wanted my opinion on?

M Yeah, I'm still wondering if I should buy it for my wife.

W Well, it's on sale now.

M How big is the discount?

W I think it's 35% off.

M Thanks, I'll take a look!

Q What is the woman mainly doing in the conversation?

(a) Negotiating for a better discount on a watch

(b) Offering to lower the price on a gift for the man's wife

(c) Informing the man of a deal on a watch he showed her

(d) Telling the man that the watch he gave his wife is now on sale

38

M How are the wedding plans going?

W Pretty well. I just have to tie up some loose ends.

M Have you finalized the seating chart?

W Mostly—I'm just waiting on guests who haven't responded yet.

M I see. And your floral arrangements are all set?

W Yes. I just need to get bridesmaids' gifts.

Q Which is correct about the woman according to the conversation?

(a) Her wedding preparations are finished.

(b) She has not started the seating arrangement.

(c) All of her guests have responded.

(d) She has decided on the flowers for the wedding.

39

W Did you see that new action film?

M Yeah, on Monday. I wasn't impressed, though.

W Really? I enjoyed it.

M The action scenes were really boring.

W I bet you went just because you loved the book.

M Yeah, and I do like the lead actor, too.

Q Which is correct about the man according to the conversation?

(a) He saw the action film on Sunday.

(b) He only enjoyed the movie's action scenes.

(c) He disliked the book the film was based on.

(d) He is a fan of the film's main star.

40

M Can I send this letter to Germany by air?

W Sure. That's one dollar and 45 cents.

M I'd like to ship this parcel there too, but to someone else.

W Would you prefer air mail or surface mail?

M Surface is fine.

W OK. Just write the parcel's contents on this customs form.

Q Which is correct according to the conversation?

(a) The man requests air mail for both the parcel and the letter.

(b) Both pieces of mail will be shipped to Germany.

(c) The parcel and the letter have the same recipient.

(d) Only the letter requires customs forms.

41

W Are Sid and Katy joining us on tomorrow's hike?

M Just Katy. Sid injured his ankle going down the stairs yesterday.

W Didn't he hurt it earlier this spring?

M Yeah, playing soccer. But it's the left ankle this time, not the right.

W Wow. Both ankles injured in just six months?

M I know. I hope he recovers as quickly as last time.

Q Which is correct about Sid according to the conversation?

(a) Neither he nor Katy will join the hike.

(b) He hurt his left ankle yesterday.

(c) His most recent injury is from playing soccer.

(d) Both his ankles are currently injured.

42

M Excuse me. Is there a cafeteria in this building?

W No, but there's a restaurant on Harbor Avenue.

M I just started working here, so I'm not sure where that is.

W It's just one block north.

M OK, thanks. And does this building have an ATM?

W Yes, next to the convenience store in the lobby.

Q Which is correct according to the conversation?

(a) The building has a cafeteria on the first floor.

(b) The man has been working in the building for years.

(c) Harbor Avenue is one block south of the building.

(d) The building has an ATM and a convenience store.

43

W Great job arranging the promotional display.

M Thanks. It was a fun new challenge.

W Most people don't get the design right the first time, but you're a natural!

M I'd love to do it again.

W Then we'll start assigning you to do displays from now on.

M That'd be great!

Q What can be inferred about the man from the conversation?

(a) He taught the woman how to design promotional displays.

(b) He is inexperienced in display design.

(c) He had several earlier designs rejected by the woman.

(d) He is the woman's supervisor.

44

M Does your restaurant have an evacuation plan?

W Yes. There's a flight of stairs for emergency use.

M Only one? How would people escape?

W This building has four emergency staircases in addition to ours.

M I see. And they're all easily accessible from here?

W Yes. Everyone could escape safely.

Q What can be inferred from the conversation?

(a) The restaurant is not prepared for emergencies.

(b) The whole building is occupied by the restaurant.

(c) The restaurant is not on the ground floor.

(d) The man is an employee of the restaurant.

45

W   I heard you went to the amusement park last weekend.

M   Yeah, we had a good time, but I doubt you would've enjoyed it.

W   Actually, I've been thinking about trying a roller coaster again.

M   I thought you were done with them forever.

W   Well, I'd like to try out a smaller one.

M   I wish you'd told me. You could have joined us!

Q   What can be inferred from the conversation?

(a) The woman was invited to last weekend's amusement park trip.

(b) The woman previously had an unpleasant roller coaster ride.

(c) The man is going back to the amusement park this weekend.

(d) The man prefers to go to amusement parks by himself.

46

Although the stereotypical diamond is colorless, these valuable gemstones occur naturally in almost every color. A diamond's hue is influenced by various factors. Trace amounts of boron and nitrogen in diamonds cause the gems to look blue or yellow. Radiation exposure turns a diamond green and is also thought to be the cause of pink and red hues. Finally, deformation of a diamond's atomic structure results in a brown color, which lowers the gem's value.

Q   What is the talk mainly about?

(a) Where colored diamonds are found in nature

(b) How diamonds are processed to remove color impurities

(c) What causes diamonds to have different colors

(d) Why colored diamonds are less valuable than white ones

47

Management has recently been planning a company-wide "green team" initiative, and we're ready to begin implementing the initial steps of that plan. First, we are changing our stationery provider to Greentree Supplies, which specializes in recycled products. Second, we are switching to an electricity company that uses renewable energy. In the coming months, look forward to further improvements, including the installation of solar panels and new incentives for carpooling.

Q   What is mainly being announced?

(a) Measures the company is taking to be more environmentally friendly

(b) The company's upcoming plan to take over Greentree Supplies

(c) Restructuring of the company's "green team" employees

(d) Reasons why the company is changing its environmental policies

48

There is a growing movement to pass legislation mandating the labeling of products containing genetically modified organisms, or GMOs. But certain members of the scientific community have criticized this. These scientists claim that labeling isn't necessary. They say that genetic modification doesn't materially change foods. They also argue that there is no evidence that GMO foods pose a danger to consumers' health, and that labeling foods with a GMO mark will only alarm consumers needlessly.

Q   What is the talk mainly about?

(a) How new laws ban the labeling of GMO foods

(b) Certain scientists' resistance to GMO-labeling

(c) Scientists' rationale for advocating bans of GMO foods

(d) Why GMO foods are harmful to consumers' health

49

Attention staff: some of you have had problems installing the latest version of our security program on your computers. If you've gotten error messages, remember that you must first uninstall the previous version. You can do this by running the old version's uninstall file, which is located in your computer's applications folder. Only after running the uninstall program can you install and use the updated software.

Q   What is the speaker mainly doing in the announcement?

(a) Explaining why the company's security software has become outdated

(b) Warning employees about computers with compromised security

(c) Providing instructions to resolve a problem installing a security update

(d) Instructing employees to remove uninstallation files from their computers

50

We're here today to discuss a worrying trend in the most recent election. While overall voter turnout in provincial elections has been gradually increasing over the years, analysts found that the number of low-income voters is down 28% from the last election. What this means is that high earners constituted a significantly larger proportion of the voting population, and the voice of low-income voters has not been properly represented in this year's results.

Q   What is the speaker's main point?

(a) The number of voters in this election has decreased over the last.

(b) Many wealthier people are opting not to vote.

(c) Analysts have been ignoring a pronounced voting trend.

(d) Weak low-income voter turnout has skewed election results.

51

Bed bugs are tiny parasitic insects that live in fabrics and feed on blood. Because infestations are hard to eradicate, prevention is crucial. At home, keep rooms clutter-free, since bed bugs thrive in any environment where they can hide. Washing linens in very hot water is also wise, as this kills unhatched eggs. Finally, since these tiny critters often inhabit mattresses, covering your mattress with plastic will ensure that it remains free of bed bugs.

Q   What is the main topic of the talk?

(a) Why bed bugs prefer to live in beds and fabrics

(b) The best way to eradicate bed bugs in public spaces

(c) Methods for preventing bed bug infestations at home

(d) How bed bug infestations spread through contact

52

One interesting technique in contemporary literature involves fracturing a linear storyline and reconstructing it in surprising ways. Kurt Vonnegut's Slaughterhouse-Five exemplifies this literary tactic, as episodes from protagonist Billy Pilgrim's life are not presented chronologically. Vonnegut fragmented the time-line of Pilgrim's life and structured it so that he could effectively juxtapose occurrences which would otherwise seem unconnected. This is one of the defining characteristics of this modern novel.

Q   What is the speaker's main point about Slaughterhouse-Five?

(a) Its unusual structure was imitated in other modern novels.

(b) It distorts time to emphasize the relatedness of incongruous events.

(c) It is a modern novel that is reminiscent of older literature.

(d) The protagonist's life appears fragmented in spite of its linear storyline.

53

Everyone, I want to confirm that our company is considering moving our offices into a different building. The Human Resources Department needs more space following its recent staff increases, and the Marketing Department has had to give its conference room up to the Customer Service Department. Moreover, because each department is currently on its own floor, collaboration is inconvenient. We are searching for a suitable new space and will keep you posted.

Q   Which is correct according to the announcement?
(a) All departments in the company have recently cut their staff size.
(b) The Customer Service Department gave its conference room up to Marketing.
(c) The Human Resources and Marketing Departments are on different floors.
(d) The company has already found a new space to move into.

54

Polycythemia is a condition characterized by the overproduction of red blood cells. It develops in response to oxygen deprivation and can be an effect of certain diseases. It also occurs in hikers at high altitudes, where the atmosphere has less oxygen. Scientists researching polycythemia have begun studying the Sherpa people, who do not develop the condition despite their high-altitude habitat in Nepal's mountains. Researchers have found that this immunity to polycythemia is the result of changes in Sherpas' genetic makeup, and they are studying these changes to develop treatments for the condition.

Q   Which is correct about polycythemia according to the talk?
(a) It occurs when the body makes too few red blood cells.
(b) It causes oxygen deprivation in those with other diseases.
(c) Sherpa people have evolved so as not to develop it.
(d) Genetics has been ruled out as a way to develop treatments for it.

55

Here at the Crystal Lake Resort, we're offering a special summer's-end discount on all our outdoor team-building programs. For groups of 10 or more, we're offering 15% off to celebrate the end of the season! We have both one-day and overnight programs for all ages and backgrounds, and can accommodate groups of up to 25. Try a wilderness trekking course, take a canoe trip, or learn to sail on our very own Crystal Lake. Check out our website today!

Q   Which is correct about the Crystal Lake Resort according to the advertisement?
(a) It is only discounting select team-building programs.
(b) It is offering discounts to open the summer season.
(c) It conducts team-building programs of varying durations.
(d) It requires a minimum of 25 participants for group programs.

56

Until the nineteenth century, young boys in the West wore dresses just as girls did. This was because fabric was expensive, and dresses, unlike trousers, could have tucks sewn into the bottom edge, which could be unfolded to lengthen the garment as the child grew. When boys wore their first trousers around age seven, it was called "breeching." For boys from well-to-do families, breeching was a celebratory occasion that merited gifts of money. For boys of lesser means, breeching was a less festive milestone, signifying their eligibility to participate in paid labor.

Q   Which is correct according to the talk?
(a) In the nineteenth century boys wore dresses instead of girls.
(b) Trousers were better at accommodating young boys' growth.
(c) Boys were typically not breeched until they reached adulthood.
(d) Breeching signaled that poorer boys were ready to begin working.

57

An Indian man named Saroo who was lost to his family in 1986 recently made headlines when he found them. At age five, Saroo was separated from his elder brother on a cross-country train. He wound up in Calcutta, far from his home in Khandwa. With no idea of how to get home, he entered an orphanage and was adopted by an Australian couple. Twenty-five years later, he used Internet satellite images to scan India for familiar landmarks, finally locating his hometown. He travelled to India in 2012, and was reunited with his family there.

Q   Which is correct about Saroo according to the news report?
(a) He left Calcutta and ended up stranded in Khandwa.
(b) His adoptive parents were foreigners to India.
(c) His birth family located him using satellite images.
(d) He found that his birth family was living in Australia.

58

Attention airport bus passengers: due to an accident on the airport's main highway, all buses must take a detour along the southwest expressway. With current traffic congestion, this will add half an hour to the journey. If you would prefer to take the train, you may bring your bus ticket with your receipt to the counter for a full refund. If you choose to take the bus or do not have your receipt, we are offering a coupon for 10% off your next ride with us.

Q   What can be inferred from the announcement?
(a) There is only one road leading to the airport.
(b) The accident occurred on the highway half an hour ago.
(c) Bus ticket holders cannot get a refund without a receipt.
(d) The bus company will exchange bus tickets for train tickets.

59

In business today, we deal with more emails than ever. And we've all heard that we should strive for "inbox zero"—that magical state where we've checked and responded to every email. But I'm here to argue that inbox zero is a fruitless pursuit. I personally have abandoned it, and even though I have almost 500 unread messages, my business hasn't suffered. I've focused on the handful of messages that really matter, assuming that if someone I've ignored really wants my attention, they'll write again.

Q   Which statement would the speaker most likely agree with?
(a) Businesses should realize the importance of inbox zero.
(b) The majority of emails do not require immediate attention.
(c) It is best to ignore all emails and communicate in person.
(d) Failing to respond to all emails leads to negative consequences.

60

Last week, participants from various clinical drug trials filed a class action lawsuit against Genovian firm Wellspring Pharmaceuticals, alleging that the company engaged in gross ethical abuses. Plaintiffs have claimed that the company's research department has violated as-yet-undisclosed laws regarding human experimentation. While the proceedings are expected to be highly publicized, it is difficult to foresee the outcome, as class action lawsuits over scientific abuses have no precedent in Genovia.

Q   What can be inferred from the news report?
(a) Court proceedings have already begun in the case.
(b) The lawsuit is the first of its kind in Genovia.
(c) Human experimentation is banned in Genovia.
(d) The media is showing no interest in the lawsuit.

1

M   I'm calling for Mary. Is she there?

W   ___________________________

(a) I didn't get the message.
(b) Sorry, she's not in.
(c) She wants to talk to Mary.
(d) Sure, I'll hold.

2

W   Excuse me. Where can I find the frozen foods section?

M   ___________________________

(a) I've eaten enough.
(b) With the frozen foods.
(c) It's one aisle down.
(d) Because they're more convenient.

3

M   Would you like some strawberry shortcake?

W   ___________________________

(a) Not until I've had a piece.
(b) Thanks. It looks delicious.
(c) I'm more into shortcake.
(d) Sure, help yourself to more.

4

W   Thanks for lending me your biology notes.

M   ___________________________

(a) Sorry that I didn't take any.
(b) I really appreciate it, too.
(c) Let me know when you want them back.
(d) Sure, I hope they were helpful.

5

M   When will the next bus come?

W   ___________________________

(a) It usually stops here.
(b) Just ten minutes ago.
(c) It shouldn't be much longer.
(d) Shortly after the bus arrives.

6

W   Too bad our hotel suite's on the ground floor.

M   ___________________________

(a) Right. That's why we booked it.
(b) I know. I was hoping for a skyline view.
(c) It's because there aren't any ground floor rooms.
(d) I agree. It couldn't be better.

7

M   What did you say your husband does?

W   ___________________________

(a) No, but you've asked before.
(b) He runs the family business.
(c) He usually does, but he forgot.
(d) Yes, he's away on business.

8

W   What'd you get at the souvenir stand?

M   ___________________________

(a) On my last trip.
(b) Just some gifts.
(c) To remember my vacation.
(d) To bring you a souvenir.

9

M   Did you visit many countries on this trip?

W   ___________________________

(a) As many as I possibly can.
(b) I managed to squeeze in half a dozen.
(c) I've traveled abroad once before.
(d) Two weeks as of today.

10

W Can you believe how close yesterday's basketball game was?

M __________________________

(a) No, the turnout was less than expected.
(b) I'd like to join, but I haven't played in a long time.
(c) Yes, it was clearly a one-sided match.
(d) I know. The teams fought it out right till the end.

11

M I think I left my scarf at the restaurant last night.

W __________________________

(a) I'd show it to the waiter before you leave.
(b) Call to see if anyone found it.
(c) You should probably return it there.
(d) Take it with you when you go back.

12

W Are you sure you turned off all the lights?

M __________________________

(a) Yes, it's better to leave one on.
(b) But I could've sworn I turned them on.
(c) I'm positive. I double-checked before leaving.
(d) Probably, since I had them when I got out.

13

M Were you offended by Karen's joke earlier?

W __________________________

(a) Then she'd better not take it seriously.
(b) I just didn't find it that amusing.
(c) No, I don't really think she's upset.
(d) Me, too—I thought she was hilarious.

14

W What a beautiful day! We should've gone to the beach!

M __________________________

(a) Don't worry. We'll have other chances.
(b) But I wish you'd gone with me.
(c) The weather will clear up soon.
(d) Right. I'm glad we decided against it.

15

M How was the feedback on the draft of your term paper?

W __________________________

(a) But I haven't submitted the final version.
(b) It underscored some serious weaknesses.
(c) So I'd be able to make some changes.
(d) Writing one is a course requirement.

16

W Hannah's struggling in school.
M We should get her some help.
W What do you suggest?
M __________________________

(a) Maybe she needs a tutor.
(b) Then study a little harder.
(c) Ask her to help you after school.
(d) She's doing fine on her own.

17

M Why wasn't Amy at the meeting?
W She was excused because she claimed to be too busy.
M Is that an adequate reason?
W __________________________

(a) Then she needs more work to do.
(b) You probably just didn't see her at the meeting.
(c) The meeting couldn't go on.
(d) The boss seemed to think so.

18

W I heard your son was in a car accident.
M Yes, he was just a bit shaken up.
W So he wasn't injured?
M _______________________

(a) Thankfully, he escaped unharmed.
(b) Not until he's fully healed.
(c) It happened while he was driving.
(d) No, it wasn't his fault.

19

M Why don't you visit a clinic for that cough?
W I just need some rest. It'll clear up.
M It could be more serious than you think.
W _______________________

(a) But I don't want to get a cough.
(b) Take some medicine for it.
(c) I'll go if I'm not better by tomorrow.
(d) Wait until you stop coughing.

20

W That guy just threw his trash into the river!
M People often do that here.
W Don't they care about the environment?
M _______________________

(a) Not as much as they should.
(b) My mistake, it won't happen again.
(c) At least he didn't toss it into the river.
(d) Maybe he found it in the garbage.

21

M How was your trip to China?
W I wish I'd gone there on my own.
M You didn't enjoy the group tour?
W _______________________

(a) That's why I decided not to go there.
(b) Agreed. Group tours are the way to go.
(c) It was a bit too regimented for my taste.
(d) Just so I didn't have to go by myself.

22

W Have you found a date for the dance?
M I'm still looking.
W I have a friend who might be interested.
M _______________________

(a) Great! Set me up with her, please.
(b) Sure. I'll ask around for you.
(c) Then you should bring a date.
(d) I don't know anyone single.

23

M Excuse me. Didn't you go to Pineridge High School?
W I did. Have we met before?
M I'm Rob Hudson. You used to hang out with my sister Alice.
W _______________________

(a) I don't know. Let's see if she can make it.
(b) Then I must've mistaken her for someone else.
(c) Oh, right. We were inseparable back then.
(d) Yes, that's my sister sitting over there.

24

W This cafeteria line is endless!
M Let's try the other dining hall.
W Won't it be just as crowded?
M _______________________

(a) It can't be worse than this.
(b) Thank goodness we missed the crowds.
(c) Only after everyone leaves.
(d) Not if both of us eat first.

25

M Want to go for a walk in the park?
W Sure, but I should finish this essay first.
M When should we go then?
W _______________________

(a) In an hour, give or take.
(b) After we get back from the walk.
(c) It takes fifteen minutes to get there.
(d) As long as I'm working on it.

26

W   We're holding a fundraiser this Saturday.

M   To raise money for what?

W   Underprivileged kids. Interested in volunteering?

M   _______________________

(a) Sure, I'll ask if they're available.
(b) Definitely—count me in.
(c) Actually, we have enough volunteers.
(d) The kids sure appreciated your help.

27

M   Have you mailed the Christmas cards?

W   No, I need to write a few more.

M   But they need to be mailed today to arrive on time.

W   _______________________

(a) Good thing I haven't mailed them yet.
(b) Then I'll hold off on shipping.
(c) I'll hurry and send them out today, then.
(d) I didn't know they were arriving tomorrow.

28

W   How did your son enjoy his visit to the zoo?

M   He couldn't get enough of the animals.

W   Was it his first experience there?

M   _______________________

(a) No, my father took me there.
(b) Yeah, that's why he was so excited.
(c) The zoo would have been better.
(d) Not yet—maybe next time.

29

M   Wasn't that election documentary fascinating?

W   Maybe if you're knowledgeable about politics.

M   But you keep up with the news, don't you?

W   _______________________

(a) Still, too much of the program went over my head.
(b) Sure, I'll notify you if I hear anything.
(c) Well, I wish it had addressed politics.
(d) Yeah. I can't wait to see it.

30

W   Have you seen the poetry quotes posted on subways?

M   Isn't it nice? The transit authority replaced some ads with them.

W   Yeah, but doesn't that mean some revenue has been lost?

M   _______________________

(a) Really? It's great the earnings increased that much.
(b) I don't think the ads will cover it.
(c) Maybe, but I think it's totally worth it.
(d) It's being used to fund projects like this.

31

M   Hi, Phillips Furniture? Can I change an order I made?

W   Certainly! What was your name?

M   Adam Carroll.

W   You bought a mahogany end table?

M   That's right. I'd like to purchase one more.

W   Sure, no problem. They should arrive together tomorrow.

Q   What is the man mainly doing in the conversation?
(a) Adding an item to an order
(b) Replacing an item on an order
(c) Inquiring about the delivery date
(d) Changing the name on a delivery form

32

W   How's the yard work going?

M   Terrible! My lawn's been overtaken by weeds.

W   Why don't you just pull them out?

M   That would be a lot of work.

W   Then you could try some herbicide.

M   OK. I'll give that a try.

Q   What is the woman mainly doing in the conversation?
(a) Suggesting ways to remove weeds from a lawn
(b) Advising the man not to use herbicides
(c) Arguing that weeding gardens is better than using herbicides
(d) Offering to help the man pull his weeds

33

M   Welcome back from vacation!

W   Thanks. I'm still exhausted from the flight.

M   How long was it?

W   Nine hours, and I didn't get any sleep.

M   That's a long one.

W   Yeah, it'll take a while to get back to normal.

Q   What is the woman mainly complaining about?

(a) Having to cut her vacation short

(b) Having to wait for a late flight

(c) Her difficulty recovering from her trip

(d) Her need to rest on her vacation

34

W   We missed a delivery while we were out.

M   Let's go to the post office to get it.

W   Nah. They'll deliver the package tomorrow.

M   The post office is closed tomorrow.

W   Then it can wait until the next day.

M   I'd rather go now. I can't wait that long.

Q   What is the man mainly doing in the conversation?

(a) Insisting that they leave after their package is delivered

(b) Suggesting that they send their package tomorrow

(c) Trying to convince the woman they should pick up a package

(d) Scheduling the time for a package delivery

35

M   I'm finished painting the living room. How does it look?

W   It looks a little thin. How many coats did you apply?

M   Two. That should have been enough.

W   Did you use a primer?

M   No. I didn't think it was necessary.

W   That explains why the old color's coming through.

Q   What is the woman mainly trying to do in the conversation?

(a) Determine why the paint on the walls looks thin

(b) Persuade the man to paint the other rooms of the house

(c) Discover why the man decided to paint the living room

(d) Prevent the man from applying another coat of paint

36

W   I want to go to this concert, but it's sold out.

M   Maybe someone's selling tickets online.

W   But ticket resellers charge too much.

M   Not always. Sometimes they just can't go.

W   So they sell their tickets at face value?

M   Right. Anyway, it couldn't hurt to look.

Q   What is the man mainly advising the woman to do?

(a) Avoid purchasing overpriced tickets from resellers

(b) Arrive at the show early to look for extra tickets

(c) Sell her tickets online for their face value

(d) Find people online selling tickets they cannot use

37

M   I don't understand your love for abstract art.

W   It's always had an emotional impact on me.

M   But it doesn't have recognizable subjects.

W   That's just it. You simply experience the feeling it creates.

M   A lot of the images are ugly, though.

W   Even so, there are powerful ideas behind those images.

Q   What is the woman mainly doing in the conversation?

(a) Arguing that abstract art engages the mind rather than the emotions

(b) Defending the appeal abstract art has for her

(c) Describing how abstract art is created

(d) Challenging the man's support for abstract art

38

W You got a new cell phone! Is that the latest model?

M I wanted to save money, so I bought the next to latest one.

W How long will it be before you've paid for it?

M Actually, I paid the full price in advance—no installment plan.

W Isn't it more expensive to do it that way?

M Sure, but I can terminate my contract without a penalty later.

Q Which is correct about the man according to the conversation?

(a) He purchased the most recent cell phone model.

(b) He saved money by signing up for an installment plan.

(c) He passed up a discount by paying for his phone up front.

(d) He is liable for a penalty if he cancels his phone contract.

39

M What smells so delicious? Is it roast beef?

W Good guess. But it's actually a pork roast.

M Wow. What's the occasion?

W Nothing special. I just wanted to try a new recipe.

M Should I run out and get some cake for dessert?

W No need. I've already baked a pie.

Q Which is correct about the woman according to the conversation?

(a) She is preparing a meal of roast beef.

(b) She is cooking for a special event.

(c) She has never used this recipe before.

(d) She has not made any plans for dessert.

40

W I think we should apply for a loan to fix the car.

M But there's so much paperwork involved.

W It's not that hard. We can do it online.

M But what if we get denied after all that work?

W We won't. We have decent jobs and no debts.

M All right, but only because interest rates are so low now.

Q Which is correct according to the conversation?

(a) The woman wants the loan to purchase a new car.

(b) Loan applications can be submitted via the web.

(c) The man and woman are currently unemployed.

(d) Interest rates are at their peak at the moment.

41

M How much are you asking for your home?

W We'd like at least $219,000.

M That much, huh? Was it appraised by a professional?

W No, but it's competitively priced.

M Have you gotten any offers?

W There was a bid for $210,000, but we're not budging one bit.

Q Which is correct about the woman according to the conversation?

(a) She has listed her home for $210,000.

(b) She has had her house appraised by a realtor.

(c) She has yet to receive an offer on her home.

(d) She is unwilling to reduce her asking price.

42

W　My favorite baseball player was caught using steroids.

M　Again? He received a fifty-game suspension for his first offense, right?

W　Yeah. This is the second time, so he got twice that.

M　That's it? He should be banned from the sport.

W　He will if he gets caught again. He also lost his record for the most hits.

M　Wow, what a shame!

Q　Which is correct about the baseball player according to the conversation?

(a) He had been caught for steroids twice before.

(b) He has been suspended for the next fifty games.

(c) He will receive a lifetime ban if he commits an additional offense.

(d) He will retain his record for the most hits.

43

M　I didn't get the research position at Stenella University.

W　I'm sorry. I know you've always wanted to work there.

M　Yes. Dan White got it. He's more qualified.

W　Well, Stenella will have other openings, right?

M　Right. I can always apply there again later.

W　And by that time you'll have even more relevant experience.

Q　What can be inferred about the man from the conversation?

(a) He is familiar with Dan White's credentials.

(b) He had no experience related to the position.

(c) He is planning to quit his research career.

(d) He currently works for Stenella University.

44

W　Will it take long to set up a camp site for tonight?

M　Getting the tent ready will take me an hour.

W　Well, we should do it before it starts getting dark.

M　But this isn't really a suitable place to camp.

W　Then why don't we just rent a cabin tonight?

M　OK, but we'll definitely use the tent tomorrow.

Q　What can be inferred from the conversation?

(a) The light outside is too dim to set up the tent.

(b) The man and woman cannot afford to rent a cabin.

(c) The man has never set up the tent before.

(d) The trip is scheduled to last more than one day.

45

M　Have you finished the novel for our book club?

W　Not yet. I've been bogged down by work.

M　The discussion takes place next week.

W　Don't worry. I don't plan on going anywhere this weekend.

M　Good, because we enjoy your insights.

W　I already have plenty to say, and I'll have more when I'm through.

Q　What can be inferred about the woman from the conversation?

(a) She has yet to start reading the club's latest novel selection.

(b) She plans to spend the weekend reading the book.

(c) She is attending the club's discussion for the first time.

(d) She does not expect to complete the novel in time.

46

With the state's new carbon tax coming into effect this spring, many are concerned that lower income people will see their cost of living rise. It is important to emphasize that people earning below a minimum threshold will be exempt from the new policy. Also, those earning only slightly more will be eligible for tax credits to offset the cost of their payments. The tax will not place a financial burden on people already struggling to make ends meet.

Q   What is the main purpose of the talk?
(a) To present the benefits of a new tax proposal
(b) To explain why a recent tax increase was repealed
(c) To describe the effect of a tax on household incomes
(d) To ease fears that a new tax will harm low-income people

47

The Glenville Arts Center has installed new automated ticketing kiosks for people who have made online reservations. These devices are easy to use. Simply input the confirmation number received when the tickets were reserved online. After checking the seat assignments, click "Enter," and swipe the credit card that was used to pay for the tickets. The kiosk will then issue the tickets along with a receipt.

Q   What is the main purpose of the announcement?
(a) To urge people to confirm their reservations online
(b) To describe how to retrieve tickets from new kiosks
(c) To inform customers of payment options for tickets
(d) To explain how to reserve concert tickets online

48

Susan Gould's first album was a hit with its emotional lyrics perfectly matching her impassioned vocal style. Her follow-up effort, Ghostlife, keeps to the musical style of that recording, captivating listeners with rustic banjo sounds, but the songs are devoid of the poignancy of her debut. Throughout Ghostlife, Gould's vocals lack genuine emotion, and her lyrics, despite touching on heartbreak and divorce, seem more formulaic than from the heart.

Q   What is the speaker's main point about Susan Gould?
(a) Her emotional singing style has limited her success.
(b) Her lyrics have addressed sadder topics over time.
(c) Her singing style is not suited to emotional songs.
(d) Her latest recording lacks the passion of her previous one.

49

While the first step in alleviating poverty in the developing world is providing adequate food and shelter, a long-term solution to the problem must focus on other issues. One of these is access to fuel. When people spend all their time and money seeking fuel, they cannot use these resources for things with more enduring benefits. Providing people with fuel for cooking, for example, would allow them to focus their time and money on education or business. This would do more in the long run to break the cycle of poverty.

Q   What is the speaker's main point?
(a) Rising fuel costs have increased poverty worldwide.
(b) Access to fuel can help people escape chronic poverty.
(c) Fuel donations are misused in poor countries.
(d) The search for new fuel reserves is rarely successful.

50

The famous Prague Castle in the Czech Republic incorporates over a thousand years of European architecture. While it was built as a simple fortress, its inhabitants gradually added other buildings for a variety of purposes. Many of these were constructed centuries apart, using the style popular at the time. This means the castle now serves as a valuable reference for a range of different periods in the region's architectural history—showcasing Romanesque, Gothic, Neoclassical, and other styles.

Q   What is the main topic of the talk?
(a) The reason Prague Castle was rebuilt in different styles
(b) How the use of Prague Castle has changed over time
(c) The efforts to preserve the architecture of Prague Castle
(d) How Prague Castle displays several architectural styles

51

The phenomenal success of the original Grand Master video game has inspired a decade of hit sequels. However, the game's plot has run its course, and its world has been fully explored by the game's developers. Now is the time to bring the series to its conclusion. The forthcoming installment in the series will be the final one. The creators of Grand Master would like to thank the game's developers for their hard work over the years.

Q   What is mainly being announced about the Grand Master series?
(a) The decline of its popularity since its initial release
(b) Its revision in response to complaints
(c) The creation of a different game based on it
(d) Its discontinuance after the next installment

52

The English poet Percy Bysshe Shelley wrote The Masque of Anarchy in response to a massacre of innocent civilians at a political rally. In the poem, he calls on people to gather in opposition to those in power. But he also advises people not to fight back against violent attempts to repress them. By remaining passive, he claims, people can shame those who protect the powerful, such as the cavalry responsible for the massacre. This shame, he says, will force the army to abandon its leaders and thereby initiate a radical change to the power structure of society.

Q   What is the speaker's main point about The Masque of Anarchy?
(a) It promotes armed resistance to repressive governments backed by the army.
(b) It urges people to lobby powerful political leaders to reform the military.
(c) It asserts that oppressive leaders are shamed when the military attacks civilians.
(d) It advocates using passive resistance to oppression to overthrow the powerful.

53

Paramount Travel is offering a new guided walking tour of the old sections of historic Port Drummond. The tours run twice per day—once in the morning and once in the evening—every Tuesday, Thursday, Saturday, and Sunday. Each tour is two hours long and follows an identical course. Morning walks are $40 and evenings are $50. Special group rates are available for bookings of six or more people if booked five days in advance. Come see the city from a new perspective—book your walking tour today!

Q   Which is correct about Paramount Travel's walking tour according to the advertisement?
(a) It is available at two separate times seven days per week.
(b) It takes the same route in both the morning and evening.
(c) The morning tour costs more than the evening one.
(d) Special rates are offered to groups of five people.

54

Today's meeting is about a change to employees' schedules. With business slow this year, we have looked at cost-cutting measures and decided to close for one additional day per week, bringing our workweek to four days. This will mean less pay across the board, as there will be fewer hours to be worked, but everyone's hourly rate will remain unchanged. Plus, we will be able to avoid any layoffs. Please understand that this policy is in the interest of everyone keeping their jobs and current health benefits.

Q   Which is correct about the company according to the announcement?
(a) It has opted to cut four days from its schedule.
(b) It is maintaining workers' current hourly rate of pay.
(c) It plans to reduce the number of its employees.
(d) It is cutting the health benefits offered to workers.

55

A study of fossils from a prehistoric wombat has shed new light on the species. Previously believed to have roamed the forest floor, the species is now thought to have been primarily a tree-dweller. Its extremely long forearms and short hind legs suggest it spent its time dangling from trees like modern orangutans. And an analysis of its jawbone and teeth reveals that it consumed foliage rather than meat. The species likely died out as the temperate rainforests that covered its home in Australia gave way to an increasingly dry climate.

Q   Which is correct about the prehistoric wombat according to the talk?
(a) Scientists now believe it dwelled mainly on the forest floor.
(b) Fossils reveal it had relatively long hind legs and short forearms.
(c) It is thought to have subsisted on a diet of both plants and meat.
(d) Evidence suggests it was wiped out by an ever more arid climate.

56

The municipal government has launched a lawsuit against CityCable for monopolistic business practices. The company has been the sole provider of cable TV services in the city since 2010, when it purchased its only competitor, Smoothview Cable. Since then, CityCable has hiked its fees by 25%. Residents wanting to subscribe to cable TV services have had no choice but to pay up, and the company's subscriber numbers, along with its revenues, have grown steadily. The city government claims competition needs to be restored to the industry.

Q   Which is correct according to the news report?
(a) CityCable was purchased by Smoothview Cable in 2010.
(b) Smoothview is currently the city's only cable TV services provider.
(c) Cable TV services in the city cost 25% more now than in 2010.
(d) The number of cable TV subscribers has declined because of the fee hikes.

57

The development of a new synthetic polymer may revolutionize the field of skin prosthetics. Because it contains nickel, this material is able to detect pressure and conduct electricity in much the same way human skin communicates sensations of pressure to the brain. Furthermore, when cut, it is capable of "healing" spontaneously. It can repair itself within minutes and with minimal loss in its electrical conductivity, and it can do so without external stimuli such as heat or light.

Q   Which is correct about the new synthetic polymer according to the lecture?
(a) Physical pressure blocks its ability to conduct electricity.
(b) It is capable of repairing itself after being damaged.
(c) Slicing it causes it to lose a substantial amount of conductivity.
(d) It requires external stimuli such as heat for regeneration.

58

There is a problem with the way history is taught in high schools. Studying history should give students access to centuries of experience, and it is experience that informs judgment. However, students spend so much time cramming names and dates that they don't even realize history has a practical application. What students should be doing is using history's examples to analyze and discuss current issues. This would make the study of history not only more relevant to their lives but also more useful.

Q   Which statement would the speaker mostly likely agree with?
(a) The study of history is inherently impractical.
(b) The way history is taught in schools has changed recently.
(c) Studying history should help students understand current issues.
(d) Teachers should challenge students' memories in history class.

59

Native fishermen on the Hawaiian island of Maui have voiced opposition to a proposal to help endangered monk seals. The plan would see federal officials bring a small number of the seals to Maui from other islands to the north. This is expected to increase their reproduction. The fishermen are against the proposal because they believe the plan would lead to restricted fishing rights. They argue that the government's priority should be the livelihoods of native fishermen.

Q   What can be inferred about Hawaiian monk seals from the report?
(a) Federal officials greatly overestimate their numbers on Maui.
(b) The plan calls for them to be moved to areas without fishing.
(c) Native fishermen view them as a threat to their livelihoods.
(d) They are more common in Maui than the islands to the north.

60

Adjusting clocks seasonally to shift daylight hours from the morning to the evening, called Daylight Saving Time, was first adopted by Germany in 1916. In the midst of World War I, the country was facing frequent shortages of fuel. By shifting daylight hours to the evening, the government reduced the number of hours people needed to light their homes—and people hardly noticed the darker mornings, since they usually slept through the early part of the day anyway.

Q   What can be inferred about Daylight Saving Time from the talk?
(a) It resulted in increased demand for fuels.
(b) It encouraged people to sleep more hours each day.
(c) It caused a public outcry in Germany when it was implemented.
(d) It was conceived as a way of reducing energy consumption.

서울대 최신기출 · 1

Listening Comprehension

1 (c)	2 (a)	3 (b)	4 (b)	5 (c)	6 (b)	7 (b)	8 (c)	9 (b)	10 (c)
11 (a)	12 (c)	13 (a)	14 (b)	15 (c)	16 (a)	17 (c)	18 (b)	19 (a)	20 (a)
21 (b)	22 (b)	23 (d)	24 (a)	25 (a)	26 (b)	27 (b)	28 (b)	29 (a)	30 (b)
31 (b)	32 (a)	33 (b)	34 (d)	35 (c)	36 (c)	37 (a)	38 (b)	39 (a)	40 (b)
41 (b)	42 (b)	43 (d)	44 (b)	45 (b)	46 (d)	47 (c)	48 (a)	49 (a)	50 (a)
51 (b)	52 (d)	53 (d)	54 (a)	55 (d)	56 (c)	57 (c)	58 (d)	59 (b)	60 (b)

Grammar

1 (d)	2 (a)	3 (c)	4 (b)	5 (b)	6 (d)	7 (c)	8 (a)	9 (b)	10 (a)
11 (c)	12 (a)	13 (c)	14 (c)	15 (a)	16 (c)	17 (c)	18 (a)	19 (c)	20 (d)
21 (d)	22 (b)	23 (d)	24 (b)	25 (a)	26 (b)	27 (a)	28 (a)	29 (b)	30 (a)
31 (c)	32 (d)	33 (d)	34 (d)	35 (a)	36 (a)	37 (b)	38 (c)	39 (d)	40 (a)
41 (a)	42 (a)	43 (c)	44 (c)	45 (b)	46 (c)	47 (c)	48 (c)	49 (c)	50 (b)

Vocabulary

1 (b)	2 (b)	3 (a)	4 (b)	5 (b)	6 (a)	7 (b)	8 (b)	9 (b)	10 (b)
11 (d)	12 (a)	13 (a)	14 (c)	15 (b)	16 (c)	17 (a)	18 (b)	19 (b)	20 (b)
21 (a)	22 (d)	23 (d)	24 (c)	25 (b)	26 (c)	27 (a)	28 (c)	29 (a)	30 (b)
31 (a)	32 (d)	33 (c)	34 (a)	35 (b)	36 (c)	37 (c)	38 (c)	39 (d)	40 (b)
41 (d)	42 (a)	43 (a)	44 (c)	45 (a)	46 (d)	47 (a)	48 (b)	49 (a)	50 (d)

Reading Comprehension

1 (d)	2 (c)	3 (d)	4 (d)	5 (b)	6 (d)	7 (b)	8 (c)	9 (d)	10 (c)
11 (d)	12 (d)	13 (b)	14 (b)	15 (c)	16 (b)	17 (c)	18 (a)	19 (c)	20 (c)
21 (a)	22 (d)	23 (d)	24 (d)	25 (b)	26 (a)	27 (c)	28 (c)	29 (b)	30 (d)
31 (d)	32 (c)	33 (d)	34 (b)	35 (b)	36 (d)	37 (a)	38 (a)	39 (b)	40 (c)

Listening Comprehension

1 (c)	2 (c)	3 (a)	4 (b)	5 (c)	6 (b)	7 (a)	8 (b)	9 (a)	10 (b)
11 (b)	12 (a)	13 (c)	14 (c)	15 (c)	16 (a)	17 (c)	18 (d)	19 (a)	20 (c)
21 (c)	22 (b)	23 (b)	24 (d)	25 (b)	26 (d)	27 (a)	28 (c)	29 (a)	30 (b)
31 (c)	32 (a)	33 (a)	34 (b)	35 (c)	36 (b)	37 (c)	38 (c)	39 (a)	40 (b)
41 (d)	42 (c)	43 (d)	44 (b)	45 (c)	46 (b)	47 (b)	48 (d)	49 (c)	50 (a)
51 (a)	52 (d)	53 (a)	54 (c)	55 (b)	56 (b)	57 (c)	58 (c)	59 (b)	60 (c)

Grammar

1 (c)	2 (b)	3 (c)	4 (c)	5 (c)	6 (d)	7 (c)	8 (c)	9 (a)	10 (d)
11 (c)	12 (d)	13 (c)	14 (d)	15 (a)	16 (c)	17 (b)	18 (c)	19 (d)	20 (c)
21 (d)	22 (b)	23 (c)	24 (d)	25 (c)	26 (d)	27 (d)	28 (d)	29 (d)	30 (b)
31 (a)	32 (a)	33 (d)	34 (c)	35 (a)	36 (c)	37 (c)	38 (c)	39 (b)	40 (b)
41 (d)	42 (b)	43 (d)	44 (c)	45 (c)	46 (c)	47 (d)	48 (c)	49 (a)	50 (b)

Vocabulary

1 (d)	2 (b)	3 (d)	4 (d)	5 (c)	6 (d)	7 (d)	8 (d)	9 (c)	10 (c)
11 (a)	12 (c)	13 (d)	14 (a)	15 (d)	16 (d)	17 (c)	18 (a)	19 (a)	20 (d)
21 (b)	22 (d)	23 (c)	24 (a)	25 (a)	26 (c)	27 (a)	28 (b)	29 (a)	30 (a)
31 (b)	32 (a)	33 (b)	34 (d)	35 (c)	36 (a)	37 (d)	38 (d)	39 (d)	40 (b)
41 (d)	42 (a)	43 (d)	44 (a)	45 (d)	46 (a)	47 (c)	48 (b)	49 (b)	50 (d)

Reading Comprehension

1 (a)	2 (d)	3 (d)	4 (a)	5 (a)	6 (a)	7 (c)	8 (c)	9 (d)	10 (b)
11 (b)	12 (c)	13 (c)	14 (b)	15 (d)	16 (a)	17 (d)	18 (a)	19 (c)	20 (b)
21 (d)	22 (d)	23 (c)	24 (c)	25 (b)	26 (c)	27 (b)	28 (c)	29 (c)	30 (c)
31 (c)	32 (d)	33 (c)	34 (a)	35 (b)	36 (b)	37 (c)	38 (c)	39 (b)	40 (b)

서울대 최신기출·3

Listening Comprehension

1 (a)	2 (d)	3 (c)	4 (a)	5 (b)	6 (d)	7 (c)	8 (b)	9 (d)	10 (b)
11 (d)	12 (a)	13 (c)	14 (b)	15 (b)	16 (b)	17 (b)	18 (a)	19 (b)	20 (a)
21 (a)	22 (b)	23 (b)	24 (d)	25 (b)	26 (d)	27 (b)	28 (c)	29 (a)	30 (a)
31 (d)	32 (d)	33 (c)	34 (c)	35 (b)	36 (b)	37 (a)	38 (d)	39 (d)	40 (d)
41 (b)	42 (b)	43 (a)	44 (c)	45 (a)	46 (d)	47 (b)	48 (a)	49 (d)	50 (a)
51 (d)	52 (c)	53 (b)	54 (a)	55 (d)	56 (c)	57 (c)	58 (b)	59 (d)	60 (c)

Grammar

1 (a)	2 (c)	3 (b)	4 (c)	5 (a)	6 (c)	7 (c)	8 (b)	9 (d)	10 (a)
11 (b)	12 (a)	13 (a)	14 (d)	15 (d)	16 (a)	17 (a)	18 (a)	19 (a)	20 (c)
21 (a)	22 (b)	23 (b)	24 (c)	25 (c)	26 (b)	27 (d)	28 (d)	29 (c)	30 (c)
31 (a)	32 (c)	33 (a)	34 (a)	35 (d)	36 (a)	37 (a)	38 (c)	39 (b)	40 (b)
41 (d)	42 (d)	43 (c)	44 (b)	45 (b)	46 (c)	47 (c)	48 (a)	49 (b)	50 (b)

Vocabulary

1 (d)	2 (a)	3 (c)	4 (b)	5 (d)	6 (b)	7 (b)	8 (a)	9 (b)	10 (c)
11 (b)	12 (d)	13 (c)	14 (a)	15 (b)	16 (d)	17 (a)	18 (a)	19 (a)	20 (a)
21 (b)	22 (a)	23 (c)	24 (b)	25 (b)	26 (d)	27 (b)	28 (d)	29 (a)	30 (b)
31 (c)	32 (d)	33 (b)	34 (a)	35 (c)	36 (d)	37 (c)	38 (c)	39 (d)	40 (b)
41 (b)	42 (b)	43 (d)	44 (d)	45 (d)	46 (b)	47 (c)	48 (d)	49 (d)	50 (b)

Reading Comprehension

1 (a)	2 (d)	3 (c)	4 (a)	5 (d)	6 (d)	7 (b)	8 (a)	9 (d)	10 (c)
11 (a)	12 (d)	13 (b)	14 (d)	15 (d)	16 (d)	17 (c)	18 (a)	19 (c)	20 (a)
21 (b)	22 (b)	23 (b)	24 (c)	25 (b)	26 (d)	27 (b)	28 (b)	29 (c)	30 (a)
31 (b)	32 (d)	33 (c)	34 (d)	35 (d)	36 (a)	37 (a)	38 (d)	39 (c)	40 (b)

Listening Comprehension

1 (d)	2 (b)	3 (c)	4 (c)	5 (a)	6 (b)	7 (c)	8 (a)	9 (b)	10 (b)
11 (a)	12 (b)	13 (c)	14 (d)	15 (a)	16 (b)	17 (c)	18 (b)	19 (b)	20 (a)
21 (b)	22 (b)	23 (a)	24 (b)	25 (a)	26 (c)	27 (c)	28 (b)	29 (b)	30 (a)
31 (b)	32 (a)	33 (a)	34 (a)	35 (a)	36 (b)	37 (b)	38 (c)	39 (d)	40 (c)
41 (c)	42 (c)	43 (c)	44 (c)	45 (b)	46 (b)	47 (c)	48 (a)	49 (c)	50 (b)
51 (b)	52 (b)	53 (c)	54 (c)	55 (d)	56 (b)	57 (b)	58 (a)	59 (c)	60 (b)

Grammar

1 (b)	2 (b)	3 (a)	4 (c)	5 (a)	6 (b)	7 (a)	8 (a)	9 (d)	10 (a)
11 (d)	12 (d)	13 (d)	14 (a)	15 (d)	16 (c)	17 (b)	18 (b)	19 (c)	20 (d)
21 (d)	22 (c)	23 (d)	24 (d)	25 (a)	26 (a)	27 (c)	28 (d)	29 (d)	30 (a)
31 (d)	32 (c)	33 (d)	34 (c)	35 (d)	36 (b)	37 (c)	38 (b)	39 (c)	40 (c)
41 (a)	42 (b)	43 (a)	44 (b)	45 (b)	46 (c)	47 (d)	48 (a)	49 (d)	50 (c)

Vocabulary

1 (a)	2 (b)	3 (a)	4 (a)	5 (a)	6 (b)	7 (c)	8 (a)	9 (c)	10 (d)
11 (a)	12 (c)	13 (a)	14 (d)	15 (b)	16 (c)	17 (c)	18 (a)	19 (c)	20 (b)
21 (d)	22 (d)	23 (a)	24 (d)	25 (b)	26 (d)	27 (a)	28 (b)	29 (c)	30 (c)
31 (c)	32 (b)	33 (a)	34 (a)	35 (d)	36 (a)	37 (c)	38 (a)	39 (c)	40 (b)
41 (b)	42 (d)	43 (b)	44 (a)	45 (b)	46 (b)	47 (b)	48 (d)	49 (d)	50 (a)

Reading Comprehension

1 (b)	2 (c)	3 (b)	4 (c)	5 (b)	6 (c)	7 (d)	8 (d)	9 (d)	10 (a)
11 (a)	12 (c)	13 (b)	14 (c)	15 (c)	16 (b)	17 (d)	18 (d)	19 (c)	20 (a)
21 (a)	22 (d)	23 (d)	24 (b)	25 (a)	26 (b)	27 (b)	28 (b)	29 (d)	30 (c)
31 (b)	32 (d)	33 (a)	34 (c)	35 (d)	36 (a)	37 (c)	38 (c)	39 (b)	40 (c)

Listening *Comprehension*

1 (a)	2 (c)	3 (a)	4 (c)	5 (c)	6 (d)	7 (d)	8 (a)	9 (a)	10 (d)
11 (b)	12 (d)	13 (a)	14 (b)	15 (d)	16 (b)	17 (a)	18 (a)	19 (d)	20 (a)
21 (b)	22 (d)	23 (d)	24 (a)	25 (c)	26 (d)	27 (b)	28 (c)	29 (a)	30 (b)
31 (a)	32 (a)	33 (b)	34 (b)	35 (c)	36 (b)	37 (c)	38 (d)	39 (d)	40 (b)
41 (b)	42 (d)	43 (b)	44 (c)	45 (b)	46 (c)	47 (a)	48 (b)	49 (c)	50 (d)
51 (c)	52 (b)	53 (c)	54 (c)	55 (c)	56 (d)	57 (b)	58 (c)	59 (b)	60 (b)

Grammar

1 (c)	2 (b)	3 (c)	4 (b)	5 (b)	6 (d)	7 (a)	8 (d)	9 (c)	10 (b)
11 (c)	12 (a)	13 (a)	14 (a)	15 (b)	16 (a)	17 (b)	18 (c)	19 (b)	20 (b)
21 (c)	22 (c)	23 (c)	24 (a)	25 (b)	26 (b)	27 (c)	28 (a)	29 (a)	30 (b)
31 (a)	32 (b)	33 (c)	34 (a)	35 (a)	36 (b)	37 (d)	38 (a)	39 (d)	40 (d)
41 (d)	42 (b)	43 (b)	44 (b)	45 (c)	46 (d)	47 (c)	48 (a)	49 (a)	50 (d)

Vocabulary

1 (b)	2 (d)	3 (d)	4 (c)	5 (d)	6 (c)	7 (c)	8 (b)	9 (a)	10 (a)
11 (d)	12 (c)	13 (d)	14 (a)	15 (c)	16 (d)	17 (a)	18 (c)	19 (a)	20 (a)
21 (a)	22 (c)	23 (d)	24 (b)	25 (c)	26 (c)	27 (b)	28 (a)	29 (c)	30 (c)
31 (a)	32 (a)	33 (b)	34 (c)	35 (c)	36 (b)	37 (c)	38 (d)	39 (c)	40 (c)
41 (a)	42 (d)	43 (b)	44 (d)	45 (b)	46 (a)	47 (d)	48 (a)	49 (a)	50 (b)

Reading *Comprehension*

1 (d)	2 (a)	3 (b)	4 (c)	5 (c)	6 (b)	7 (b)	8 (c)	9 (a)	10 (a)
11 (d)	12 (a)	13 (a)	14 (c)	15 (d)	16 (c)	17 (d)	18 (d)	19 (c)	20 (c)
21 (a)	22 (a)	23 (a)	24 (c)	25 (a)	26 (d)	27 (c)	28 (d)	29 (b)	30 (c)
31 (c)	32 (b)	33 (b)	34 (d)	35 (b)	36 (d)	37 (b)	38 (b)	39 (d)	40 (c)

Listening Comprehension

1 (b)	2 (c)	3 (b)	4 (d)	5 (c)	6 (b)	7 (b)	8 (b)	9 (b)	10 (d)
11 (b)	12 (c)	13 (b)	14 (a)	15 (b)	16 (a)	17 (d)	18 (a)	19 (c)	20 (a)
21 (c)	22 (a)	23 (c)	24 (a)	25 (a)	26 (b)	27 (c)	28 (b)	29 (a)	30 (c)
31 (a)	32 (a)	33 (c)	34 (c)	35 (a)	36 (d)	37 (b)	38 (c)	39 (c)	40 (b)
41 (d)	42 (c)	43 (a)	44 (d)	45 (b)	46 (d)	47 (b)	48 (d)	49 (b)	50 (d)
51 (d)	52 (d)	53 (b)	54 (b)	55 (d)	56 (c)	57 (b)	58 (c)	59 (c)	60 (d)

Grammar

1 (a)	2 (d)	3 (a)	4 (b)	5 (d)	6 (c)	7 (d)	8 (b)	9 (b)	10 (b)
11 (d)	12 (b)	13 (a)	14 (b)	15 (d)	16 (a)	17 (c)	18 (c)	19 (a)	20 (a)
21 (b)	22 (d)	23 (c)	24 (b)	25 (d)	26 (d)	27 (c)	28 (d)	29 (c)	30 (a)
31 (d)	32 (c)	33 (c)	34 (b)	35 (a)	36 (b)	37 (a)	38 (d)	39 (b)	40 (c)
41 (d)	42 (b)	43 (b)	44 (c)	45 (c)	46 (c)	47 (a)	48 (d)	49 (c)	50 (d)

Vocabulary

1 (c)	2 (b)	3 (c)	4 (b)	5 (c)	6 (b)	7 (c)	8 (d)	9 (c)	10 (b)
11 (d)	12 (a)	13 (d)	14 (b)	15 (a)	16 (c)	17 (b)	18 (b)	19 (c)	20 (c)
21 (a)	22 (a)	23 (c)	24 (b)	25 (c)	26 (d)	27 (a)	28 (b)	29 (b)	30 (c)
31 (a)	32 (d)	33 (d)	34 (d)	35 (a)	36 (a)	37 (c)	38 (c)	39 (d)	40 (a)
41 (c)	42 (b)	43 (a)	44 (b)	45 (a)	46 (d)	47 (c)	48 (a)	49 (c)	50 (c)

Reading Comprehension

1 (d)	2 (a)	3 (d)	4 (d)	5 (b)	6 (c)	7 (b)	8 (a)	9 (a)	10 (b)
11 (b)	12 (a)	13 (d)	14 (c)	15 (d)	16 (b)	17 (c)	18 (b)	19 (a)	20 (c)
21 (d)	22 (d)	23 (c)	24 (a)	25 (c)	26 (d)	27 (d)	28 (a)	29 (c)	30 (b)
31 (c)	32 (c)	33 (a)	34 (b)	35 (b)	36 (d)	37 (d)	38 (d)	39 (c)	40 (c)

등급	점수	영역	능력검정기준(Description)
1⁺급 Level 1⁺	901~990	전반	외국인으로서 최상급 수준의 의사소통 능력 교양 있는 원어민에 버금가는 정도로 의사소통이 가능하고 전문분야 업무에 대처할 수 있음 (Native Level of Communicative Competence)
1급 Level 1	801~900	전반	외국인으로서 거의 최상급 수준의 의사소통 능력 단기간 집중 교육을 받으면 대부분의 의사소통이 가능하고 전문분야 업무에 별 무리 없이 대처할 수 있음 (Near-Native Level of Communicative Competence)
2⁺급 Level 2⁺	701~800	전반	외국인으로서 상급 수준의 의사소통 능력 단기간 집중 교육을 받으면 일반분야 업무를 큰 어려움 없이 수행할 수 있음 (Advanced Level of Communicative Competence)
2급 Level 2	601~700	전반	외국인으로서 중상급 수준의 의사소통 능력 중장기간 집중 교육을 받으면 일반분야 업무를 큰 어려움 없이 수행할 수 있음 (High Intermediate Level of Communicative Competence)
3⁺급 Level 3⁺	501~600	전반	외국인으로서 중급 수준의 의사소통 능력 중장기간 집중 교육을 받으면 한정된 분야의 업무를 큰 어려움 없이 수행할 수 있음 (Mid Intermediate Level of Communicative Competence)
3급 Level 3	401~500	전반	외국인으로서 중하급 수준의 의사소통 능력 중장기간 집중 교육을 받으면 한정된 분야의 업무를 다소 미흡하지만 큰 지장 없이 수행할 수 있음 (Low Intermediate Level of Communicative Competence)
4⁺급 Level 4⁺	301~400	전반	외국인으로서 하급 수준의 의사소통 능력 장기간의 집중 교육을 받으면 한정된 분야의 업무를 대체로 어렵게 수행할 수 있음 (Novice Level of Communicative Competence)
4급 Level 4	201~300		
5⁺급 Level 5⁺	101~200	전반	외국인으로서 최하급 수준의 의사소통 능력 단편적인 지식만을 갖추고 있어 의사소통이 거의 불가능함 (Near-Zero Level of Communicative Competence)
5급 Level 5	10~100		

앞면(Side1)

TEPS

Test of English Proficiency
developed by
Seoul National University

수험번호 Registration No.

성명 Name 한글 / 한자

문 제 지 번 호
Test Booklet No.

감독관확인란

청 해 Listening Comprehension	문 법 Grammar	어 휘 Vocabulary	독 해 Reading Comprehension

주 민 등 록 번 호 National ID No.

고사실란 Room No.

수 험 번 호 Registration No.

비밀번호 Password

좌석번호 Seat No.

서 약 | 본인은 필기구 및 기재오류와 답안지 훼손으로 인한 책임을 지고, 부정행위 처리규정을 준수할 것을 서약합니다.

답안작성시 유의사항

1. 답안 작성은 반드시 **컴퓨터용 싸인펜**을 사용해야 합니다.

2. 답안을 정정할 경우 수정테이프(수정액 불가)를 사용해야 합니다.

3. 본 답안지는 컴퓨터로 처리되므로 훼손해서는 안되며, 답안지 하단의 타이밍마크(|||)를 찢거나, 낙서 등으로 인한 훼손시 불이익이 발생할 수 있습니다.

4. 답안은 문항당 정답을 1개만 골라 ● 와 같이 정확히 기재해야 하며, 필기구 오류나 본인의 부주의로 잘못 표기한 경우에는 당 관리위원회의 OMR판독기의 판독결과에 따르며, 그 결과는 본인이 책임집니다.

Good ●   Bad ◐ ◑ ● ⊗ ◓

5. 감독관의 확인이 없는 답안지는 무효처리됩니다.

뒷면(Side2)

TEPS
Test of English Proficiency
developed by
Seoul National University

성 영문

명 서명

응시일자 : 20　년　월　일

<부정행위 및 규정위반 처리규정>

1. 모든 부정행위 및 규정위반 적발 및 이에 대한 조치는 TEPS관리위원회의 처리규정에 따라 이루어집니다.

2. 부정행위 및 규정위반 행위는 현장 적발 뿐만 아니라 사후에도 적발될 수 있으며 모두 동일한 조치가 취해집니다.

3. 부정행위 적발 시 당해 성적은 무효화되며 사안에 따라 최대 5년까지 TEPS관리위원회에서 주관하는 모든 시험의 응시자격이 제한됩니다.

4. 문제지 이외에 메모를 하는 행위와 시험 문제의 일부 또는 전부를 유출하거나 공개하는 경우 부정행위로 처리됩니다.

5. 각 파트별 시간을 준수하지 않거나, 시험 종료 후 답안 작성을 계속할 경우 규정위반으로 처리됩니다.

성　명 (성·이름순으로 기재)

EX HONG GIL DONG

(이름 기재란: A B C D E F G H I J K L M N O P Q R S T U V W X Y Z 마킹란)

단체구분

학생	일반
◯	◯

질문란

1. 귀하의 TEPS 응시목적은?
   - (a) 입사지원
   - (b) 인사정책
   - (c) 개인실력측정
   - (d) 입시
   - (e) 국가고시 지원
   - (f) 기타

2. 귀하의 영어권 체류 경험은?
   - (a) 없다
   - (b) 6개월 미만
   - (c) 6개월 이상 1년 미만
   - (d) 1년 이상 3년 미만
   - (e) 3년 이상 5년 미만
   - (f) 5년 이상

3. 귀하께서 응시하고 계신 고사장에 대한 만족도는?
   - (a) 0점
   - (b) 1점
   - (c) 2점
   - (d) 3점
   - (e) 4점
   - (f) 5점

4. 최근 2년내 TEPS 응시횟수는?
   - (a) 없다
   - (b) 1회
   - (c) 2회
   - (d) 3회
   - (e) 4회
   - (f) 5회 이상

학력 / 전공 / 직업

학력			전공	직업
	재학	졸업		
초등학교	◯	◯	인 문 학 ◯	공 무 원 ◯
중 학 교	◯	◯	사회과학·법학 ◯	고시준비 ◯
고 등 학 교	◯	◯	경제학·경영학 ◯	교　사 ◯
전 문 대 학	◯	◯	자 연 과 학 ◯	군　인 ◯
대 학 교	◯	◯	의학·약학·간호학 ◯	의 료 인 ◯
대 학 원	◯	◯	공 　 학 ◯	자 영 업 ◯
			교 육 학 ◯	학 　 생 ◯
			음악·미술·체육 ◯	회 사 원 ◯
			기 　 타 ◯	무 　 직 ◯
				기 　 타 ◯

직종 / 직책

직 종		직 책	
고 위 임 직 원 ◯	무 　 역 ◯	임 　 원 ◯	
전문직 (과학·공학) ◯	외 　 환 ◯	부 　 장 ◯	
전 문 직 (교육) ◯	자 　 금 ◯	차 　 장 ◯	
전문직(법률·회계·금융) ◯	공 　 무 ◯	과 　 장 ◯	
기 　 술 　 직 ◯	업 　 무 ◯	대 　 리 ◯	
영 　 업 ◯	품 질 관 리 ◯	계 　 장 ◯	
홍 　 보 ◯	전 　 산 ◯	사 　 원 ◯	
총 　 무 ◯	행 　 정 　 직 ◯	인 　 턴 ◯	
인 　 사 ◯	생 산 관 리 ◯	기 　 타 ◯	
경 　 리 ◯	서 비 스 ◯		
기 　 획 ◯	기 　 타 ◯		
구 　 매 ◯			

TEPS

Test of English Proficiency
developed by
Seoul National University

수험번호
Registration No.

성명
Name
한글
한자

문제지번호
Test Booklet No.

감독관확인란

청 해
Listening Comprehension

문 법
Grammar

어 휘
Vocabulary

독 해
Reading Comprehension

주 민 등 록 번 호
National ID No.

고사실란
Room No.

수 험 번 호
Registration No.

비밀번호
Password

좌석번호
Seat No.

서 약	본인은 필기구 및 기재오류와 답안지 훼손으로 인한 책임을 지고, 부정행위 처리규정을 준수할 것을 서약합니다.

답안작성시 유의사항

1. 답안 작성은 반드시 **컴퓨터용 싸인펜**을 사용해야 합니다.
2. 답안을 정정할 경우 수정테이프(수정액 불가)를 사용해야 합니다.
3. 본 답안지는 컴퓨터로 처리되므로 훼손해서는 안되며, 답안지 하단의 타이밍마크(|||)를 찢거나, 낙서 등으로 인한 훼손시 불이익이 발생할 수 있습니다.
4. 답안은 문항당 정답을 1개만 골라 ●와 같이 정확히 기재해야 하며, 필기구 오류나 본인의 부주의로 잘못 표기한 경우에는 당 관리위원회의 OMR판독기의 판독결과에 따르며, 그 결과는 본인이 책임집니다.
   - Good ● Bad
5. 감독관의 확인이 없는 답안지는 무효처리됩니다.

TEPS
Test of English Proficiency
developed by
Seoul National University

성 영문
명 서명

응시일자 : 20   년   월   일

〈부정행위 및 규정위반 처리규정〉

1. 모든 부정행위 및 규정위반 적발 및 이에 대한 조치는 TEPS관리위원회의 처리규정에 따라 이루어집니다.

2. 부정행위 및 규정위반 행위는 현장 적발 뿐만 아니라 사후에도 적발될 수 있으며 모두 동일한 조치가 취해집니다.

3. 부정행위 적발 시 당해 성적은 무효화되며 사안에 따라 최대 5년까지 TEPS관리위원회에서 주관하는 모든 시험의 응시자격이 제한됩니다.

4. 문제지 이외에 메모를 하는 행위와 시험 문제의 일부 또는 전부를 유출하거나 공개하는 경우 부정행위로 처리됩니다.

5. 각 파트별 시간을 준수하지 않거나, 시험 종료 후 답안 작성을 계속할 경우 규정위반으로 처리됩니다.

성   명 (성·이름순으로 기재)

EX HONG GIL DONG

(A B C D E F G H I J K L M N O P Q R S T U V W X Y Z 마킹란)

단체구분

학생	일반
◯	◯

질문란

1. 귀하의 TEPS 응시목적은?
   - ⓐ 입사지원
   - ⓑ 인사정책
   - ⓒ 개인실력측정
   - ⓓ 입시
   - ⓔ 국가고시 지원
   - ⓕ 기타

2. 귀하의 영어권 체류 경험은?
   - ⓐ 없다
   - ⓑ 6개월 미만
   - ⓒ 6개월 이상 1년 미만
   - ⓓ 1년 이상 3년 미만
   - ⓔ 3년 이상 5년 미만
   - ⓕ 5년 이상

3. 귀하께서 응시하고 계신 고사장에 대한 만족도는?
   - ⓐ 0점
   - ⓑ 1점
   - ⓒ 2점
   - ⓓ 3점
   - ⓔ 4점
   - ⓕ 5점

4. 최근 2년내 TEPS 응시횟수는?
   - ⓐ 없다
   - ⓑ 1회
   - ⓒ 2회
   - ⓓ 3회
   - ⓔ 4회
   - ⓕ 5회 이상

학력 / 전공 / 직업

학력	재학	졸업	전공		직업	
초등학교	◯	◯	인문학	◯	공무원	◯
중학교	◯	◯	사회과학·법학	◯	고시준비	◯
고등학교	◯	◯	경제학·경영학	◯	교사	◯
전문대학	◯	◯	자연과학	◯	군인	◯
대학교	◯	◯	의학·약학·간호학	◯	의료인	◯
대학원	◯	◯	공학	◯	자영업	◯
			교육학	◯	학생	◯
			음악·미술·체육	◯	회사원	◯
			기타	◯	무직	◯
					기타	◯

직종 / 직책

직종			직책	
고위임직원	◯	무역	◯	임원	◯
전문직(과학.공학)	◯	외환	◯	부장	◯
전문직(교육)	◯	자금	◯	차장	◯
전문직(법률.회계.금융)	◯	공무	◯	과장	◯
기술직	◯	업무	◯	대리	◯
영업	◯	품질관리	◯	계장	◯
홍보	◯	전산	◯	사원	◯
총무	◯	행정직	◯	인턴	◯
인사	◯	생산관리	◯	기타	◯
경리	◯	서비스	◯		
기획	◯	기타	◯		
구매	◯				

TEPS

Test of English Proficiency
developed by
Seoul National University

수험번호 Registration No.

성명 Name 한글 한자

문제지번호 Test Booklet No.

감독관확인란

청 해 Listening Comprehension

문 법 Grammar

어 휘 Vocabulary

독 해 Reading Comprehension

주 민 등 록 번 호 National ID No.

고사실란 Room No.

수 험 번 호 Registration No.

비밀번호 Password

좌석번호 Seat No.

서 약 본인은 필기구 및 기재오류와 답안지 훼손으로 인한 책임을 지고, 부정행위 처리규정을 준수할 것을 서약합니다.

답안작성시 유의사항

1. 답안 작성은 반드시 **컴퓨터용 싸인펜**을 사용해야 합니다.
2. 답안을 정정할 경우 수정테이프(수정액 불가)를 사용해야 합니다.
3. 본 답안지는 컴퓨터로 처리되므로 훼손해서는 안되며, 답안지 하단의 타이밍마크(|||)를 찢거나, 낙서 등으로 인한 훼손시 불이익이 발생할 수 있습니다.
4. 답안은 문항당 정답을 1개만 골라 ■와 같이 정확히 기재해야 하며, 필기구 오류나 본인의 부주의로 잘못 표기한 경우에는 당 관리위원회의 OMR판독기의 판독결과에 따르며, 그 결과는 본인이 책임집니다.

Good ■ Bad |) |∙ |) |X |Ø

5. 감독관의 확인이 없는 답안지는 무효처리됩니다.

뒷면(Side2)

TEPS

Test of English Proficiency
developed by
Seoul National University

성	영문	
명	서명	

응시일자 : 20   년   월   일

〈부정행위 및 규정위반 처리규정〉

1. 모든 부정행위 및 규정위반 적발 및 이에 대한 조치는 TEPS관리위원회의 처리규정에 따라 이루어집니다.

2. 부정행위 및 규정위반 행위는 현장 적발 뿐만 아니라 사후에도 적발될 수 있으며 모두 동일한 조치가 취해집니다.

3. 부정행위 적발 시 당해 성적은 무효화되며 사안에 따라 최대 5년까지 TEPS관리위원회에서 주관하는 모든 시험의 응시자격이 제한됩니다.

4. 문제지 이외에 메모를 하는 행위와 시험 문제의 일부 또는 전부를 유출하거나 공개하는 경우 부정행위로 처리됩니다.

5. 각 파트별 시간을 준수하지 않거나, 시험 종료 후 답안 작성을 계속할 경우 규정위반으로 처리됩니다.

성   명 (성·이름순으로 기재)

EX HONG GIL DONG

A	A	A	A	A	A	A	A	A	A	A	A	A	A	A	A	A	A	A
B	B	B	B	B	B	B	B	B	B	B	B	B	B	B	B	B	B	B
C	C	C	C	C	C	C	C	C	C	C	C	C	C	C	C	C	C	C
D	D	D	D	D	D	D	D	D	D	D	D	D	D	D	D	D	D	D
E	E	E	E	E	E	E	E	E	E	E	E	E	E	E	E	E	E	E
F	F	F	F	F	F	F	F	F	F	F	F	F	F	F	F	F	F	F
G	G	G	G	G	G	G	G	G	G	G	G	G	G	G	G	G	G	G
H	H	H	H	H	H	H	H	H	H	H	H	H	H	H	H	H	H	H
I	I	I	I	I	I	I	I	I	I	I	I	I	I	I	I	I	I	I
J	J	J	J	J	J	J	J	J	J	J	J	J	J	J	J	J	J	J
K	K	K	K	K	K	K	K	K	K	K	K	K	K	K	K	K	K	K
L	L	L	L	L	L	L	L	L	L	L	L	L	L	L	L	L	L	L
M	M	M	M	M	M	M	M	M	M	M	M	M	M	M	M	M	M	M
N	N	N	N	N	N	N	N	N	N	N	N	N	N	N	N	N	N	N
O	O	O	O	O	O	O	O	O	O	O	O	O	O	O	O	O	O	O
P	P	P	P	P	P	P	P	P	P	P	P	P	P	P	P	P	P	P
Q	Q	Q	Q	Q	Q	Q	Q	Q	Q	Q	Q	Q	Q	Q	Q	Q	Q	Q
R	R	R	R	R	R	R	R	R	R	R	R	R	R	R	R	R	R	R
S	S	S	S	S	S	S	S	S	S	S	S	S	S	S	S	S	S	S
T	T	T	T	T	T	T	T	T	T	T	T	T	T	T	T	T	T	T
U	U	U	U	U	U	U	U	U	U	U	U	U	U	U	U	U	U	U
V	V	V	V	V	V	V	V	V	V	V	V	V	V	V	V	V	V	V
W	W	W	W	W	W	W	W	W	W	W	W	W	W	W	W	W	W	W
X	X	X	X	X	X	X	X	X	X	X	X	X	X	X	X	X	X	X
Y	Y	Y	Y	Y	Y	Y	Y	Y	Y	Y	Y	Y	Y	Y	Y	Y	Y	Y
Z	Z	Z	Z	Z	Z	Z	Z	Z	Z	Z	Z	Z	Z	Z	Z	Z	Z	Z

단체 구분

학생	일반
○	○

질 문 란

1. 귀하의 TEPS 응시목적은?
   - (a) 입사지원 (b) 인사정책
   - (c) 개인실력측정 (d) 입시
   - (e) 국가고시 지원 (f) 기타

2. 귀하의 영어권 체류 경험은?
   - (a) 없다 (b) 6개월 미만
   - (c) 6개월 이상 1년 미만 (d) 1년 이상 3년 미만
   - (e) 3년 이상 5년 미만 (f) 5년 이상

3. 귀하께서 응시하고 계신 고사장에 대한 만족도는?
   - (a) 0점 (b) 1점
   - (c) 2점 (d) 3점
   - (e) 4점 (f) 5점

4. 최근 2년내 TEPS 응시횟수는?
   - (a) 없다 (b) 1회
   - (c) 2회 (d) 3회
   - (e) 4회 (f) 5회 이상

학력 / 전공 / 직업

학력	재학	졸업	전공	직업
초등학교	○	○	인 문 학 ○	공 무 원 ○
중 학 교	○	○	사회과학·법학 ○	고시준비 ○
고등학교	○	○	경제학·경영학 ○	교 사 ○
전문대학	○	○	자 연 과 학 ○	군 인 ○
대 학 교	○	○	의학·약학·간호학 ○	의 료 인 ○
대 학 원	○	○	공 학 ○	자 영 업 ○
			교 육 학 ○	학 생 ○
			음악·미술·체육 ○	회 사 원 ○
			기 타 ○	무 직 ○
				기 타 ○

직종 / 직책

직 종		직 책	
고 위 임 직 원 ○	무 역 ○	임 원 ○	
전문직(과학.공학) ○	외 환 ○	부 장 ○	
전 문 직 (교 육) ○	자 금 ○	차 장 ○	
전문직(법률.회계.금융) ○	공 무 ○	과 장 ○	
기 술 직 ○	업 무 ○	대 리 ○	
영 업 ○	품 질 관 리 ○	계 장 ○	
홍 보 ○	전 산 ○	사 원 ○	
총 무 ○	행 정 직 ○	인 턴 ○	
인 사 ○	생 산 관 리 ○	기 타 ○	
경 리 ○	서 비 스 ○		
기 획 ○	기 타 ○		
구 매 ○			

TEPS

Test of English Proficiency
developed by
Seoul National University

앞면(Side1)

청해 Listening Comprehension

문법 Grammar

어휘 Vocabulary

독해 Reading Comprehension

수험번호 Registration No.
성명 Name 한글 한자

문제지번호 Test Booklet No.
감독관확인란

주민등록번호 National ID No.

수험번호 Registration No.

비밀번호 Password

고사실란 Room No.

좌석번호 Seat No.

서약

본인은 필기구 및 기재오류와 답안지 훼손으로 인한 책임을 지고, 부정행위 처리규정을 준수할 것을 서약합니다.

답안작성시 유의사항

1. 답안 작성은 반드시 **컴퓨터용 싸인펜**을 사용해야 합니다.
2. 답안을 정정할 경우 수정테이프(수정액 불가)를 사용해야 합니다.
3. 본 답안지는 컴퓨터로 처리되므로 훼손해서는 안되며, 답안지 하단의 타이밍마크(▮)를 찢거나, 낙서 등으로 인한 훼손시 불이익을 받을 수 있습니다.
4. 답안은 문항당 정답을 1개만 골라 ● 와 같이 정확히 기재해야 하며, 필기구 오류나 본인의 부주의로 잘못 표기한 경우에는 단 관리위원회의 OMR판독기의 판독결과에 따르므로, 그 결과는 본인이 책임집니다.

   Good ● Bad ◖ ◑ ◐ ✕ ✓

5. 감독관의 확인이 없는 답안지는 무효처리됩니다.

유의사항

TEPS

Test of English Proficiency
developed by
Seoul National University

성	영문	
명	서명	

응시일자 : 20 년 월 일

<부정행위 및 규정위반 처리규정>

1. 모든 부정행위 및 규정위반 적발 및 이에 대한 조치는 TEPS관리위원회의 처리규정에 따라 이루어집니다.

2. 부정행위 및 규정위반 행위는 현장 적발 뿐만 아니라 사후에도 적발될 수 있으며 모두 동일한 조치가 취해집니다.

3. 부정행위 적발 시 당해 성적은 무효화되며 사안에 따라 최대 5년까지 TEPS관리위원회에서 주관하는 모든 시험의 응시자격이 제한됩니다.

4. 문제지 이외에 메모를 하는 행위와 시험 문제의 일부 또는 전부를 유출하거나 공개하는 경우 부정행위로 처리됩니다.

5. 각 파트별 시간을 준수하지 않거나, 시험 종료 후 답안 작성을 계속할 경우 규정위반으로 처리됩니다.

성 명 (성·이름순으로 기재)

EX HONG GIL DONG

(A~Z 마킹란)

단체구분

학생	일반
○	○

질 문 란

1. 귀하의 TEPS 응시목적은?

- ⓐ 입사지원 ⓑ 인사정책
- ⓒ 개인실력측정 ⓓ 입시
- ⓔ 국가고시 지원 ⓕ 기타

2. 귀하의 영어권 체류 경험은?

- ⓐ 없다 ⓑ 6개월 미만
- ⓒ 6개월 이상 1년 미만 ⓓ 1년 이상 3년 미만
- ⓔ 3년 이상 5년 미만 ⓕ 5년 이상

3. 귀하께서 응시하고 계신 고사장에 대한 만족도는?

- ⓐ 0점 ⓑ 1점
- ⓒ 2점 ⓓ 3점
- ⓔ 4점 ⓕ 5점

4. 최근 2년내 TEPS 응시횟수는?

- ⓐ 없다 ⓑ 1회
- ⓒ 2회 ⓓ 3회
- ⓔ 4회 ⓕ 5회 이상

학력 / 전공 / 직업

학력	재학	졸업	전공	직업
초등학교	○	○	인 문 학 ○	공 무 원 ○
중 학 교	○	○	사회과학·법학 ○	고시준비 ○
고등학교	○	○	경제학·경영학 ○	교 사 ○
전문대학	○	○	자 연 과 학 ○	군 인 ○
대 학 교	○	○	의학·약학·간호학 ○	의 료 인 ○
대 학 원	○	○	공 학 ○	자 영 업 ○
			교 육 학 ○	학 생 ○
			음악·미술·체육 ○	회 사 원 ○
			기 타 ○	무 직 ○
				기 타 ○

직종 / 직책

직 종		직 책	
고 위 임 직 원 ○	무 역 ○	임 원 ○
전문직(과학.공학) ○	외 환 ○	부 장 ○
전 문 직 (교육) ○	자 금 ○	차 장 ○
전문직(법률.회계.금융) ○	공 무 ○	과 장 ○
기 술 직 ○	업 무 ○	대 리 ○
영 업 ○	품 질 관 리 ○	계 장 ○
홍 보 ○	전 산 ○	사 원 ○
총 무 ○	행 정 직 ○	인 턴 ○
인 사 ○	생 산 관 리 ○	기 타 ○
경 리 ○	서 비 스 ○	
기 획 ○	기 타 ○	
구 매 ○		

앞면(Side1)

TEPS

Test of English Proficiency
developed by
Seoul National University

수험번호 / Registration No.

성명 / Name — 한글 / 한자

문제지번호 / Test Booklet No.

감독관확인란

| 청　해 / Listening Comprehension | 문　법 / Grammar | 어　휘 / Vocabulary | 독　해 / Reading Comprehension |

주 민 등 록 번 호 / National ID No.

고사실란 / Room No.

수 험 번 호 / Registration No.

비밀번호 / Password

좌석번호 / Seat No.

| 서　약 | 본인은 필기구 및 기재오류와 답안지 훼손으로 인한 책임을 지고, 부정행위 처리규정을 준수할 것을 서약합니다. |

답안작성시 유의사항

1. 답안 작성은 반드시 **컴퓨터용 싸인펜**을 사용해야 합니다.

2. 답안을 정정할 경우 수정테이프(수정액 불가)를 사용해야 합니다.

3. 본 답안지는 컴퓨터로 처리되므로 훼손해서는 안되며, 답안지 하단의 타이밍마크(|||)를 찢거나, 낙서 등으로 인한 훼손시 불이익이 발생할 수 있습니다.

4. 답안은 문항당 정답을 1개만 골라 ● 와 같이 정확히 기재해야 하며, 필기구 오류나 본인의 부주의로 잘못 표기한 경우에는 당 관리위원회의 OMR판독기의 판독결과에 따르며, 그 결과는 본인이 책임집니다.

Good ●　　Bad ◖ ◔ ◉ ✗ ✓

5. 감독관의 확인이 없는 답안지는 무효처리됩니다.

TEPS

Test of English Proficiency
developed by
Seoul National University

성	영문	
명	서명	

응시일자 : 20   년   월   일

<부정행위 및 규정위반 처리규정>

1. 모든 부정행위 및 규정위반 적발 및 이에 대한 조치는 TEPS관리위원회의 처리규정에 따라 이루어집니다.

2. 부정행위 및 규정위반 행위는 현장 적발 뿐만 아니라 사후에도 적발될 수 있으며 모두 동일한 조치가 취해집니다.

3. 부정행위 적발 시 당해 성적은 무효화되며 사안에 따라 최대 5년까지 TEPS관리위원회에서 주관하는 모든 시험의 응시자격이 제한됩니다.

4. 문제지 이외에 메모를 하는 행위와 시험 문제의 일부 또는 전부를 유출하거나 공개하는 경우 부정행위로 처리됩니다.

5. 각 파트별 시간을 준수하지 않거나, 시험 종료 후 답안 작성을 계속할 경우 규정위반으로 처리됩니다.

성 명 (성·이름순으로 기재)

EX HONG GIL DONG

A B C D E F G H I J K L M N O P Q R S T U V W X Y Z

(각 칸마다 A~Z 마킹란)

단 체 구 분

학생	일반
○	○

질 문 란

1. 귀하의 TEPS 응시목적은?
   - ⓐ 입사지원
   - ⓑ 인사정책
   - ⓒ 개인실력측정
   - ⓓ 입시
   - ⓔ 국가고시 지원
   - ⓕ 기타

2. 귀하의 영어권 체류 경험은?
   - ⓐ 없다
   - ⓑ 6개월 미만
   - ⓒ 6개월 이상 1년 미만
   - ⓓ 1년 이상 3년 미만
   - ⓔ 3년 이상 5년 미만
   - ⓕ 5년 이상

3. 귀하께서 응시하고 계신 고사장에 대한 만족도는?
   - ⓐ 0점
   - ⓑ 1점
   - ⓒ 2점
   - ⓓ 3점
   - ⓔ 4점
   - ⓕ 5점

4. 최근 2년내 TEPS 응시횟수는?
   - ⓐ 없다
   - ⓑ 1회
   - ⓒ 2회
   - ⓓ 3회
   - ⓔ 4회
   - ⓕ 5회 이상

학 력 / 전 공 / 직 업

학력	재학	졸업	전공	직업
초등학교	○	○	인 문 학	공 무 원 ○
중 학 교	○	○	사회과학·법학	고시준비 ○
고등학교	○	○	경제학·경영학	교 사 ○
전문대학	○	○	자 연 과 학	군 인 ○
대 학 교	○	○	의학·약학·간호학	의 료 인 ○
대 학 원	○	○	공 학	자 영 업 ○
			교 육 학	학 생 ○
			음악·미술·체육	회 사 원 ○
			기 타	무 직 ○
				기 타 ○

직 종 / 직 책

직종		직책	
고 위 임 직 원	무 역 ○	임 원 ○	
전문직(과학.공학)	외 환 ○	부 장 ○	
전 문 직 (교육)	자 금 ○	차 장 ○	
전문직(법률.회계.금융)	공 무 ○	과 장 ○	
기 술 직	업 무 ○	대 리 ○	
영 업	품 질 관 리 ○	계 장 ○	
홍 보	전 산 ○	사 원 ○	
총 무	행 정 직 ○	인 턴 ○	
인 사	생 산 관 리 ○	기 타 ○	
경 리	서 비 스 ○		
기 획	기 타 ○		
구 매 ○			

앞면(Side1)

TEPS

Test of English Proficiency
developed by
Seoul National University

수험번호 Registration No.
성명 Name | 한글 | 한자
문제지번호 Test Booklet No.
감독관확인란

청해 Listening Comprehension

문법 Grammar

어휘 Vocabulary

독해 Reading Comprehension

주민등록번호 National ID No.
고사실란 Room No.
수험번호 Registration No.
비밀번호 Password
좌석번호 Seat No.

서 약

본인은 필기구 및 기재오류와 답안지 훼손으로 인한 책임을 지고, 부정행위 처리규정을 준수할 것을 서약합니다.

답안작성시 유의사항

1. 답안 작성은 반드시 **컴퓨터용 싸인펜**을 사용해야 합니다.
2. 답안을 정정할 경우 수정테이프(수정액 불가)를 사용해야 합니다.
3. 본 답안지는 컴퓨터로 처리되므로 훼손해서는 안되며, 답안지 하단의 타이밍마크(|||)를 찢거나, 낙서 등으로 인한 훼손시 불이익이 발생할 수 있습니다.
4. 답안은 문항당 정답을 1개만 골라 ● 와 같이 정확히 기재해야 하며, 필기구 오류나 본인의 부주의로 잘못 표기한 경우에는 당 관리위원회의 OMR판독기의 판독결과에 따르며, 그 결과는 본인이 책임집니다.
5. 감독관의 확인이 없는 답안지는 무효처리됩니다.

Good ●   Bad ◖ · ◗ ⊗ ◍

TEPS

Test of English Proficiency
developed by
Seoul National University

성	영문
명	서명

응시일자 : 20   년   월   일

<부정행위 및 규정위반 처리규정>

1. 모든 부정행위 및 규정위반 적발 및 이에 대한 조치는 TEPS관리위원회의 처리규정에 따라 이루어집니다.

2. 부정행위 및 규정위반 행위는 현장 적발 뿐만 아니라 사후에도 적발될 수 있으며 모두 동일한 조치가 취해집니다.

3. 부정행위 적발 시 당해 성적은 무효화되며 사안에 따라 최대 5년까지 TEPS관리위원회에서 주관하는 모든 시험의 응시자격이 제한됩니다.

4. 문제지 이외에 메모를 하는 행위와 시험 문제의 일부 또는 전부를 유출하거나 공개하는 경우 부정행위로 처리됩니다.

5. 각 파트별 시간을 준수하지 않거나, 시험 종료 후 답안 작성을 계속할 경우 규정위반으로 처리됩니다.

성 명 (성·이름순으로 기재)

EX HONG GIL DONG

A B C D E F G H I J K L M N O P Q R S T U V W X Y Z

단 체 구 분

학생	일반
○	○

질 문 란

1. 귀하의 TEPS 응시목적은?
   - a 입사지원
   - b 인사정책
   - c 개인실력측정
   - d 입시
   - e 국가고시 지원
   - f 기타

2. 귀하의 영어권 체류 경험은?
   - a 없다
   - b 6개월 미만
   - c 6개월 이상 1년 미만
   - d 1년 이상 3년 미만
   - e 3년 이상 5년 미만
   - f 5년 이상

3. 귀하께서 응시하고 계신 고사장에 대한 만족도는?
   - a 0점
   - b 1점
   - c 2점
   - d 3점
   - e 4점
   - f 5점

4. 최근 2년내 TEPS 응시횟수는?
   - a 없다
   - b 1회
   - c 2회
   - d 3회
   - e 4회
   - f 5회 이상

학 력

	재학	졸업
초등학교	○	
중 학 교	○	
고 등 학 교	○	
전 문 대 학	○	
대 학 교	○	
대 학 원	○	

전 공

인 문 학	○
사회과학·법학	○
경제학·경영학	○
자 연 과 학	○
의학·약학·간호학	○
공 학	○
교 육 학	○
음악·미술·체육	○
기 타	○

직 업

공 무 원	○
고시준비	○
교 사	○
군 인	○
의 료 인	○
자 영 업	○
학 생	○
회 사 원	○
무 직	○
기 타	○

직 종

고 위 임 직 원	○
전문직(과학·공학)	○
전 문 직 (교육)	○
전문직(법률·회계·금융)	○
기 술 직	○
영 업	○
홍 보	○
총 무	○
인 사	○
경 리	○
기 획	○
구 매	○
무 역	○
외 환	○
자 금	○
공 무	○
업 무	○
품 질 관 리	○
전 산	○
행 정 직	○
생 산 관 리	○
서 비 스	○
기 타	○

직 책

임 원	○
부 장	○
차 장	○
과 장	○
대 리	○
계 장	○
사 원	○
인 턴	○
기 타	○

SINCE 1999
ALL PASS

- 1999년 정기시험 최초 시행
- 2018년 뉴텝스 시행 (총점 600점 변경)
- 국내 대학 수시, 편입, 졸업인증 활용
- 전문대학원 입시 반영
- 공무원 선발 및 국가자격시험 대체
- 공공기관, 기업 채용 및 인사고과 활용

텝스로 올패스!

고교부터 대학(원), 취업, 승진을 잇는
대한민국 대표 영어시험 TEPS

 02.886.3330     www.teps.or.kr   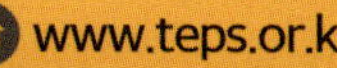  www.facebook.com/teps4u    @teps

실제 기출 어휘와 예문을 그대로 수록한

서울대 최신기출
NEW TEPS VOCA

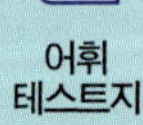

www.nexusbook.com

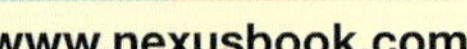

서울대 최신기출 NEW TEPS VOCA | 넥서스 TEPS연구소·문덕 지음 | 536쪽 | 17,500원

뉴텝스도 역시 넥서스!

그냥 믿고 따라와 봐!

마스터편 실전 500+

독해 정일상, 넥서스TEPS연구소 지음 | 17,500원　**문법** 테스 김 지음 | 15,000원　**청해** 라보혜, 넥서스TEPS연구소 지음 | 18,000원

500점

실력편 실전 400+

독해 정일상, 넥서스TEPS연구소 지음 | 18,000원　**문법** 넥서스TEPS연구소 지음 | 15,000원　**청해** 라보혜, 넥서스TEPS연구소 지음 | 17,000원

400점

기본편 실전 300+

독해 정일상, 넥서스TEPS연구소 지음 | 19,000원　**문법** 장보금, 써니 박 지음 | 17,500원　**청해** 이기헌 지음 | 19,800원

300점

입문편 실전 250+

독해 넥서스TEPS연구소 지음 | 18,000원　**문법** 넥서스TEPS연구소 지음 | 15,000원　**청해** 넥서스TEPS연구소 지음 | 18,000원

넥서스
NEW TEPS
시리즈

목표 점수 달성을 위한
뉴텝스 기본서 + 실전서

뉴텝스 실전 완벽 대비
Actual Test 수록

고득점의 감을 확실하게 잡아 주는
상세한 해설 제공

모바일 단어장, 어휘 테스트 등
다양한 부가자료 제공